Stormy Weather

The New Hampshire Primary and Presidential Politics

Dante J. Scala

palgrave
macmillan

First published 2003 by
PALGRAVE MACMILLAN™
175 Fifth Avenue, New York, N.Y. 10010 and
Houndmills, Basingstoke, Hampshire, England RG21 6XS.
Companies and representatives throughout the world.

PALGRAVE MACMILLAN is the global academic imprint of the Palgrave Macmillan
division of St. Martin's Press, LLC and of Palgrave Macmillan Ltd. Macmillan®is a registered
trademark in the United States, United Kingdom and other countries. Palgrave is a registered
trademark in the European Union and other countries.

ISBN 0-312-29622-3 hardback

Library of Congress Cataloging-in-Publication Data
Scala, Dante J.
   Stormy weather : the New Hampshire primary and presidential politics / by Dante J. Scala.
      p. cm.
   Includes bibliographical references.
   ISBN 0-312-29622-3 (alk. paper)
   1. Primaries--New Hampshire. 2. Democratic Party (N.H.) 3. Presidents--United
States--Nomination. I. Title.

JK2075.N42S33 2003
324.273'0154'09742--dc22   2003062319

A catalogue record for this book is available from the British Library.

Design by planettheo.com

First edition: November 2003
10 9 8 7 6 5 4 3 2 1

Printed in the United States of America.

For my mother,
and for the memory of my father.

Contents

Acknowledgements

When I told one of my interviewees, Jane Wood, about my project, she compared me to an Eagle Scout candidate who had taken on the job of painting a rather long fence. Covering a span of some thirty years in the life of the New Hampshire presidential primary, and in the life of the New Hampshire Democratic Party, has proven to be quite a task. Luckily, I had a lot of people helping me with the paint job, and I would like to thank them now.

First, my research has been greatly assisted by the New Hampshire Institute of Politics at Saint Anselm College, where I am fortunate enough to be a research fellow. The institute has offered both time and funding to me to pursue my research, and both commodities have been invaluable.

Bill Gardner, New Hampshire's secretary of state, and New Hampshire political historian Charles Brereton were very kind to a new kid on the block when I arrived here in 1999. Brereton's book on the presidential primary, *First in the Nation,* was quite helpful to me then and remained so in this project.

In the course of researching this book, I conducted several dozen interviews with participants in the New Hampshire primary, past and present. Those I interviewed were uniformly generous with their insights and experience. The interviews were an education in themselves, and I hope that I convey some small part of the knowledge I gained from them.

An important part of this book is an investigation into the political demographics of New Hampshire. This would not have been possible without the unflagging assistance of Thomas Duffy (an alumnus of Saint Anselm College) and New Hampshire's Office of State Planning. Martin Capodice also offered valuable advice in studying census data on white-collar and blue-collar workers.

Over the past two summers, student research assistants here at the institute have aided me with my research. Jennifer Durant, Jennifer Doherty, Keith Luter, and Melissa Surawski all worked diligently and skillfully. A special thanks to Mr. Luter and Ms. Surawski for their careful work in deciphering census maps and their aid in creating demographic profiles of New Hampshire's city wards. Lindsay Hanson and Jason Crawford provided some very helpful pinch-hitting in the late innings.

I am blessed with fine colleagues at Saint Anselm College. Dale Kuehne and Paul Manuel, in particular, have been full of enthusiasm and sound advice as I struggled with this book. Donald Cox, Ward Holder, Brother Isaac Murphy, O.S.B., and Beth Salerno made the tasks of research much less solitary and much more fun. Lorie Cochran consistently made day-to-day business easier.

I have worked hard over the past four years to become the second-most knowledgeable person on New Hampshire politics here at Saint Anselm. I am fortunate to have the most knowledgeable person, Michael Dupre of the Sociology Department, as my colleague and friend.

Several of my colleagues in the study of presidential nomination politics were kind enough to read various drafts of my work. To Emmett Buell, Rhodes Cook, Bill Mayer, Patricia Southwell, and Constantine Spiliotes, I say thanks.

David Pervin, my editor at Palgrave Macmillan, has done a hundred things to improve this book, and a lot more of which I am blissfully unaware. He also has shown exceptional patience to a rookie author.

I share with Henry Olsen of the Manhattan Institute a love of baseball, American politics, and the numbers that help us understand them better. This book was born out of countless e-mails between us. Again and again, Henry's dictum, "Why guess when you can look it up?" has driven my research forward, and for that he has my thanks and continued friendship.

Finally, my wife, Julie Alig, continued her uncanny knack of assuring me I could do something when all evidence pointed in the opposite direction. For that and much more, she has, as always, my love. Our son, William Hector, was born during the final stages of this book and has thus far refrained from comment on it.

CHAPTER ONE

New Hampshire and the Presidency

In January 1999, one year before Democratic voters began choosing their party's nominee for the highest office in the land, the long-range forecast for Vice President Al Gore's presidential campaign was clear, sunny skies. Up in New Hampshire, the home of the first-in-the-nation presidential primary, all the signs pointed toward good weather: Gore possessed the backing of party regulars both nationally and in New Hampshire, most notably the support of Governor Jeanne Shaheen, the top Democratic office-holder. He enjoyed all the privileges and prerogatives of the vice presidency, including a widespread network of fund-raisers. And despite the scandals of the Clinton administration, Gore could claim to be the steward of eight years of peace and prosperity. And surely Democrats held Gore, the number-two man on a ticket that had returned their party to the White House, in a special place in their hearts.

No leading member of the Democratic Party seemed interested in mustering a challenge to Gore. The only blip on the long-range radar screen was the seemingly quixotic campaign of a retired Democratic senator from New Jersey: Bill Bradley, a three-term U.S. senator best known for his professional basketball career as a New York Knickerbocker and his mastery of arcane subjects such as federal tax policy. Often mentioned as a possible contender for the presidency, Bradley had weathered a close call in his 1990 run for a third term as senator and later decided against running for a fourth term in 1996, declaring that politics was "broken."

Back in January 1999, the Bradley challenge to the Gore campaign seemed like little more than a snow squall in New Hampshire. One of the few who saw something more dangerous was a veteran stormwatcher, Joseph Keefe, chair of the state Democratic Party during the mid-1990s and former candidate for the First Congressional District. Keefe, a Gore supporter, was sizing up the opponent, and he was wary of what he saw. In a January 29 memo, Keefe detailed to Gore campaign operatives his concerns:

> . . . the dynamic of this race has changed dramatically of late, with the thinning of the field to two candidates and Bill Bradley's maiden voyage (as an announced candidate) to NH. Bradley is signing people up—even people who have been Clinton/Gore loyalists. While I am not sounding a note of panic, neither do I want to underestimate the significance of what is going on.[1]

Keefe then offered his assessment of the early buzz surrounding Bradley's candidacy: Bradley was both "fairly well known" for a presidential candidate and "seen as cerebral and independent." He "generally strikes people as an interesting and likable figure," especially within the Democratic party establishment. While most voters still did not know much about Bradley, this relative anonymity only piqued their curiosity. In contrast, while Gore had visited New Hampshire frequently, "I honestly don't think we can say that there is as much interest in the Vice President—a known commodity in many respects—as there is in Bradley right now."

Furthermore, Keefe added, Bradley was on the move in New Hampshire and apparently making inroads:

> Bradley is also campaigning. This wasn't a testing the waters trip. He was putting the hard sell on activists, one on one (so to speak), and was directly asking for their support. We should realize that his ability to come up here and do that—while the Vice President is hampered by the exigencies of office, the

immobility of having to travel with an entourage on Air Force Two, the legalities associated with official visits to NH, where it is difficult to do politics and people cannot be asked directly for their support, etc.—gives Bradley certain advantages over us at the present juncture. Essentially, he is campaigning and we're not.[2]

Bradley's early moves in a game that would last a full year, had already changed the dynamics of the contest, Keefe advised. Previously, the Gore campaign had planned to set up shop in New Hampshire in May 1999—an ample eight months before the primary—and begin a full-blown campaign in September. That plan needed to be scrapped, said Keefe: "It was in our interest to have the campaign start as late as possible. Unfortunately, we would no longer be right if we continued to adhere to this strategy. We no longer control (unilaterally at least) the pace of the race."[3]

Bradley the retired basketball star doubtless would have appreciated Keefe's point that the team that dictates the pace of the game can often overcome other weaknesses. The ability of an underdog to turn the tables on a stronger foe and start to dictate the rhythm of the campaign is at the core of the strange political alchemy of the New Hampshire primary.

Seven months later, just after Labor Day, the Bradley squall had grown into a major nor'easter, and Keefe was writing another memo to the Gore campaign leadership. Two separate polls had indicated that Bradley was running even with Gore in New Hampshire, and the buzz surrounding the challenger had reached the ears of the Washington, D.C.–based national political media. But Keefe's ears had long been attuned to the sound and fury of the Bradley campaign, and he did his best to cut through the noise for the benefit of Gore's operatives. The fact that Bradley had risen so far, so fast actually held some good news for the reeling campaign of the vice president. Along with the spiking poll numbers came rising expectations for the challenger: "now [Bradley] almost has to win or he could be in trouble," Keefe observed.[4] Still, the polls signaled the day of reckoning for the Gore campaign's underestimation of the Bradley threat. "I have never felt that the Gore campaign has taken Bradley as seriously as he should be taken," Keefe wrote. "I can tell you, however, that from the beginning he was taken seriously in New Hampshire. People were curious about him. They wanted to meet him. They like his message—what little of it there is—because it's a little offbeat but serious; a thoughtful, as opposed to an impassioned, insurgency but an insurgency just the same."[5]

Time and time again, insurgency has been the watchword for the modern New Hampshire Democratic presidential primary. The key question in primary after primary has been not "Who's ahead?" but rather "Who's coming from behind?" This is because New Hampshire, time and time again, has been the best, often the last, chance for the "outs" in the Democratic Party to challenge the "ins" for the grand prize of the presidential nomination. As Keefe put it in his January 1999 memo: "The history of the NH Primary, at least on the Democratic side, demonstrates a bias in favor of the insurgent candidacies of perceived outsiders/underdogs . . . challenging the party and political establishments."[6]

By February 1, the day of the 2000 New Hampshire primary, expectations for Gore's campaign had been so battered by the Bradley storm that the national media hailed the four-point margin of victory as a significant success for the vice president. The insurgent came just a few thousand votes short of the upset, winning 47 percent of the vote. Ad hoc explanations were plentiful for the potency of the Bradley insurgency in New Hampshire: deep ambivalence and "Clinton fatigue" among the Democratic faithful; an initially clumsy, bureaucratic Gore campaign; Bradley's assiduous wooing of primary voters through time-honored New Hampshire methods of personal campaigning such as town-hall meetings; and the stereotypical quirkiness of the New Hampshire primary voter. All those factors indeed may have influenced the strength and duration of the Bradley storm that reached its peak in New Hampshire and dissipated weeks later. They do not, however, explain the presence of the Bradley storm itself, especially when one notices the presence of similar political patterns over New Hampshire in previous primary years. Time and again, two major factions in the Democratic Party, traditional working-class voters and reform-minded elites, have clashed in the Granite State. And every four years, pundits and political observers express surprise over the political storms that occur when those two fronts collide. But there is always a quite predictable chance of politically stormy weather in this notoriously unconventional first-in-the-nation primary state. Time and again, candidates have planned campaign strategies and tactics—

from debates over campaign messages, to efforts at the grassroots level, to GOTV (get out the vote) efforts—in the hopes of riding a New Hampshire storm and gaining momentum that would translate into their party's nomination.

New Hampshire and the Changing Presidential Nomination System

The fact that candidates for the highest office in the land must pass muster with the residents of New Hampshire, a small New England state, is one of the greatest eccentricities of the American electoral calendar. This eccentricity is embraced by those who consider New Hampshire the last bastion of grassroots politics in the presidential selection process, a place where a politician seeking the highest office in the land must look a voter in the eye, shake hands, and answer questions on a one-to-one basis. Critics dismiss the New Hampshire primary as an annoying appendix to the presidential nomination process, a model of grassroots democracy now much more myth than reality. They charge that the primary gives vastly disproportionate influence to a relatively small group of voters who are unrepresentative of the national electorate, pointing to the Granite State's peculiarly libertarian brand of conservatism, its aversion to taxes, and its homogeneous, white population.

That such a small state came to play such a large role in choosing major-party nominees for president—and thus a significant role in choosing the next occupant of the White House—is a uniquely American story of the idiosyncrasies of local politics mixing with national trends to produce an unforeseen development. When the state's political elites scheduled the presidential primary to coincide with Town Meeting Day in March,[7] they did so in order to save the money and trouble of holding two separate events. Not in their wildest dreams did the frugal Yankees realize that they were gaining squatter's rights to the most valuable real estate in presidential nomination politics.

For all its rich tradition and considerable attention, the New Hampshire presidential primary is a relatively recent development. Indeed, presidential primaries based on the idea that rank-and-file members of political parties, rather than party leaders, should be the ones to choose nominees for political office is a fairly new wrinkle in American politics. Over the past two hundred years, America's political parties have lurched in fits and starts toward democratization in choosing a presidential nominee.[8]

The first party mechanism for nominating a presidential candidate was the caucus. The fight between Federalists and Republicans, the first political parties in the United States, for control of the national government in 1796 gave each great incentive to unify their members behind a single candidate for the presidency; they also had to settle the question of who within the party would hold the power of choosing a nominee. The party elites faced a dilemma that would arise again and again throughout the history of the nomination process: how to keep control of the nomination process while ensuring the unity and enthusiasm of the party faithful for the nominee.

The first solution to this problem came from the Republicans, the party of Jefferson, and it handed over the power of nomination to a select few. From 1800 to 1824, Republican members of Congress met or caucused every four years to choose the party's candidate for president. During this period, the Republicans' main opponent, the Federalist Party, fell to the status of a regional party and no longer presented a viable challenge. With reduced incentive to combine forces against a common foe, the Republicans began to fight among themselves. In the face of factional bickering between the once-dominant Virginia wing of the party and the emerging power in New York and Pennsylvania, the Republicans' congressional caucus was doomed to impotence. Leading up to the 1824 elections, the Republican Party, rather than unifying behind the candidate nominated by the caucus, Secretary of the Treasury William Crawford of Georgia, splintered as other Republican presidential nominees emerged to challenge him. Secretary of State John Quincy Adams of Massachusetts, Speaker of the House Henry Clay of Kentucky, and military hero Senator Andrew Jackson of Tennessee all ran campaigns with the backing of the nomination of their own state legislatures. With multiple candidates running in the general election, Jackson won a plurality of the popular vote, but no candidate emerged with a majority of the votes in the electoral college. The decision, for the only time in American history, went to the House of Representatives, where Adams won the day—to the howls of Jackson's infuriated supporters.

Soon after, Jackson began a successful effort to unseat Adams in 1828. Jackson's supporters, the nucleus of the modern Democratic Party, created a new method to choose presidential candidates, a convention designed to provide for input from all corners of the party, not just the Washington elite. The convention, first held in 1840, simultaneously centralized and decentralized presidential politics. On one hand, the emergence of a presidential nominee from the convention ensured that there would be a clear, national standard-bearer who took his mandate from the party base. But that mandate was generated through a decentralized process that took into account the preferences of local politicians, the electability of candidates, and the sectional balance of tickets, which would be important as the divisions between the North and the South increased.

The real centers of power at the convention, as in the political party itself, were state and local party organizations. Parties allocated a certain number of delegates to the states based on each state's number of voters and the corresponding number of votes it held in the electoral college. Power flowed upward, from local or state party meetings (caucuses) and local conventions, to state conventions, and ultimately to the national convention. Delegates either were chosen by caucuses or were appointed by the governor or a state party leader. The procedure for selecting delegates varied significantly from state to state: Some state parties opted for a relatively open process, while in others the party bosses ensured that they would dole out delegate privileges.

Delegates to the convention were chosen based on their representing the interests of their state, or at least its political leaders, and not because they favored a particular candidate. In theory, they enjoyed some independence of judgment when it came to selecting a nominee. In practice, state party leaders kept a tight leash on the discretion of their delegates and used them as bargaining chips in sessions with other party chieftains from other states. The Democratic Party provided that the state parties had a formal right to bind their delegates to a particular choice of nominee.

Those choices often were made in the infamous smoke-filled back rooms of the convention, where party leaders negotiated which candidate would be most likely to win the election and to protect their interests—not always the same thing. Negotiations over the nomination were often long and convoluted, and while party bosses wheeled and dealed behind the scenes, delegates voted again and again on the convention floor. Vote trading and other complex machinations were customary features of conventions. The Democratic convention became the butt of jokes in 1924 when delegates took 103 ballots (and two weeks) to choose a nominee. "A second-hand convention is one of the hardest things to get rid of in the world," the humorist Will Rogers quipped.

New Hampshire and the Presidential Primary

By the end of the nineteenth century, however, familiarity with the party bosses' machinations and machines had bred contempt among reformers. Progressive Era critics of the presidential nomination system charged that the process was corrupt and closed to the influence of the public, with the result that party spirit—a polite reference to the interests of party leaders—had triumphed over the political principle of democratic choice resting on the voice of the people. The reformers argued that the conventions had resulted in mediocre candidates and thus the people's choice was being constrained and indeed manipulated. Reformers proposed bypassing the bosses and giving the choice of presidential nominees to the people via the use of direct primaries, in which voters would cast ballots for the candidates of their choice. Wisconsin, led by progressive Governor Robert LaFollette, was a trailblazer in this movement, passing a direct primary law in 1905. By 1916, twenty-five states had adopted presidential primaries.

Among these states was New Hampshire, whose movement to a primary system was motivated by local concerns. During the first decade of the twentieth century, reformers battled to open up the political system to popular control and were opposed by the Republican Party establishment and its corporate ally, the Boston and Maine (B & M) Railroad, which maintained control over the Republican Party by means of the state party convention. At the 1906 state convention, for instance, party delegates were quite willing to trade, sell, or exchange their voting power in return for various forms of remuneration from the party machine. Public outcry led to the end of such "proxy" voting and the creation of an open primary for the 1910 state election, in which rank-and-file members of the party could cast their ballots for their choice of nominee.[9]

New Hampshire's Democrats, who took advantage of a split between progressive and establishment Republicans to gain control of the state government in 1913, expanded the primary system to include popular election of delegates to the national party conventions. The primary date was at first slated for the third Tuesday in May 1916, but was moved up to the second Tuesday in March, to coincide with Town Meeting Day on which residents of New Hampshire hamlets decided local issues by direct democracy.[10] In 1916, the Granite State held the second-in-the-nation primary behind Indiana, a status it shared with Minnesota. New Hampshire took first place in 1920, when Indiana moved its date to May and Minnesota discarded its primary. Thus, through an accident of local convenience, New Hampshire became the state with the first primary.

The end result of Progressive Era reforms to the nomination process was a mixed bag. As late as 1920, only one-third of the states employed primaries as their mode of selection. Most delegates arriving at the convention were not bound to vote for any nominee, and state and local party organizations maintained their power to engage in back-room deals. Since the nomination was decided only at the convention, the final selection of a presidential nominee remained in the hands of political leaders rather than rank-and-file party members.

The importance of presidential primaries was thus based less on the number of delegates a candidate won and more on the aura of electability that a primary victor would gain in the eyes of the party bosses. This was true as late as 1960, when both John F. Kennedy and Hubert Humphrey saw primaries in Wisconsin and West Virginia as opportunities to win over skeptical party leaders from various states. Theodore H. White, in the classic *The Making of the President 1960,* captured the limited role of primaries when he wrote that Kennedy and Humphrey realized "if they could not at the primaries prove their strength in the hearts of Americans, the Party bosses would cut their hearts out in the back rooms of Los Angeles," where the convention was held. White highlighted that the candidates then, as now, had to craft a message meant to appeal to various constituencies: "first, the folksy audience of the primary state to be won directly, along with the local delegates that could be harvested in the primary victory (this, of course, was the least of their considerations); next, the national audience, as the nation first paid its attention to the combat and assessed the men; and, last, there were the bosses of the big Eastern states and the smaller organized states who would coldly watch the race to observe the performance of political horseflesh."[11]

If the aura of electability was of central importance on primary performance, doing well in New Hampshire, the first primary, took on added importance: A candidate doing better than expected immediately gained publicity, and perhaps even credibility. This was apparent in 1952, for example, the first time in New Hampshire that primary voters voted for a candidate listed on the ballot, rather than, as previously, a local delegate who might or might not be committed to a particular candidate.[12]

A freshman senator from Tennessee, Estes Kefauver, smelled an opportunity in the Yankee North. Kefauver, who had been running against entrenched power since his first campaign against a machine-backed state senator, had gained national attention as chairman of the Senate Special Committee to Investigate Interstate Crime. The committee's nationally televised hearings in 1950 and 1951 "became the most discussed topic in the country, and to millions the crime committee members became overnight celebrities."[13] The hearings also made Kefauver a marked man in the eyes of party regulars, who labeled him a maverick disloyal to his party.[14] Armed with his newfound notoriety, Kefauver declared his intentions to seek the support of the Democratic voters of New Hampshire for their party's presidential nomination.

The incumbent Democratic president, Harry Truman, was less than impressed with Kefauver's challenge, let alone with the primary itself. At a White House press conference in January 1952, Truman said, "all these primaries are just eyewash when the convention meets, as you will find out."[15] The president's remarks, predictably enough, provoked the ire of fiercely independent New Hampshire residents. The mood was summed up by the *Keene Sentinel* in Cheshire County, New Hampshire:

> The primaries are indeed eyewash. They are meant to clear the eyes of the delegates of the trash thrown in them by professional convention-rousers. They rest the bloodshot eyes of delegates who have been subjected to the pressures of machine politicians and allow them to see more clearly. . . . It's time the

voters, not the smoke-filled rooms of convention halls, decided who was to get the nomination.[16]

Confident of his support among party leaders, not least because he was the product of the party machine in Missouri, Truman almost withdrew his name from the New Hampshire ballot. He was dissuaded from doing so by the national party chairman, who thought a win in New Hampshire would bolster the flagging administration.[17]

The ensuing campaign established what became a classic model of a New Hampshire presidential primary: a grassroots insurgency pitted against an establishment candidate supported by party regulars. To be sure, in 1952 the state Democratic Party was a weak minority in decline, having recently lost races for governor, U.S. senator, and both of the state's seats in the House of Representatives. What there was of party organization, however, was squarely behind Truman; the party leadership wanted to keep a lock on coveted spots in the delegation to the convention, as well as on the role of national committeeman to the party. All in all, the slate of people on the ballot as delegates committed to Truman was far more prominent than the names committed to his challenger.[18] Kefauver countered the opposition of the state party leadership with the force of his own personality and a break from tradition—rather than waiting for the party to come to him with the nomination, he went to the New Hampshire party faithful to ask for their support. One prominent Cheshire County Democrat, Pat Russell, recalled a Kefauver visit to the southwest corner of the state:

> probably a hundred people came to see him. . . . I was very impressed with him. Number one, he looked you right in the eye when he was talking to you . . . he went up to every single person in the hall, introduced himself, asked their name . . . came back to the beginning of the line and said, "it's really nice to have met you, Pat" . . . to remember somebody's name, which he did, all around the hall . . . I was certainly impressed.[19]

Turnout at such events was sometimes less than inspiring: An event in the city of Keene drew only 30 people, another in Claremont, just 60.[20] Nonetheless, after each meet-and-greet, the Kefauver campaign gathered the names of people the senator had met, and Kefauver's traveling secretary mailed each of the senator's new acquaintances "a friendly note signed 'Estes.'" This early example of grassroots campaigning generated attention and gained support for Kefauver.

The campaign for the incumbent president, in contrast, was a lackluster affair, a fatal combination of indifference and overconfidence. Problems started with Truman himself, who was at best ambivalent about the campaign: "The attempt to arouse interest in an absent and reluctant candidate . . . seemed to be ill-fated from the start," noted William Dunfey, a longtime state party leader, in his history of the state Democratic Party.[21] Three weeks before the primary, Democratic National Committeeman Emmett Kelley declared that state Democratic leaders "will leave no stone unturned to guarantee a victory for President Truman." Political experts forecasted a Truman triumph. But Truman's campaign in the Granite State only got off the ground in the last ten days prior to the day of the primary, with a headquarters in Manchester, a phone bank, distribution of leaflets, and political leaders coming to speak in support of the president's reelection.[22] On Town Meeting Day, March 11, Kefauver cruised to a relatively easy victory, with 54.6 percent of the vote; his slate of delegates to the national party convention also triumphed in a clean sweep.[23]

That Kefauver won so convincingly actually worked against him under the "mixed system" of presidential nominations, which weighed the opinions of party elites more heavily than the votes of the party rank-and-file. Myrtle McIntyre, a leading supporter of Kefauver, recalled that the senator "actually was quite upset the night that he was winning the primary against Truman. He didn't want to win—he wanted to make a darn good showing. But he won and when he did that got all the pols nationwide mad at him."[24]

Kefauver's worries were justified. Truman's announcement a few weeks after New Hampshire that he would not seek reelection did not automatically make Kefauver the party's heir apparent—quite the contrary. Even after his victories in New Hampshire and most of the other primaries held prior to the convention, the insurgent senator had only about 40 percent of the 616 delegates he required to secure the nomination. At the national convention, Kefauver led all other candidates on the first ballot with 340 votes but never came close to securing a majority of delegates. As his campaign sputtered, the candidacy of Adlai

Stevenson, the governor of Illinois, gained momentum among the party's leadership, winning the nomination on the third ballot. Stevenson had not entered a single primary, but he had more important factors in his favor than Kefauver: a reputation as a centrist; the approval of labor; acceptance by the southern wing of the party; solid links with the party leadership on the East Coast; and perhaps most of all, the personal seal of approval of Truman himself.[25]

Kefauver's run as an insurgent and his appeal in New Hampshire was prototypical, even though his campaign was derailed by the rules of the nomination process favoring the party bosses. No other insurgents emerged among the Democrats, however, for more than a decade. In 1960, John Kennedy convinced party bosses that he was a viable candidate by entering selected primaries, especially in Protestant West Virginia. In 1964, Lyndon Johnson faced no opposition within the party after succeeding the assassinated Kennedy in November 1963. It would take the contentious, virulent, and ultimately violent presidential season of 1968 to break open the presidential nomination process. The 1968 primaries illuminated all the weaknesses of the mixed system of presidential nominations in which a candidate generated significant support but was denied the nomination. The 1968 insurgent, Senator Eugene McCarthy of Minnesota, like Kefauver before him, was unable to capitalize on his success in the primaries. The discontent resulted in new rules, more democratic in character, and in the emergence of New Hampshire as a key battlefield in the presidential nomination process.

In 1968, at the height of the Vietnam War, McCarthy aimed to show strength among the Democratic Party by entering selected primaries in specific states; New Hampshire was not on the initial target list. For McCarthy, Massachusetts, Wisconsin, Nebraska, Oregon, and California all appeared to be better opportunities to make a mark than the Granite State, which was perceived as hawkish and so reliant on military spending at the Portsmouth Naval Yard and Pease Air Base that "any anti-Vietnam crusade could be construed by many of the state's workers as a threat to job security."[26]

But New Hampshire activists supporting his candidacy suggested that virtue could be made of the difficulties the state presented to the insurgent: Given that expectations were so low for McCarthy in New Hampshire—President Lyndon Johnson's political team had already said McCarthy could carry no more than

10 percent of the vote—even a relatively poor performance would boost the campaign, and a victory would have "major national repercussions."[27]

McCarthy took the counsel of the local activists. Meanwhile Johnson, confident of the advantages of incumbency and of the support of the party bosses, abided by the traditional axiom that an early declaration of candidacy was a sign of weakness. Thus, Johnson's name did not appear on the ballot, nor did he make any personal appearances in the state; instead, he had his campaign team stage a write-in campaign, as had been done in the 1964 primary.[28] On primary day, March 12, McCarthy indeed showed much better than expected, and his 8 percent loss to the incumbent president helped jump start his campaign. McCarthy's strong showing was trumpeted nationally as a severe blow to Johnson. By the end of March, Johnson announced he would not seek a second term.

McCarthy's success and Johnson's surprise departure was an earthquake that radically reshaped the contours of the race for the Democratic nomination, and the McCarthy campaign was not the better for it. Johnson's vice president, Hubert Humphrey, entered the race for the nomination as the new candidate of the party establishment. With the race now wide open, Senator Robert Kennedy of New York joined in, positioning himself as the insurgent, thus competing for the same constituency as McCarthy; just moments after declaring victory in the California primary, he was assassinated. Humphrey did not run in any contested primaries, instead relying successfully on the power of party bosses to get him enough delegates to win the nomination. And like Kefauver before him, McCarthy found that his primary victories ultimately held little value when it came to the prize of the nomination. As the party bosses rallied around Humphrey, those insurgents whose hopes had been raised by McCarthy protested. As Humphrey accepted the nomination in Chicago in the summer of 1968, police battles with antiwar demonstrators outside the convention hall were broadcast around the country.

Cries of foul were plentiful after the nomination of Humphrey, which was declared illegitimate by the New Politics movement, a combination of the left wing of the Democratic Party and the anti–Vietnam War movement. Their main charge was that Humphrey, with the aid of party bosses, had circumvented the will of the rank-and-file members of the Democratic Party by manipulating the rules to the advantage of their favored candidate. In response to these charges, the Democratic Party created a special Commission on Party Structure and Delegate Selection at the convention to reform the nomination process. The commission (eventually called the McGovern-Fraser Commission after Senator George McGovern of South Dakota and Congressman Donald Fraser of Minnesota) reworked the rules for delegate selection in time for the next presidential election cycle in 1972. To pull the teeth of the party bosses and render them powerless to decide the party's presidential nominee, the commission established a series of requirements for state parties to follow if they wanted their delegates to be seated at the next quadrennial national convention—a significant shift from the laissez-faire attitude the national parties had historically taken when it came to the selection of convention delegates. Among the requirements were: a ban on proxy voting in which one party member was allowed to cast a ballot for another; abolition of the unit rule that gave the candidate with the most votes in the state all the delegates of that state; and the end of the practice of automatically making the party elite ex-officio delegates. (The party rethought this matter in 1982, and created a bloc of "superdelegates" composed of officeholders who were not pledged to any candidate, in order to give elected officials more of a voice in the party's nomination process.) All state parties were to establish written rules outlining the delegate selection process explicitly, and all delegates were to be selected in the same calendar year as the national convention. Party meetings were to be held at uniform times and on uniform dates, in easily accessible public places, and with public notice. In sum, to make the presidential nomination process as transparent and democratic as possible, the McGovern-Fraser Commission yanked it out of the insider world of the party bosses and thrust it into the public spotlight. As a result, the nomination now went to the candidate most successful in winning the support of the party activists and ordinary voters who attended primaries and caucuses.[29]

McGovern himself was the first candidate to take advantage of these new rules that undermined the party bosses. In 1972, he successfully upended the candidate with the blessing of the party establishment, Senator Edmund Muskie of Maine. As in 1968, the first events on the nomination calendar, including the New Hampshire primary, played a significant role. In January 1972, McGovern finished a closer-than-expected second to Muskie in the Iowa caucuses[30] and followed up this surprise weeks later with another strong second-place finish to Muskie in New Hampshire, the nation's first primary. After the tottering Muskie campaign collapsed in the Florida primary, McGovern moved from insurgent to legitimate contender and went on to secure his party's nomination in a major rebuff to the party leadership. Once again, New Hampshire had made a great noise completely out of proportion to its size, and its primary was allied with the forces of democracy and reform running wild in the Democratic party machinery.

The glare of the presidential spotlight was not to everyone's liking in New Hampshire. State Representative Jim Splaine, sponsor of state legislation in 1975 and 1999 mandating that New Hampshire remain first, explained that the Granite State's political elite disagreed on the merits of keeping New Hampshire first.[31] Senator Ted Kennedy of Massachusetts was talking of running for the Democratic presidential nomination in 1976, and the idea of a regional New England primary had some support in New Hampshire as a way to support his candidacy. Second, New Hampshire Democrats were wary of another bruising primary battle. The 1968 primary was a "civil war" among the state's Democrats, Splaine said, and 1972 replicated the experience. Democrats who supported rival candidates in those years sometimes did not talk to one another for years afterward. Some of New Hampshire's political elite asked, "Why do we want to do this to ourselves again?" Splaine recalled. One of the strongest arguments for the legislation was the economic windfall the primary brought to the state— estimated, at the time, at $8 million, which spoke volumes in the fiscally conservative state.

While the procedural changes before 1972 had changed the rules of the game in primary politics, concern remained that big money could determine the process by providing such support to a candidate that he or she could overwhelm others without such resources, thereby impairing democracy. In response to the scandals of Watergate, Congress passed a series of new laws meant to wring out the corrupting influence of big money from the campaign system. The Federal Election Campaign Act of 1971, amended in 1974, brought significant changes to campaign finance. Contribution limits were imposed ($1,000 for individuals, $5,000 for political action committees), as well as overall and state-by-state spending limits for candidates who accepted government funding.[32] In an attempt to level the playing field somewhat, federal matching funds were offered to all candidates who met certain minimum requirements.[33] All monies raised and spent by presidential candidates were to be accounted for and disclosed. Again, reformers equated a better, fairer political system with a more transparent, democratic system.[34]

These important, indeed fundamental, changes in the election process generated considerable uncertainty and speculation among political analysts and potential candidates. To be sure, the goal of increased democracy through enhanced power to the people had been met, as had the objective of diminishing the impact of big money. Presumably this would benefit not the party establishment's candidate but instead enhance the opportunities for outsiders. But just as possibly, wide open contests would result in no candidate acquiring a majority of delegates, thus triggering a return to the brokered conventions of old, in which the party leaders put their heads together and emerged from the infamous smoke-filled rooms with a compromise candidate. One thing was for sure: Candidate strategy had to change to adapt to this new environment, although it still was unclear how and to what extent.[35]

The campaign that best understood the implications of the new rules wound up with a large advantage over its rivals. As early as November 1972, Hamilton Jordan wrote a lengthy memo outlining a strategy for Jimmy Carter, then a relatively unknown governor of Georgia considering a run in the 1976 primaries. Hamilton argued that the first part of any strategy was a series of impressive showings in early contests like Iowa and New Hampshire, which would transform the nationally obscure southern governor to a recognized front runner for the Democratic nomination. The second part of Jordan's strategy was proving that Carter's popularity extended outside the South with victories in "medium-size states." Next, Carter had to establish himself as a "major contender" for the nomination in an early contest in a "large industrial and traditionally Democratic" state. And last but not least, Carter had to "demonstrate consistent strength in all primaries entered."[36]

The success of the Carter strategy rested heavily on early success generating momentum to create credibility and exposure. In turn, these could lead to increased support, including financial, from a broad range of people—as was now necessary, given the changes in funding rules. As prominent New

Hampshire Democrat and Carter supporter Bill Shaheen put it later, Carter "really didn't have a lot of money" immediately after New Hampshire, but in the weeks after his win there, "all that publicity, all that momentum, plus all that money" came "pouring in." [37] Carter had become an "anomaly" who made people stop and say, "Whoa! I had better start looking at this guy!" Jimmy Carter's successful run through the gauntlet of the 1976 primaries prompted an assessment of just how much the parties' methods of selecting presidential nominees had changed. In many ways, the basic strategy outlined by Hamilton and pursued with success by Carter became the model for future aspirants to their party's presidential nomination.

Carter's capture of the 1976 Democratic nomination was all the more remarkable given the very small voter base with which he began. Carter won New Hampshire with just 28 percent of the vote, which came mainly from moderate to conservative Democrats. If the other conservative Democrat in the race, Senator Henry "Scoop" Jackson of Washington, had not skipped New Hampshire, Carter might well have lost New Hampshire to Mo Udall, the liberal congressman from Arizona. Whereas prior to the McGovern-Fraser reforms, party bosses tended to settle on a candidate acceptable to various groups within the party, Carter's campaign had shown that it was now equally if not more important for presidential candidates to mobilize factions—groups that use political parties as vehicles to pursue their interests—rather than to build coalitions in order to win the nomination. Factions, argues political scientist Nelson Polsby, allow the perceived needs of citizens to be expressed in one clear voice, and thus are the core atoms of any complex political system. They are the building blocks of political parties, providing them with the loyal support of their members, which adds to the party's mass base. Factions also contribute the ideological underpinnings to party programs, as well as the organizational infrastructure as intermediaries between a party's leaders and its followers. [38]

Coalitions are alliances of factions, coming into existence to pursue interests common to each of the allies. These alliances do not spring from the "natural bedrock interests," but from the allies' calculation of long-term advantage in a complex political world. When no faction is large enough to achieve its goals without assistance, factions have an incentive to cooperate in coalitions. [39] Historically, political parties have performed the task of coalition building, as they are made up of various factions within a bigger or smaller "tent." In the past, strong party organization had the power to ensure unity, or at least to promote compromises and alliances among its members. Absent strong party organization, however, factions are likely to narrowly pursue their self-interest and to regard other groups, even within the same nominal party, as rivals, never as potential allies.[40]

By 1976, the reforms to the presidential nomination process had so severely weakened political parties that the coordination of factions and coalition building behind a single candidate were no longer possible. The nomination process had thus become an unfettered free-for-all, with every candidate and faction for themselves. The candidate had to distinguish himself from his competitors, build organizations, and get more of his supporters out to vote—all while hoping that his rivals wound up competing less successfully for the same share of the vote in another wing of the party and that the targeted factions were sufficient in number to lead either to a majority or at least to a strong showing.[41] In short, absent a unifying party, the electorate was increasingly seen as segments to be added, rather than an undifferentiated whole. Given this view, the presidential nomination process was increasingly becoming wide open, and, once again, New Hampshire was a catalyst for this intraparty anarchy.

New Hampshire and Momentum

Carter's success in the 1976 primary, starting with Iowa and New Hampshire, codified what had been suspected in the wake of the 1968 and 1972 campaigns: New Hampshire was no longer simply a test of strength for front runner and contender, it now *bestowed* strength on candidates who performed well there and fueled the campaign's efforts in subsequent primaries. Furthermore, the energy that New Hampshire provided the fortunate candidate seemed wildly disproportionate to its small electorate and the tiny number of convention delegates it provided to the winner.[42]

The fuel New Hampshire has provided, in a word, is "momentum." Momentum sometimes takes on a mystical, ill-defined quality for observers and participants in a campaign, something akin to "team chemistry" in sports. A losing team is often said to suffer from bad chemistry among its members, but that chemistry magically transforms when the same team has a winning streak. Candidates often claim to have momentum until results at the polls prove otherwise.

The outstanding example of momentum turning a loser into a winner is the 1984 campaign of Senator Gary Hart of Colorado. In the year before the New Hampshire primary, Hart was clearly stuck in the second tier of candidates, struggling to emerge from the shadow of two party heavyweights, former vice president Walter Mondale and the astronaut-turned-politician, Senator John Glenn of Ohio. The outstanding characteristic of Hart's otherwise lackluster national effort was a dedicated cadre of volunteers and operatives in New Hampshire (led by future governor Jeanne Shaheen); indeed, without his New Hampshire organization, it is fair to say that Hart had no national campaign.

The nomination cycle's first contest in Iowa seemingly provided little to cheer Hart's supporters. Hart won 14.8 percent of the vote in the caucuses—roughly 30 points behind Walter Mondale's 44.5 percent. Mondale's supposed main challenger, however, fared even worse: Glenn limped into sixth place in Iowa, carrying just 5.3 percent of the vote.[43] And as a result, Hart's 30-point loss was magically transformed into a victory as the candidates moved on to New Hampshire. Hart shot past Mondale in the week after Iowa to thrash him in New Hampshire; the momentum from that victory set up a battle royal for the nomination that lasted until the final primaries of the season in New Jersey and California.

How did Hart's modest second-place finish in Iowa and victory in New Hampshire yield so much momentum for his campaign? In the fluid, dynamic environment of a presidential nomination contest, argued political scientist John Aldrich,[44] a candidate can gain momentum quickly from the type of short-term electoral success Hart experienced. In the presidential primaries, a candidate's momentum is judged on a weekly, even daily, basis by the answer to a single question: What is the likelihood that the candidate will go on to win the support of a majority of the delegates to the party's national convention and the nomination? A candidate is said to have momentum if that likelihood is on the rise. In the course of the campaign, that likelihood will rise and fall as political handicappers compare a candidate's progress in relation to his competitors and consider what opportunities are left for the candidate to pick up more delegates.[45] According to the handicappers in the 1984 horse race, then, what truly mattered in Iowa was that Hart finished second, regardless of whether he finished 3 points or 30 points behind Mondale. By finishing second, Hart had boosted his likelihood of winning the nomination, and Glenn had severely damaged his chances.[46]

One difficulty with attributing momentum to any candidate, however, is the fact that there is no single, observable measure of the likelihood of a candidate capturing the nomination. Observers, such as the national media, then must resort to surrogate measures of a candidate's strength[47]; in Hart's case, some argue the media may have measured the insurgent's strength rather generously in their desire to cover a competitive race.[48] Media attention along with financial contributions and standings in the polls are the three main measurements of momentum.[49] Often these measures all affect one another in a cyclical manner. A flurry of stories on a candidate boosts name recognition; increased name recognition leads to better standings in the polls; and better showings in the polls prompt more contributors to send funds to the campaign. In the week between Iowa and New Hampshire, Hart enjoyed both the media spotlight and the simultaneous acceleration in the polls, while Mondale was tagged as the tortoise to Hart's hare. At a certain point, the momentum may be seen as ineluctable as the candidate takes on, or is given, an "aura of success."[50]

A candidate gains that aura by exceeding expectations or a series of markers that observers such as the national media lay down as criteria for successful results. The media's expectations are often criticized as arbitrary, especially by those candidates who fail to meet them or feel that the media have been too lenient on their opponents. Expectations, however, do have their roots in a comparison of assumptions about how a candidate will do—based on evidence such as historical precedents, poll standings, results from neighboring states, and the efforts of campaigns—with how a candidate actually does.[51] Expectations and momentum are a zero-sum game: a *better than expected performance* fuels momentum, increasing the candidate's likelihood of winning the nomination while reducing that of the opponent; *performing no better than expectations but no worse* means the candidate remains moving at the same pace toward the nomination, with little advantage for either the candidate or the opponent; *performing worse than expectations* puts the brakes on a candidate's momentum, harming his chances of winning the nomination and advancing those of the opponent.[52]

Momentum can thus be fleeting, an important consideration given that the presidential nomination "process" is really more a series of loosely connected electoral contests held at irregular intervals over a prolonged period of time. Each state has its own peculiarities, its own set of factions and differing proportions of factions, so that momentum created in one primary can be dashed as the successful message employed there backfires in subsequent states.

Momentum can be a valuable addition to the other types of resources that a candidate carries with him into the presidential nomination process.[53] Some of these, such as a candidate's ideological reputation or his inherent abilities as a campaigner, are established prior to the beginning of the campaign. A candidate's liberalism, for example, will aid him in a liberal state but harm him in a conservative one. The availability of vital resources—money, attention from the media, and overall popularity—may depend on the success of the candidate's campaign, such as a strong performance in a competitive primary that attracts media coverage. With all other factors equal, candidates with more resources will do better than candidates with fewer resources, and early success can generate increased resources, such as the backing of donors who prefer to send their donations to perceived winners.[54]

The 1984 nomination cycle confirmed for observers that early primaries like New Hampshire can play a crucial role in affecting the rest of the campaign. An unknown like Hart who does well can suddenly break from the pack while favorites who perform poorly can come up lame. Nothing succeeds like exceeding expectations: Candidates who perform better than expected in one primary are more likely to repeat or improve on that performance in subsequent primaries. In contrast, initial stumbles are highly unlikely to be forgiven: Candidates who perform worse than expected in one event are more likely to repeat their fate and do even worse in subsequent primaries.

New Hampshire's Role in 2004

Making sense of the postreform presidential nomination process has been a frustrating exercise for political scientists and historians. One reason for their difficulties is that new wrinkles in the process emerge every four years; another is the very small number of electoral events they have to study—sixteen in all, eight Democratic and eight Republican, including the elections of 1972, 1976, 1980, 1984, 1988, 1992, 1996, and 2000. The number of cases is still lower when one takes into account elections when an incumbent was involved, such as 1984 and 1996.[55] Nonetheless, amid all the noise and tumult of the process, analysts of the presidential nomination process have discerned the rhythms of the primary season and postulated the relative importance of the New Hampshire primary within the ebb and flow of primary politics. Analyst Rhodes Cook, for example, has divided the nomination process into five stages[56]; in the first two, New Hampshire plays a prominent role.

First Stage: The Exhibition Season

Also referred to as the invisible primary, this is the period that extends from the morning after a general presidential election, until the first contests in Iowa and New Hampshire more than three years later. "The exhibition season is a building and testing period," Cook wrote, "in which candidates are free to fashion campaign themes and to discover which constituencies are receptive to their appeals."[57] Key tasks include fund-raising; the early stages of organization building in various primary states; and seeking the support of key interest groups such as labor unions.[58] Although no votes are cast in the exhibition season, the games played at this time clearly count on the candidate's record.

The ability to raise money is one of the chief benchmarks for a successful campaign during the exhibition season. Conventional political wisdom places the prerequisite amount for a viable primary campaign at roughly $20 million. Candidates with lots of cash on hand have obvious advantages in a nomination campaign, including the capability to pay for staffers, to put advertising on the airwaves, and to garner valuable data from polling. Money alone may not necessarily decide a nomination, but money does make it possible for a candidate to employ certain means that help to secure a victory, such as advance polling.

The task of raising campaign funds, however, has been greatly complicated by the campaign finance reforms of the 1970s. Prior to these reforms, a presidential candidate was able to rely on a small group of wealthy donors to provide invaluable seed money for the initial stages of a campaign. After the reforms, which placed a ceiling of $1,000 on individual donations (now raised to $2,000 for the 2004 election cycle, after the passage of the McCain-Feingold campaign finance reform legislation), reliance on a few fat-cat donors was no longer possible. In order to run a viable campaign, presidential candidates instead have to collect thousands upon thousands of donations, in addition to obtaining matching public funding. Campaigns employ a variety of strategies to accomplish this daunting task.[59] While insurgent ideological candidates can patch together a viable campaign by using direct mail or even 1-800 numbers, candidates who can raise money in thousand-dollar increments, as opposed to hundred-dollar increments, undoubtedly are able to raise large amounts of money more efficiently while still being eligible for matching public financing as well. The ability to raise funds is, in many ways, the first real contest of the nomination season. During the exhibition season prior to the 2000 Republican primary, Lamar Alexander, Elizabeth Dole, and former vice president Dan Quayle closed up their campaigns before a single vote was cast, blaming fund-raising troubles.

Cash on hand is also valuable to an aspiring presidential nominee as an outward sign of a viable campaign during a period of time when such signals are weak and easily distorted. Hard information on how well a campaign is actually doing or how it will do when votes are cast in primaries is hard to come by during the "invisible primary." Inevitably, public opinion polls are taken. Attributing much credence to them is foolhardy, however, given that the respondents to these polls know little and perhaps care even less about the presidential nomination process at such an early stage. Straw polls—essentially political party fund-raisers in which ticket holders are allowed to cast votes for their favorite candidate—are another dubious method of gauging the strength of potential nominees during this period. Given the dearth of real political news, however, such events can take on inflated importance, especially if the news media and major candidates take them seriously. The run-up to the 2000 primaries is a case in point. In August 1999, GOP front runner George W. Bush announced that he would take part in the Iowa Republican Party's August straw poll and do his best to win it. Media attention intensified and the stakes increased for all participants, especially potential challengers to Bush; longtime presidential aspirant Lamar Alexander threw in the towel after finishing sixth.

Much media speculation inevitably focuses on how candidates are doing in the first-in-the-nation primary in New Hampshire. Thus, in addition to fund-raising trips to money centers such as New York and California, New Hampshire's Manchester International Airport is a frequent stop for candidates playing in the exhibition season. One weekend in fall 2002, for instance, Senator John Edwards of North Carolina did no fewer than a dozen events in a three-day tour of the state, beginning with a speech at the state Democratic Party's annual Jefferson-Jackson dinner Friday night in Manchester. The events ranged widely in size and were held all over the state, from the smallest, a coffee with four or five people, to house parties with dozens of people, including one at the home of Peter Burling, leader of the Democratic delegation in the New Hampshire House of Representatives. At one point during Edwards's whirlwind weekend, the van taking the candidate from Claremont to Cornish in western New Hampshire got lost. Edwards's political consultant, Nick Baldick, himself a New Hampshire primary veteran, chalked this up as par for the course: "This is New Hampshire," he said. "There are no signs. People are going to get lost."[60]

For many aspiring presidential candidates, a trip to New Hampshire is indeed similar to an educated business traveler's first voyage to a far-off land. The traveler needs to accomplish a number of things on his first visit. He needs to make acquaintances and discover friends. He needs a base of operations that will run and expand while he is away on business elsewhere. Most of all, though, the traveler needs a guide from among the natives. But how should he choose? Dayton Duncan, veteran New Hampshire activist and author of *Grass Roots,* a book on activists in the 1988 presidential campaign, described the dilemma of finding good advice this way:

> You're a wealthy Englishman going big-game hunting in a foreign country. . . .
> [You] might be very good at firing your big gun. But you're in a foreign country,
> and [depending on] which guides you hire when you arrive, they might lead
> you to where you get a good shot off, or they might lead you to where all you
> get is malaria. And part of it is, before you made your choice of guides, had
> you done some previous work on that, of trying to determine who the guides
> ought to be? Or, do you also just have innate, common sense or innate political
> ability to figure it out?[61]

Answering these questions, Duncan said, is key to this first stage of the New Hampshire primary: the competition among the candidates to lure activists and build an organization. This contest ends by the close of September or early October, months before the primary; by this time, the courtship of activists is mostly complete, and organizations are well along in their setup. Courting activists is more an art than a science, in part because there are as many motivations that draw activists to candidates as there are activists, said Manchester Democratic party chair Ray Buckley:

> Some people just like personal attention. If you're running for president, and you call this person once a week for six months, you've got him. Other people, they want you to be the . . . craziest liberal. Another person, it's because you're on a particular committee in the Senate, and so you did something on an issue, they're attracted on the issue. . . . They happened to have been at an event, and you gave an amazing speech, and you showed charisma, so the person was excited by that. You get this one person in, because they know forty other activists, you happen to get that whole clique.[62]

Unlike the early days of the New Hampshire primary, candidates must now undertake this competition in the media spotlight, knowing that their every move is scrutinized by the political cognoscenti. When the New Hampshire Democratic Party held a fund-raising dinner in February 2003, for instance, the list of presidential candidate attendees made not just the *Manchester Union Leader* but also ABC News.com's "The Note," a daily must-read for the national political elite. American politics today, including media coverage of politics, "lends itself to endless speculation, and gum-chewing, and thumb-sucking about what's going to happen, versus real reporting on what actually is happening," Duncan said. In that type of environment, grassroots campaigning in New Hampshire is important in part because of the image such action conveys to the watching media. "Having that as your backdrop to how you're campaigning is a good backdrop to have. It also saves you from getting a rap going, particularly early on, that you're doing it wrong."

The fact that the New Hampshire primary comes first on the calendar also means that there is an inordinately long period of buildup toward that event.

During the months prior to the day when actual voters cast ballots, Duncan observed, "there's no reality against which to base how well you're doing." During that period of time, early polling and media analysis fill the vacuum:

It's all perception, both in polls and whether Jack Germond thinks you're doing a good job or not, or whether other columnists [do]. . . . You don't know; it's impossible to tell because that's the whole thing—nobody has voted yet. We're the first time that voters actually go to a voting booth and cast their opinion. Up until then, it's all . . . speculation to a certain extent. And it's all analysis freed from any reality.

Much of the campaign that happens prior to October of the year before the New Hampshire primary—about four months before ballots are cast— may have little impact on the final results, Duncan said. Bill Clinton, for example, did not even announce his candidacy for the 1992 presidential nomination until the fall of 1991. But any campaign manager who pursues the strategy of making New Hampshire wait, let alone ignores it, would also have to be up to the task of convincing contributors, whose funding is vital to the campaign after New Hampshire, that the campaign is viable. Duncan imagined such a conversation between a campaign manager and a potential donor: "'Yeah, I know we've got a couple bad columns in the *Washington Post,* and the *New York Times* says that nothing's happening in New Hampshire for our guy. But trust me, we don't need to do that yet.' I don't know anyone that can probably stand it." For a presidential candidate in New Hampshire, grassroots politicking gives a campaign an aura that catches the eye of "the contributor in Los Angeles, and Dallas, and New York City, for whom New Hampshire is this inexplicable, infuriating place," Duncan said. "It's as if you're not a real candidate for president of the United States unless you're doing something in New Hampshire." In order to raise money and to be the national candidate "in that long period in which nothing is happening" except in Iowa, New Hampshire, and inside the circles of party fund-raisers, the better a candidate is perceived to be doing in New Hampshire, the more likely he is "to raise the money that makes you more likely to raise more money, to make you more likely to be presumed as a 'real candidate.'" In contrast, a candidate viewed as poorly funded who is also seen as "hapless in New Hampshire" has few viable options, Duncan said.

Second Stage: The Media Fishbowl

The seemingly interminable exhibition season finally ends in January of the year of the presidential election, when Iowa holds its caucuses and, soon after, New Hampshire its primary.

The Iowa caucuses are both inconclusive and definitive for candidates' fortunes. On one hand, the January caucuses held in precincts across the state do not actually award convention delegates to candidates; this occurs months later at state party conventions. On the other hand, and more important, the Iowa caucuses are "the gateway to a long and complex nomination process, and all players and all observers very much want whatever information they can glean" from the results, however transitory they may be.[63] The media turn their attention from speculation on a candidate's prospects to analysis of the verdict from actual voters: "Iowa results, plus media spin"[64] set the story line for New Hampshire and establish the roles of front runner, lead challenger (or challengers), and the remaining bit players who have the unenviable parts of long shots or also-rans.

For the week between the Iowa caucuses and New Hampshire's first-in-the-nation primary, the attention of the national political media descends on New Hampshire in a deluge. "That week is full of electricity," said Pat Griffin, executive vice president for the advertising firm O'Neil Griffin Bodi and a veteran of several political campaigns. In jest, he compared the last week before the primary to being on the set of *Doctor Zhivago:*

> All these Washington types buy their mukluks . . . to come up once every four years. . . . They come up and say, "My God, where can I get my hair done? Where can I find arugula salad?" . . . Go to [Manchester restaurant] Richard's Bistro at night, they're all at the same places, [saying] "My goodness, can you believe this tundra where these people live?"[65]

The national political media venture into the tundra—at least as far as Manchester and its environs, if not the seacoast or the Connecticut River valley or the North Country—because the people who live there possess something they want dearly: information on how actual voters feel about the presidential candidates. The Iowa caucuses, in which participants have to devote hours of time on a single evening, are usually low-turnout events attended by party faithful, in which strong organizations are often vital to a good showing. The New Hampshire primary, in contrast, turns out a much higher percentage of voters, and candidates must therefore be able to appeal to a variety of constituencies.[66] Iowa and New Hampshire together, plus the media's interpretations of those two contests, winnow the field to a front runner and one or, at most, two or three challengers. Since the modern nomination process was instituted in 1972, no nominee has ever finished out of the money—that is, lower than third place—in either Iowa or New Hampshire.[67]

Thus, while candidates spend increasing amounts of time running for the presidential nomination, their campaigns often falter and disappear before most voters have had a chance to take a good look at them. Even before the 2000 cycle, scholars expressed concern over a so-called rush to judgment on candidates once the business of delegate selection actually begins.[68] As a result of the winnowing effects of Iowa and New Hampshire, many candidates drop out long before the great majority of primary voters have had a chance to express their opinions of them. While the media often attribute these early departures to a supposed failure of the candidate to connect with voters, a more concrete factor is a lack of funds. Given the need for a candidate to raise money from a large number of contributors and the reluctance of most contributors to waste money on a perceived loser, most campaigns must do very well in the first contests because there will be no second chance later in the primary season. Early losers are written off by the press, which cuts off the flow of free media coverage, which makes it increasingly unlikely that they will be able to raise the money necessary to fight another day.

The Breakaway Stage[69]

After the traditional first contests in Iowa and New Hampshire, other state primaries and caucuses ensue in which the great majority of convention delegates are allocated among the candidates still competing. (Roughly four-fifths of the states that choose most of the delegates hold primaries.) The pause between the Iowa and New Hampshire stage and this third stage of the nomination season has become increasingly brief. State parties and state legislatures have tended to move up their contests closer and closer to the front of the primary calendar in pursuit of a piece of the action that Iowa and New Hampshire enjoy by voting first.

In 1976, for example, Jimmy Carter won the New Hampshire primary on February 24. In the month following New Hampshire, only five states held primaries, and just two more held primaries in April. A dozen primaries were held more than three months after New Hampshire, including contests in California, New Jersey, and Ohio as late as June 8. Carter and his operatives assumed, correctly, that Iowa and New Hampshire could slingshot the campaign through subsequent primaries, given the time they would have to capitalize on a strong early showing by gaining media attention and raising money.[70]

Current-day candidates seeking to copy the Carter strategy now face a much steeper hill to climb, even if they fare well in Iowa and New Hampshire. Since 1976, the primary calendar has become increasingly front-loaded. Eight years later, both major parties had divvied up roughly a quarter of their delegates by the middle of March. In 1988, one-third of delegates had been chosen by this point; this was the year of Super Tuesday, when eleven southern or border states held primaries in early March in an attempt to exert regional influence on the nominee. By 1996, supersized states such as New York and California had moved up to March. And in 2000, nomination contests in both parties were essentially finished just five weeks after New Hampshire.[71] On March 7, Al Gore and George W. Bush triumphed in primaries held in states across the country, including California, Georgia, Massachusetts, Maryland, Minnesota, Missouri, and New York. As the 2004 nomination season nears, indications point toward further front-loading of the primary calendar.

The front-loading of the breakaway stage has left the *mop-up stage,* which includes contests held from mid-March to mid-June, increasingly irrelevant. Since 1976, the candidate with the most delegates by mid-March has won the party's nomination.[72] Finally, *conventions,* once the place where nominations were decided among party bosses, have become rubber stamps of the primary process, as well as made-for-television venues where the party presents its message for the general election season.

New Hampshire—Always First, Sometimes Right

Given the number of states crowding in on the first-in-the-nation primary, one might well ask: Has New Hampshire lost its punch? Certainly New Hampshire's reputation for early and accurate prognostication has been called into question. The state's political elite once boasted that New Hampshire was "always first, always right," alluding to the fact that no candidate had been elected president without first weathering a New England winter and emerging victorious in New Hampshire.

The New Hampshire primary may have reached its height of perceived influence during the 1988 presidential nomination season, said New Hampshire secretary of state William Gardner, the official in charge of scheduling and running the primary.[73] In that election season, both eventual nominees, Republican George H. W. Bush and Democrat Michael Dukakis, lost the Iowa caucuses, but then won New Hampshire and eventually the nomination. Since then, candidates twice have been successful in shrugging off a New Hampshire loss and rebounding to win the nomination of their party.

The first blemish on New Hampshire's clean slate appeared in 1992, when Bill Clinton finished second to former Massachusetts senator Paul Tsongas in the Democratic primary yet went on to win his party's nomination and ultimately the presidency. A second mark on New Hampshire's record appeared in 2000, when George W. Bush suffered an 18-point loss to John McCain. That night, at his concession speech at Saint Anselm College in Manchester, he called his defeat a bump in the road and went on to win his party's nomination and the presidency. On the Democratic side, despite a quite well-funded campaign, Bill Bradley was not able to gain any momentum in subsequent primaries after a close New Hampshire contest with Vice President Al Gore.

Scholars still attribute a significant, if not decisive, role to the New Hampshire primary in deciding a party's presidential nominee. In addition, scholars speculate that a shorter, more concentrated primary season may actually increase the potential power of New Hampshire by increasing the possibility of an underdog scoring an early upset, staggering a front runner, and riding his campaign's momentum to the nomination before media and voter scrutiny has a chance to focus.[74]

Other scholars of the presidential nomination process argue that regardless of front-loading, tumultuous primary seasons are things of the past because political parties have long since regained control of the nomination process. While political parties no longer have the same organizational structure as before the reforms of the early 1970s, and party chieftains no longer decide the nominee in the smoke-filled rooms of yore, the "loose networks of office holders, activists, and other committed partisans" who influence or control resources such as funds, expertise, and "credible cues" or endorsements are able to give favored candidates the assistance they need to significantly improve, if not guarantee, their prospects of victory.[75] For all the candidates who have ventured to New Hampshire for the Democratic primary in hopes of unseating the front runner, no candidate has succeeded in duplicating the unexpected successes of Carter or McGovern—although Gary Hart came close to doing so in 1984.[76]

Where does all this leave New Hampshire in 2004? One Granite State political observer, lobbyist and Richard Gephardt supporter James Demers, predicted that the task of winnowing the candidates, traditionally attributed to New Hampshire, will likely take place prior to that primary. "I think we will see candidates announce their intentions of running," Demers said, "and never make it to the New Hampshire primary."[77] Candidates touted as contenders may well drop out as the primary approaches and they struggle to put together the infrastructure of resources and organization needed to run a viable national presidential campaign. Demers argued that as states bunch their primaries, there will be less opportunity for the bump provided by New Hampshire to generate momentum, thus increasing the importance of "the ability to put a national campaign together, and have the ability to raise the resources before the New Hampshire primary takes place, or it just won't happen." "It's no longer the time of Jimmy Carter," said activist Dayton Duncan. A modest campaign cannot focus all its resources on a New Hampshire victory and then move the campaign to the next target, slowly building a presidential campaign. With the front-loading of the primary, "so much happens immediately afterwards," he said.

Nevertheless, New Hampshire remains important in this front-loaded system in two different ways. One, if a candidate wins in New Hampshire, he automatically is one of the candidates to be seriously considered. A lower-funded candidate, without a New Hampshire victory, is finished, Duncan observed. A front-running candidate with heavy funding might be able to withstand a loss in New Hampshire, but if he wins New Hampshire, the nomination is his.

Second, front-loading has done nothing to diminish the importance of New Hampshire, Duncan said, and will not until some candidate makes the daring move to declare (by word or deed) that New Hampshire is in fact unimportant. New Hampshire used to be seen as the predictor of who would win the presidency; but after Bill Clinton and George W. Bush, it is now only *an* indicator of future success—not *the* indicator.

Perhaps one of the reasons New Hampshire has been and remains an indicator is that it is an early testing ground of candidates' organizational skills, charisma, and appeal to the broad range of the relevant electorate. For, notwithstanding its idiosyncrasies—and what state is not idiosyncratic?—New Hampshire's populace is composed of various factions that have their analogues in the rest of the nation. How a candidate crafts a message to appeal to those factions or constituencies in New Hampshire does affect how they will be perceived thereafter. New Hampshire's ability to determine the nomination may be in question; that it is an early indicator of how a candidate plans on running a campaign and the likely chances of the success of that message, however, is not.

CHAPTER TWO

Weather Patterns

The morning of the 2000 New Hampshire primary was a sunny one, but not for Vice President Al Gore and his operatives. Early exit polls showed that Gore had frittered away a lead over his challenger, Bill Bradley, and was trailing the insurgent. A campaign that took months to build suddenly had just hours to redeem itself. To salvage a victory, Gore's multimillion-dollar campaign now depended on decidedly low-tech devices: sound trucks, shoe leather, and knuckles on doors.

For Gore, salvation on primary day would come not from the quietly prosperous bedroom communities of southern New Hampshire. Nor would it emerge from the college towns of Durham and Hanover. Those places by and large belonged to Bill Bradley, who was rolling up a lead among wealthy, educated Democrats and independents. Gore's hopes lay elsewhere, in places that some say belong to New Hampshire's past. The vice president's sound trucks and "pull teams" were hitting the streets of working-class wards in cities such as Manchester, Somersworth, Dover, Berlin, and Nashua. "It wasn't individual voters that we were really pulling out," said Gore's New Hampshire state director, Nick Baldick, "we were pulling out a demographic"—the blue-collar, working-class voters of New Hampshire's Democratic Party.[1] As the January sun set over New Hampshire, the working-class wards carried the afternoon and the primary, and arguably the Democratic presidential nomination for Al Gore.

Ballots cast in the 2000 New Hampshire Democratic presidential primary, by county

County	Ballots cast	Percentage of total vote
Hillsborough	48,936	31.2 %
Rockingham	34,315	21.9
Merrimack	18,468	11.8
Strafford	15,791	10.1
Cheshire	9,960	6.3
Grafton	9,640	6.1
Belknap	6,049	3.9
Sullivan	4,992	3.2
Carroll	4,400	2.8
Coos	4,311	2.7

Rhodes Cook, *United States Presidential Primary Elections, 1968-1996: A Handbook of Election Statistics.* Copyright © Congressional Quarterly Press.

The political storm that brewed during the 2000 New Hampshire primary had its own unique characteristics, but its occurrence should not have come as a surprise. The storm was one of a series of naturally occurring phenomena in New Hampshire Democratic primaries over the past three decades. The battles are memorable: McGovern vs. Muskie in 1972 generated the storm; so did Udall vs. Carter in 1976; Hart vs. Mondale in 1984; Tsongas vs. Clinton in 1992; and Bradley vs. Gore in 2000. And just as meteorologists successfully predict storms when warm fronts and cold fronts collide, so political analysts can predict the likelihood of political insurgencies in New Hampshire primaries because of the presence of two distinct factions within the state's Democratic primary voting population: working-class voters and upscale, educated reformers. These factions tend to have different preferences. Working-class voters focus on bread-and-butter issues such as jobs and economic security while elites are attracted to candidates who buck the establishment, promising to reform the party and move it in new directions. Presidential candidates can attempt to appeal to one faction or another, or they may try to bridge the gap between the two. Any strategy tailored exclusively to New Hampshire voters, however, entails risks in subsequent primaries in states with demographics distinct from those in the first-in-the-nation primary.[2]

Candidates in the 2004 New Hampshire Democratic primary will continue to set sail into stormy weather—and in the absence of a competitive Republican primary, this book focuses on understanding the unique forces that generate Democratic turbulence. Ongoing demographic shifts in the Democratic primary electorate mirror trends statewide and indicate the growth of a significant bloc of elite, reform-minded Democrats and the simultaneous decline in the relative voting power of people from the gritty mill cities, once the hallmark of New Hampshire Democratic politics. Notwithstanding this decline, the interests and concerns of this group of voters remain a force to reckon with, and no candidate can ignore them. These two blocs of voters are the Scylla and Charybdis between which future Democratic contenders in the Granite State must successfully navigate.

A Tour of the Backyard:
The Geography of the New Hampshire Democratic Party

When presidential campaigns arrive in this "small backyard," as activist and author Dayton Duncan put it, its particular quirks and idiosyncrasies, its history and background pose a challenge.[3] Duncan points out that a good and smart candidate who takes the time to understand New Hampshire's peculiarities and fashions a strategy accordingly will do well, but a candidate who confuses the backyard with a backwater is sunk. Crucial to understanding the lay of the land is the history of the Democratic party in New Hampshire.

Storms are so strong in the state's presidential primary in part because the state party that hosts it is so weak: The stronger the state political party, the less likely for disputes and differences to create turmoil. For most of its history, the New Hampshire Democratic Party has been a weak minority party. Further, as one-time party chairman William Dunfey put it, it has been a "malignant

minority," often unable to reconcile its internal conflicts in order to present a
united front against the majority Republicans.[4]

As a result, presidential candidates campaigning in this state have frequently
found themselves playing in a truly open field, albeit one that often resembles a
rugby scrum. In New Hampshire, the Democratic primary has tended to favor
the spoiler and the underdog, in part because the Democratic Party has been the
minority party for so long, Duncan said. The Democrats have never won
consistently so the party hierarchy has typically been weak and poorly developed.
For instance, Duncan pointed out, Democrats rarely have controlled the office
of the governor, whose traditional role is to impose order on the party through
a combination of incentives and punishments for party members. Their highest
elected officials have tended to be minority leaders in the state house and senate,
or perhaps an executive councilor.[5] Without powerful elected officials to impose
discipline on the party, Duncan said, it is more open to "maverick runs" during
presidential primary years. By contrast, the Republican primary generally has
been "more royalist," tilted toward coronating the favorite and the front runner,
although John McCain clearly was an exception to this rule in 2000. Since
Republicans have been the majority party in New Hampshire for so long, those
within the party generally have followed a pecking order, moving their way up
the political hierarchy. While Republican primaries tend to confirm the line of
succession, Duncan said, the Democratic primaries resemble more of an "open
brawl."

Historically, the key split in the state Democratic party has been between
city and town. This division has overlapped with conflicts between immigrants, largely Irish and French Canadian, in urban industrial areas such as
Manchester and Nashua, and the Protestants who populated the small rural
towns of the state.

The Democrats enjoyed their greatest period of success as a party of the
towns. In the early nineteenth century, this party of "the farmers, backwoods-
men, and laborers" supported Andrew Jackson's presidency and aided Franklin
Pierce, the only American president born in New Hampshire, in his rise to
power.[6] Led by the Concord Clique, a group of party leaders headquartered
in Concord, the state's capital, New Hampshire Democrats maintained
possession of political offices and "took deep root in rural areas of the state."[7]

The golden age of the Democrats ended in the mid-1850s, a casualty of the national conflict over slavery. Pierce and his northern Democratic colleagues had failed to understand "the violent anti-sectional feelings and prejudices that his native New England had developed against the South."[8] Elected president in 1852, Pierce was stigmatized by his appeasement of southern interests and failed to gain renomination from the national party. Back home, New Hampshire Democratic leaders who had supported Pierce's efforts to maintain the Union faced opposition from an alliance of factions that became the foundation of the modern Republican Party.[9] In the 1856 presidential election, New Hampshire broke from the Democratic column and cast its five electoral votes for antislavery Republican candidate John Fremont. Pierce himself was a political exile in his home state, which "refused to honor the memory of its only President" until 1913, when one of the White Mountains was renamed after him.[10]

The 1850s marked the beginning of the state Democrats' exile from power in New Hampshire, an exile that has continued (with brief but significant interruptions) until the current day. The party remained on the outside looking in, despite being the beneficiary of the influx of two major waves of immigration in the nineteenth and early twentieth centuries: first the Irish and then the French Canadians.[11] Many of the Irish gained employment building New Hampshire's network of railroads prior to the Civil War, and later that century many French Canadians went to work in manufacturing, most famously at the Amoskeag Manufacturing Company in Manchester. The mills, casualties of the Great Depression and the migration of the textile industry to the South, remain the defining features of New Hampshire's largest city:

> Even today as one passes the elegant, now silent, brick factories which stretch along the Merrimack River for a mile and a half on one side and a half of a mile on the other, it is easy to imagine smoke rising from its smoke stacks, the hour tolling from its commanding clock tower, and the whistle blowing to announce the end of another twelve-hour work day. As the whirring of thousands of looms is stilled, the gigantic mill yard suddenly fills with thousands of men, women, and children—seventeen thousand in its heyday—pouring out of the gates of the world's largest textile factory.[12]

As a result of immigration and industrialization, the New Hampshire Democratic Party comprised key elements of the New Deal coalition—namely, urban workers and ethnic minorities—that propelled the national Democratic Party to majority status during the Great Depression of the 1930s.[13] Cities with relatively large manufacturing bases—Manchester and Nashua in southern Hillsborough County; Dover, Rochester, and Somersworth toward the seacoast; Claremont and Franklin in the western half of the state; and Berlin up in the North Country—provided the base for a potential Democratic comeback during the New Deal era of the 1930s and the 1940s.[14] But even the national Democratic high tide could not lift the fortunes of New Hampshire Democrats. At the top of the ticket, President Franklin Delano Roosevelt carried this state in three straight general elections, from 1936 to 1944. During this height of national Democratic dominance, New Hampshire Democrats failed to win even one of five gubernatorial elections. "The most fascinating thing about the Democrats of New Hampshire," wrote political scientist Duane Lockard in 1959, "is that a party able to win so many votes year after year is still unable to win elections."[15]

The voter base of the Democratic Party, although numerous, remained divided against itself along lines of ethnicity and religion. As the French-Canadians and the Irish rose to ascendancy in the Democratic Party, they battled both with the predominantly rural old-guard Yankee Protestant leadership and with one another for control of the political organization. As one state party chair put it, "every Democratic primary in New Hampshire is an Irish versus French-Canadian struggle."[16] In 1934, a remark offensive to the French that was wrongly attributed to the Democrats' Irish candidate for governor led to his narrow loss on election day.[17] The continued struggles for control over the party in Hillsborough County in the 1940s led to the "disintegration of the state-wide organization," and as the national party's dominance waned, the New Hampshire Democrats' golden opportunity disappeared.[18] Meanwhile, the party's rural, Protestant base continued to defect to the Republicans. In a history of the state's Democrats written in 1954, Dunfey ruefully concluded that the "paradoxical Yankee-French-Irish triangle" at the heart of the party could win back control of state political offices only under "the most favorable circumstances."[19] All in all, ethnic and religious animosity coupled with a "lack of effective leadership and strong candidates" led to continued frustration for the minority party.[20] After hitting a trough in the 1950s, however, the party enjoyed some important political successes, including the election of moderate to conservative Democrats Thomas McIntyre to the U.S. Senate in 1962 (an office he held until 1980) and John King to the governor's office.

In the last three decades of the twentieth century, New Hampshire enjoyed sharp economic growth, a surge that has slowly but surely transformed the state from one of mill towns and quiet rural life. Journalist Jules Witcover pointed out the shift in his account of the 1976 primary:

> Except for an uncommonly small percentage of blacks, however, New Hampshire is not all that unlike many other states. Contrary to the impression given by picture postcards of snowy covered bridges and white church steeples, the state is heavily industrial, and growing more so each year as plants and blue-collar workers push northward from Boston and the eastern Massachusetts complex. From Manchester and Nashua south and over to the seacoast, where most of the state's population works and lives, New Hampshire hums with the rhythms of machine and manual labor, and with considerable white-collar energy as well.[21]

From 1970 to 1980, New Hampshire's economy was the thirteenth fastest-growing in the nation, and the growth accelerated from 1980 to 1990, when it was the sixth fastest-growing state.[22] Much of this economic growth came from a shift toward nontraditional and high-technology industries such as electronics firms.[23] This growth has led to a corresponding increase in population along with a change in its character. With the movement of industry has come a substantial influx of population, as Massachusetts residents migrated across the state line to the two most adjacent counties, Rockingham and Hillsborough, in southern New Hampshire. Together, these two counties account for 61 percent of the population increase in the state over the past four decades. In addition to the growth along the border, Carroll County and the smaller towns of Merrimack County have also experienced smaller but significant population increases, which are likely explained by the attractiveness of their more rural life setting.[24]

Economic and demographic developments reshaped the state Democratic
Party as well and reinforced the old divisions between town and city in new ways.
Ethnic and religious divisions have slowly faded into memory as migration from
other states and the passing of generations drastically changed the state's
population. The split between rural and urban areas within the Democratic Party
remains, although now the lines of division are along tiers of socioeconomic
status: social class, income, occupation, and education. For the most part, New
Hampshire's manufacturing centers have remained the stronghold of working-
class Democrats, economically liberal but leaning conservative on social issues.
Meanwhile, towns surrounding these cities—the "suburbs" of New Hampshire
as well as once-rural areas undergoing development—have been centers of
another important Democratic constituency: well-educated, prosperous, culturally liberal but friendlier to business than traditional Democrats. Wealthy,
socially conscious people "who would buy an intellectual" as a presidential
candidate make up the left wing of the party, said state senator Lou D'Allesandro,
who represents parts of Manchester and neighboring Goffstown. The left wing
tends to impose a litmus test on politicians, he said, based in part on social and
educational background: "Did you graduate from the right school? Do you have
the right pedigree? After that, do you share my social concerns?"[25]

Within the state Democratic Party, the liberal insurgent candidacies of
Eugene McCarthy in 1968 and George McGovern in 1972 brought many new
people into the party and challenged its establishment, said current state
Democratic Party chair Kathy Sullivan.[26] Since then, liberal Democrats and
centrist Democrats have fought a continuing series of battles for control of the
party. A series of liberal Democratic losses in the 1980s, for example, prompted
moderates to band together to create a forerunner of the state chapter of the
moderate Democratic Leadership Council. Moderate Democrats, such as
Governor Hugh Gallen in the 1970s and Governor Jeanne Shaheen and
Congressman Dick Swett in the 1990s, have enjoyed electoral success—but
at the cost, liberals in the party charge, of abandoning or severely compromis-
ing core Democratic principles. Moderate Democrats, unsurprisingly, disagree
with the liberals' assessment. Democrats in New Hampshire, activist Bill
Shaheen said, are like Republicans in Massachusetts: "You're out of power so
long that you don't know how to lead."[27] As a result, Democrats tend to expect

"too much, too quickly, if you want to stay in power. We look at winning an election as a revolution, rather than an evolution. If we really want to lead, the changes have to be slow because people in general—Democrats, independents, Republicans . . . don't like quick change." The New Hampshire Democratic Party has become more moderate, said Shaheen, because most people want moderate, centrist positions, not extreme ones. Back in the days of McCarthy, the issue dividing liberals from moderates and conservatives was the Vietnam War, Sullivan said. Nowadays, Democrats are not divided on social issues, such as civil rights, equal rights, and social justice, but on economic issues, such as the creation of an income tax in a state that places no broad-based taxes on its citizenry.

Most recently, the division of Democrats between Al Gore and Bill Bradley in the 2000 presidential primary revealed a larger schism going deeper than the personalities or issue positions of the candidates themselves, said Manchester party chair Ray Buckley.[28] Buckley speculated that many of Bradley's supporters may not have known much about the candidate's positions on the issues, but "were just itching to get out from under the moderate leadership" of Bill Clinton, Al Gore, and Governor Jeanne Shaheen. Shaheen, an architect of Gary Hart's primary victory in 1984, won the governor's seat in 1996, the first Democrat to hold the office since Hugh Gallen in almost twenty years. She governed as a moderate Democrat, holding the line against the introduction of a broad-based income tax and refusing to overturn the state's death penalty. While Shaheen held the governor's office for three straight terms, some of the more idealistic, more doctrinaire members of the party felt that she and the party's center were not willing to do enough to support their issues, said Peter Burling, Democratic leader in the state's House of Representatives.[29] New Hampshire liberals' need to promote a more activist, progressive political agenda just "exploded onto Bill Bradley" and propelled his insurgent campaign, Buckley said. "They had been kept to the sideline for so many years, they felt." Later in 2000, the same schism emerged in the primary for state office when state senator Mark Fernald, an advocate of a state income tax, staged a challenge to incumbent Shaheen. When Shaheen ran unsuccessfully against John Sununu for Bob Smith's Senate seat in 2002, Fernald captured the party's nomination for governor but lost badly in the general election to Republican Craig Benson.

The Democratic Presidential Primary:
Candidates, Campaigns, and Outcomes

Candidates in the Democratic primary come to the state with national ambitions that they know will be affected by their performance in the Granite State. The lessons of previous candidates' performances combine with their knowledge, whether great or scant, of the lay of the political land. Any candidate has to choose a strategy to appeal to a highly informed voting population that is in the national spotlight and knows it. That spotlight also means that whatever position the candidate takes to appeal to New Hampshire's voters will receive extensive national exposure. This, in turn, can create a predicament as a candidate tries to balance the need to appeal to New Hampshire voters with the desire not to be seen later as changing, willy-nilly, his platform. Broadly speaking, presidential primary candidates have fallen into one of two camps: the reformers and the establishment.

The Reformers

That reformist candidates see themselves as part of a tradition was made clear in one of Bill Bradley's last campaign advertisements in the Granite State in 2000. Reeling from a 30-point loss in the Iowa caucuses, Bradley's campaign released an ad featuring Niki Tsongas, the widow of 1992 New Hampshire primary winner Paul Tsongas, the late U.S. senator from Massachusetts. The image reflected the reality: Bradley and Tsongas were linked by a number of common traits—both were former U.S. senators from the Northeast, both were Democrats with a reputation for fiscal prudence. Most of all, though, both Bradley and Tsongas displayed the same general theme that connected their candidacies to those of Gary Hart, Paul Simon, Morris Udall, and George McGovern: an elitist, liberal notion of reform. Each candidate had performed well in New Hampshire, and Bradley was hoping that by reminding New Hampshire's Democratic voters that he was in the same mold, he would revive his flagging campaign.

Reformist candidates have distinguished themselves in Democratic presidential contests in two ways. First, reformist candidates for the Democratic presidential nomination have placed themselves outside of the party mainstream by centering their campaign around nontraditional issues for Democrats, issues other than jobs and economic security for working families. One of Bradley's main themes, for example, was campaign finance reform; Tsongas and Simon called for fiscal reform in 1992 and 1988; Gary Hart proclaimed himself the candidate of new ideas in 1984; Morris Udall preached environmental protection in 1976; and George McGovern campaigned against the Vietnam War in 1972.

Second, reformist candidates for the Democratic presidential nomination have attempted to single themselves out by asserting that their party (more specifically, the reigning party leadership) was in need of reform and new direction. In 2000, Bradley's pitch for campaign finance reform was combined with a subtle (and sometimes not-so-subtle) attack on the integrity of Gore and the Clinton administration. In 1992, Tsongas proclaimed the virtues of fiscal responsibility as the way to return Democrats to responsible governance. In 1984, Hart portrayed himself as the catalyst to the renewal of the party and Walter Mondale as the candidate of the doomed status quo in the party. Udall took up the banner of progressivism in 1976. And in 1972, McGovern campaigned under a whole new system of rules, designed to democratize the primary process within his party, which he himself had coauthored in an effort to wrest power away from the traditional Democratic bosses.

Establishment Candidates

In the 2000 primary, Vice President Al Gore represented the other major camp of candidates in New Hampshire presidential primaries. After a shaky start to his campaign for the party nomination, Gore made a dramatic shift in image during the months before the New Hampshire primary, especially after Bradley pulled even with him in early autumn polls in New Hampshire. Shedding his image of a cool-minded, unfeeling technocrat, Gore took on the role of an aggressive populist, a fighter who would do battle for working families. Although Gore often faced the mocking of the national press for his efforts, data from exit polls of New Hampshire Democratic primary voters indicate that the vice president persuaded voters that he would fight for them.

By taking on the role of the populist, Gore joined the series of candidates who have campaigned on similar themes in the Granite State. In 1992, Bill Clinton campaigned on a platform he eventually summed up as "putting people first." In 1988, Richard Gephardt was a fierce proponent of protecting American workers from the ravages of free trade. Labor unions were chief backers of Walter Mondale's 1984 nomination. Jimmy Carter's promise to restore honesty and morality to government appealed to socially conservative working-class Democrats in 1976. And in 1972, the Democratic establishment put all its eggs in what turned out to be the fragile basket of Edmund Muskie's campaign to unify working-class and elite Democrats and defeat the Republican president, Richard Nixon.

Territorial Divides

Battles between reformer candidates and establishment candidates have reinforced the old divides between town Democrats and city Democrats in New Hampshire. Reformer candidates typically have found New Hampshire's towns, particularly those populated by well-educated, upscale Democrats, to be friendly territory for their insurgent movements. In particular, the state's university centers, such as Keene, Durham, and the upper Connecticut River valley, historically have been the base for the left wing of the party, said Burling. Establishment candidates, in contrast, have largely relied on working-class areas for their support, particularly the state's old manufacturing cities, where the socioeconomic status levels of income, education, and occupation tend to be lower. Using census data such as measures of income, education, and occupation, one may generate maps of the state that highlight ten zones, five populated largely by working-class Democrats and five by elite Democrats.[30] Over the last three decades, these zones have expanded or contracted to some degree, but overall they have largely remained stable. These zones have also been remarkably stable in their voting habits in presidential primaries. They are:

Working-class Zones

1. Rochester-Somersworth area.[31]
2. Manchester.[32] The Democrats of this city of 107,000, the largest in the state, traditionally have been more conservative than state Democrats as a whole, observed Joseph McQuaid, editor of the *Manchester Union*

Leader.[33] The blue-collar Catholic Democrats who worked in the mills were pro-union, but even the unions tended to be conservative. Manchester Democrats tend to be more hawkish on matters of national security and take more conservative positions on social issues, according to McQuaid.

3. Southwestern New Hampshire, specifically working-class areas in the westernmost counties of Cheshire and Sullivan, bordering Vermont.[34]

4. Northwestern New Hampshire, specifically working-class areas in Grafton County.[35]

5. The North Country, specifically the mill city of Berlin and neighboring towns such as Gorham.[36] This is one of the last refuges of traditional working-class voters, said Coos County party chair Paul Robitaille.[37] Democrats in this economically ailing region tend to vote along class lines and are wary of candidates who espouse gun control and environmental protection.

Elite Zones

1. Durham, the home of the state university, and the seacoast.[38]

2. Border towns adjacent to Massachusetts.[39] Many Democrats who live in the southern tier of Rockingham County tend to work in Boston, watch Boston television, read the *Boston Globe,* and spend less time in the state and more time commuting in their cars, said former state Democratic Party director Ken Robinson.[40] By and large, they also have lived in New Hampshire for a shorter amount of time than a New Hampshire resident who lives farther north.

3. Western Hillsborough County and Cheshire County.[41]

4. The area surrounding Concord, the state capital.[42]

5. Hanover, home of Dartmouth College, and adjacent towns.[43]

In each of these two zones, voters have behaved in consistent, predictable patterns over the past three decades of presidential primary politics in New Hampshire. Voters from working-class zones have consistently supported mainstream Democrats, candidates who have the blessing of the national and state party establishments, and focus on bread-and-butter issues such as jobs and economic security. In contrast, voters from elite zones have consistently backed insurgent Democrats, candidates who emphasize their desire to change the direction of the party and focus on the theme of reform.

An examination of three primaries (1972, 1984, and 2000) makes this clear. In each of these three primaries, a mainstream Democrat and an insurgent Democrat fought one-on-one battles in New Hampshire:

- *The 1972 Primary:* Senator George McGovern of South Dakota, an architect of the democratizing reforms of the party's presidential nomination process, emerged as the chief challenger to the heavy favorite, Senator Edmund Muskie of Maine.
- *The 1984 Primary:* Senator Gary Hart of Colorado, self-proclaimed candidate of new ideas for the Democratic Party, emerged from the pack of second-tier candidates. He became the alternative to former Vice President Walter Mondale of Minnesota.
- *The 2000 Primary:* A former senator, Bill Bradley of New Jersey, ran as the alternative to the sitting vice president, Al Gore.

And in each of these contests, working-class voters lined up behind the candidate of the party establishment while voters from elite areas took the side of the reformer-insurgent.

In 1972, for example, Muskie won 46 percent of the vote, compared to McGovern's 37 percent. But in the five working-class zones mentioned above, Muskie generally did considerably better than in his statewide performance, and McGovern considerably worse.

Muskie carried all five working-class zones and, in all but one, he achieved a larger margin of victory over McGovern than he did statewide. In Manchester, Muskie managed only a narrow victory over McGovern after weathering a series of attacks by the state's largest newspaper, the *Manchester Union Leader.* In all five working-class zones, McGovern performed worse than he did statewide, mostly far worse.

McGovern fared much better in more upscale areas. In all five elite zones, he did significantly better than he did statewide, ranging from just under 43

TABLE 2.1

1972 New Hampshire Democratic Presidential Primary

	Edmund Muskie	George McGovern	Muskie's Margin of Victory
STATEWIDE	46.4 (%)	37.2 (%)	9.2 (percentage points)
Working-class Zones			
Rochester-Somersworth	61.5	25.6	35.9
Manchester	35.9	32.9	3.0
Southwestern N.H.	57.8	30.6	27.2
Northwestern N.H.	41.3	21.6	19.7
North Country	58.0	27.8	30.2
Elite Zones			
Durham—seacoast	43.2	42.9	0.3
Massachusetts border	49.7	48.1	1.6
W. Hillsborough—Cheshire	32.4	49.6	-17.2
Concord area	39.2	50.5	-11.3
Hanover area	19.8	77.0	-57.2

percent in Durham and the seacoast up to a high of 77 percent in the area of Hanover.

Twelve years later, McGovern's campaign manager, Gary Hart, then a U.S. senator from Colorado, ran another type of insurgent campaign against Mondale, the establishment front runner. Gone were the wedge issues of Vietnam and social liberalism: Hart actually campaigned as a centrist, urging his party to rid itself of its image as a creature of special interests. Nonetheless, in this New Hampshire primary, the same divide between working-class Democrats and elite Democrats emerged.

With the exception of southwestern New Hampshire, Hart tended to do at least slightly worse in the working-class zones than he did statewide while Mondale typically carried a greater percentage of votes in these working-class areas than he did statewide. Hart carried four out of five of these zones, the exception being the North Country. While Hart certainly held his own among New Hampshire's working-class Democrats, he pulled far ahead of his main competitor in the zones where the state's elite Democrats live. In all five of New

TABLE 2.2

1984 New Hampshire Democratic Presidential Primary

	Gary Hart	Walter Mondale	Hart's Margin of Victory
STATEWIDE	37.3 (%)	27.9 (%)	9.4 (percentage points)
Working-class Zones			
Rochester-Somersworth	36.4	35.0	1.4
Manchester	30.9	28.7	2.2
Southwestern N.H.	40.1	32.7	7.4
Northwestern N.H.	33.5	26.4	7.1
North Country	29.9	39.3	-9.4
Elite Zones			
Durham—seacoast	39.9	23.3	16.6
Massachusetts border	56.6	32.0	24.6
W. Hillsborough—Cheshire	39.7	18.9	20.8
Concord area	47.4	17.8	29.6
Hanover area	37.9	22.5	15.4

Hampshire's elite zones, Hart carried a greater percentage of the vote than he did statewide. Hart did only slightly better than his statewide performance in the college areas of Durham and Hanover; in those towns, he split the vote with liberals such as George McGovern and Jesse Jackson. Hart performed best in the communities along the southern Interstate 93 corridor on the Massachusetts border and in the towns around the state capital of Concord in southern Merrimack County. In contrast, Mondale found the elite zones to be unfriendly territory, performing worse than he did statewide in four out of five of them.

Sixteen years later, the contest between Bradley and Gore again took on the same profile as Hart-Mondale and the earlier McGovern-Muskie primaries. Gore, the establishment candidate, found strength among working-class Democrats while the insurgent found the elite zones far more friendly territory. Just like Muskie in 1972 and Mondale in 1984, Gore did far better in the working-class zones of New Hampshire than he did statewide. And just like McGovern in 1972, Bradley's insurgent campaign plummeted among working-class voters; in all five working-class zones, he performed worse than he did statewide, usually more than 10 percentage points worse.

TABLE 2.3

2000 New Hampshire Democratic Presidential Primary

	Al Gore	Bill Bradley	Gore's Margin of Victory
STATEWIDE	49.8 (%)	45.7 (%)	4.1 (percentage points)
Working-class Zones			
Rochester-Somersworth	60.2	31.8	28.4
Manchester	59.8	32.3	27.5
Southwestern N.H.	53.9	34.3	19.6
Northwestern N.H.	49.1	42.0	7.1
North Country	57.2	32.0	25.2
Elite Zones			
Durham—seacoast	43.6	53.1	-9.5
Massachusetts border	47.3	47.8	-0.5
W. Hillsborough—Cheshire	41.8	54.7	-12.9
Concord area	43.2	52.1	-8.9
Hanover area	33.2	63.9	-30.7

In the elite zones, Bradley fared much better, winning all five, just as Hart did sixteen years earlier. He walloped Gore in the Dartmouth College area and won by nearly 10 percentage points in western Hillsborough and Cheshire counties and in the Concord area. Unlike Hart, however, Bradley won in the border towns of Massachusetts by only the smallest of margins and thus was unable to offset his heavy losses in working-class communities.

The 1972, 1984, and 2000 primaries all added to the mystique of New Hampshire and its attraction to underdogs and upsets. The patterns of the three separate storms, however, look remarkably similar. In each case, insurgents McGovern, Hart, and Bradley were quite successful in attracting the voters from elite zones of New Hampshire Democrats, who gravitated toward the anti-establishment candidate calling for reform and change within both the Democratic Party and politics. In two of the three cases, the insurgent was unable to attract many votes from working-class Democrats; in 1972 and again in 2000, working-class Democrats stuck with the establishment candidate, and both times the insurgent fell short of victory in New Hampshire. Hart, the only insurgent who won a majority of working-class zones, was the one underdog who achieved an outright victory over the establishment candidate.

The Elite Score:
Predicting Success from New Hampshire Results

Gary Hart's campaign was an example of a successful attempt to build a coalition candidacy that attracted voters from both key elements in the party. Hart's success at finding favor among both elites and working-class Democrats in New Hampshire has been the exception to the rule, however. Some candidates do well in New Hampshire without coalition building—in particular, candidates who appeal to a constituency possessing a high socioeconomic status (SES), what might be called the elite, do relatively well in New Hampshire and certainly better than expected. However, while the elite strategy might have significant payoffs in New Hampshire, it comes at the cost of appealing to the working-class segment of the population. The more a candidate relied on and appealed to the elite segment of the population, the less likely he would perform well in the remaining primaries. Thus, an insurgent's hopes inflated by success in New Hampshire have time and again deflated when he went on to other primary states. That is, with the exception of McGovern in 1972, *no candidate* whose appeal was disproportionally high among the elite went on to win the party nomination. In contrast, candidates who succeeded in appealing to both elite and working-class Democrats may not have won New Hampshire, but their balanced performance was more likely to augur success in subsequent primaries.

New Hampshire primary voting patterns, then, tell us a good deal about a presidential candidate's potential for success in subsequent nomination contests. Political analyst Rhodes Cook has claimed that results in the Granite State offer a first, often definitive, look at how candidates will do among three constituencies: suburban voters; college towns; and the mill towns where the remnants of New Hampshire's blue-collar population live.[44]

In the following section, I build on Cook's analysis by using Census Bureau data to target towns and city wards in New Hampshire where these three constituencies are most prominent. (For the purpose of this analysis, I have collapsed college-town areas and well-to-do suburbs into "elite communities," as opposed to "working-class communities.") In order to target these specific areas, I examined each town and city ward in New Hampshire for the following indicators of socioeconomic status: percentage of adults with at least a college education, percentage of adults in blue-collar and white-collar occupations, and median family income.[45] Once lists of elite communities and working-class communities were set, the Democratic primary vote results were compiled for both sets of communities. The results offer a comprehensive view of how candidates for the Democratic presidential nomination from 1968 to 2000 did among two important Democratic Party constituencies in New Hampshire.

After the vote totals were listed, a candidate's percentage of the vote in elite communities was divided by a candidate's percentage of the vote in working-class communities. The result is the candidate's "elite score." The principle behind the elite score is a simple, straightforward one: It is not merely the quantity of votes that matters to a candidate but also the source (or sources) of those votes. The meaning of the score is equally straightforward: The closer the candidate's score to 1.00, the better the candidate's potential to build a coalition among the various factions of the Democratic Party. In sum:

- *The higher the candidate's elite score was above 1.00,* the better he did among elite communities compared to his support in working-class communities.

- *The lower the candidate's elite score below 1.00,* the better the candidate fared among working-class communities compared to his support in elite communities.

- *The closer the candidate's elite score was to 1.00,* the more even was the candidate's performance in elite communities and in working-class communities. The candidate who received significant support from both groups displayed the ability to forge a coalition among different factions of the Democratic Party.

Using the elite score, one can observe how voters from elite areas of New Hampshire have eagerly backed one reformer after another in their efforts to buck the Democratic Party establishment. Although the orientation of reform has changed, the enthusiasm of elite voters for reformers has not. In the late 1960s and early 1970s, elite voters provided the backbone of the liberal, anti–Vietnam War candidacies of Eugene McCarthy and George McGovern. In the early 1980s and 1990s, they fueled the efforts of Gary Hart and Paul Tsongas to reinvent the party and lead it back toward the center. And in 2000, many elite voters in New Hampshire defected from incumbent vice president Al Gore and backed challenger Bill Bradley, who promised a departure from eight years of the Clinton-Gore status quo.

The 1968 Primary: Thunder from the Left

As allegedly unrepresentative of the entire nation as the New Hampshire electorate is, its demographics in the 1968 Democratic primary clearly pointed toward the tumult of that extraordinary year. Neither President Lyndon Johnson nor Senator Eugene McCarthy of Minnesota, the two main candidates, came remotely close to achieving a coalition; instead, each candidate tended to gather what votes he could on his side of the cleavage within the party over the Vietnam War.

Johnson's elite score was 0.62, a number that indicates his vote came mainly from working-class areas in New Hampshire. (See Table 2.4.) In those areas, Johnson carried roughly 55 percent of the vote; in elite areas of New Hampshire, Johnson ran far behind McCarthy, winning only 34 percent of the vote. While one has to take into account that Johnson did not campaign in person in New Hampshire, the defections of elite voters to the insurgent cannot be ignored. A comparison of Johnson's elite score to the scores of the other two incumbents who campaigned in New Hampshire (President Jimmy Carter in 1980 and Vice President Al Gore in 2000) indicates the difficulty that Johnson would have had uniting the party had he stayed in the race:

Johnson	0.62
Gore	0.76
Carter	0.91

1968 New Hampshire Democratic Presidential Primary

Total votes cast: 55,470

Candidate	Total Vote	Total %, all votes cast	Elite Vote	Elite %	Working-class Vote	Working-class %	Elite Score
Lyndon Johnson	27,520	49.6	1,949	34.4	13,942	55.2	0.62
Eugene McCarthy	23,269	41.9	3,291	58.1	9,076	35.9	1.62

* N.B.: Percentages in this table and subsequent tables do not add up to 100 because voters cast ballots for minor candidates or candidates of the other party. In 1968, for example, 2,532 registered Democrats cast write-in votes for Republican Richard Nixon.

Support for Eugene McCarthy, whose candidacy was centered around opposition to the American war in Vietnam, was even more skewed toward one faction of the party. With an elite score of 1.62, McCarthy did far better in elite areas than in working-class areas, though he did succeed in narrowly carrying working-class Berlin and Rochester.[46] The media often described McCarthy's campaign as a "children's crusade," referring to the thousands of students who descended on New Hampshire to work for the senator's election.[47] The point of the spear of the McCarthy movement, however, was not the college students, but the well-educated elite. By the spring before the New Hampshire primary, political action groups comprised of religious, academic, and even some business elites were slowly mainstreaming in 1967 what had been "fringe dissent" in 1966.[48]

The 1972 Primary: The Center Does Not Hold

Four years later, New Hampshire saw a virtual replay of the 1968 primary. Once again, a candidate from the left wing of the party captured the hearts and minds of New Hampshire's Democratic elite. Once again, elite voters spurned the choice of the party establishment in favor of the reformer. And once again, the support of the elite was not enough to put that candidate over the top in New Hampshire—but it was enough to establish his status as the alternate when the establishment choice faltered.

This time around, the reformer was Senator George McGovern of South Dakota, who began his campaign in single digits in preliminary straw polls and ended with an unexpectedly respectable 37 percent showing on primary day.[49] McGovern's call for reform was also an indictment of a bankrupt political elite that had led the country into the war in Vietnam, which he termed "a moral and political disaster—a terrible cancer eating away the soul of the nation."[50] McGovern also favored amnesty for those who illegally evaded the draft, took a pro-choice position on abortion, advocated reducing criminal penalties for marijuana use, and supported school integration, even by mandatory busing of students.[51]

In contrast, Senator Edmund Muskie of Maine, Hubert Humphrey's running mate in 1968, was the very model of moderation, a candidate who espoused the "politics of trust" in a speech on the eve of the 1970 midterm elections in opposition to the "politics of fear" of President Richard Nixon and the Republican Party. "I'm a man of the center," Muskie said, "but the center gradually moves left, and it's the Democratic Party that does it."[52] So while Muskie wanted to end American military action in Vietnam and took liberal positions on a variety of issues, including the environment, consumer protection, and national health insurance, the main pillar of his candidacy was his ability to beat Nixon in the fall.[53]

Muskie's campaign planned to showcase his electability by running in every single primary.[54] The strategy derailed in New Hampshire when the "Man from Maine" managed to carry only 46 percent of the vote in the state bordering his own; McGovern finished within 10 points of Muskie, at 37 percent. Muskie's elite score of 0.81, however, indicated that he indeed had far more potential to assemble a coalition of elites and working-class voters than his main competitor. (See table 2.5.) McGovern's elite score of 1.57 indicates that his support in New Hampshire overwhelmingly came from elites. Despite Muskie's problems in Manchester, where *Manchester Union Leader* editor William Loeb had launched a barrage of attacks against him, McGovern still came nowhere close to challenging the front runner among lunch-pail, working-class Democrats. McGovern's play to a specific portion of a highly polarized populace served him well in New Hampshire, and this strategy helped him to fill the vacuum in the contest when Muskie's campaign fell apart in the Florida primary that followed. It cost McGovern—and the Democrats—dearly in the presidential campaign,

1972 New Hampshire Democratic Presidential Primary

Total votes cast: 88,854

Candidate	Total Vote	Total %, all votes cast	Elite Vote	Elite %	Working-class Vote	Working-class %	Elite Score
Edmund Muskie	41,235	46.4	3,844	36.9	17,410	45.4	0.81
George McGovern	33,007	37.2	5,148	49.4	12,055	31.4	1.57
Sam Yorty	5,401	6.1	373	3.6	3,051	8.0	0.45
Wilbur Mills	3,563	4.0	182	1.7	2,352	6.1	0.28

however, as Richard Nixon's landslide was one of the most sweeping in American history.

The 1976 Primary: Carter Breaks from the Pack

By 1976, the Democrats had been out of the White House for eight years. The emotional divisions that had marked the 1972 campaign had diminished with the end of the Vietnam War, and defeat combined with the legacy of Richard Nixon's resignation in the wake of the Watergate scandal created a desire for change and clean hands. With President Gerald Ford appearing vulnerable, the opportunities for the Democrats seemed considerable. Although such an environment might have led the party to consolidate behind one candidate, instead the open field drew six major candidates to New Hampshire seeking to stake a position and gain ground.

From the pack emerged the former governor of Georgia, Jimmy Carter. With a clean reputation and a plainness that spoke of integrity, Carter positioned himself as a counter to the tarnished political class of Washington. No New Hampshire winner has ever done more with less than Jimmy Carter did in 1976. In a crowded field, Carter did not even manage to get three out of ten votes, yet his six-point victory helped to propel him to his party's nomination.

Every campaign talks about getting out their vote, but Carter's campaign in New Hampshire followed this simple motto to the letter. If the field is fairly crowded with contenders, a candidate does not necessarily need the support of multiple groups or factions to win. Facing a host of liberal candidates, Carter's strategy was to position himself as pro-reform, but in a conservative or traditional fashion. Carter was the sole moderate to conservative running in New Hampshire, since Henry "Scoop" Jackson, the conservative Democratic senator from Washington state, had decided to sit out New Hampshire and focus his efforts on later primaries—a tactical mistake that would come back to haunt him. Carter plugged in with blue-collar workers: "the rank-and-file, the shoe shop workers, the working stiffs," said Carter activist Bill Shaheen. He appealed to traditional Democrats who, after Watergate, wanted the country to go back to the normal routine.

With a small but dedicated corps in New Hampshire, Carter's campaign was based not on volume but on both precision targeting of likely Carter voters and frequent, high-quality voter contact, said longtime activist Kathy Rogers, whose first primary campaign was Carter's. Rogers offered one example of a single Carter volunteer who canvassed the towns of Allenstown and Pembroke door-to-door, visiting each voter at least three times. "She was at the polls on election day. They knew her. When they went in to vote, they had to walk by her and know that they'd seen her at their house, they liked her . . . to them, it was her [and not so much Carter]. In a lot of towns, that was the thing."[55]

Carter carried the working-class vote by almost a two-to-one margin over his nearest competitor. (See Table 2.6.) Coming behind Carter was Arizona congressman Morris Udall, whose base of support was the elite, among whom he did substantially better than Carter. This was not enough, however, for him to win the primary, and it bode poorly for his future prospects. A look at the elite score indicates that Carter with a score of .82 was better able to create a coalition than Udall whose score was a lopsided 2.26, indicating his appeal was limited to the elite faction of the party. The only candidate whose score was closer to 1.00 was write-in candidate Hubert Humphrey, with a score of 0.93; Humphrey, however, did not run an active campaign. Coming in third in the primary was Senator Birch Bayh of Indiana, but his score of .74 indicated a lack of appeal among the elite.

Carter's victory was the last hurrah for the blue-collar vote in New Hampshire. He was the last candidate to win an "open primary" (one in which

TABLE 2.6

1976 New Hampshire Democratic Presidential Primary

Total votes cast: 81,525

Candidate	Total Vote	Total %, all votes cast	Elite Vote	Elite %	Working-class Vote	Working-class %	Elite Score
Jimmy Carter	23,373	28.7%	2,970	22.5	9,815	27.6	0.82
Morris Udall	18,710	23.0%	4,127	31.2	4,906	13.8	2.26
Birch Bayh	12,510	15.3%	1,456	11.0	5,259	14.8	0.74
Fred Harris	8,863	10.9%	1,458	11.0	3,114	8.8	1.25
R. Sargent Shriver	6,743	8.3%	712	5.4	2,921	8.2	0.66
Hubert Humphrey	4,296	5.3%	569	4.3	1,643	4.6	0.93

no incumbent was running) while losing in the elite areas of the state. In subsequent primary cycles, New Hampshire's increasing prosperity was the catalyst for an ever-expanding pool of elite voters and a shrinking pool of working-class voters.

The 1980 Democratic Primary: The Incumbent Tested

Traditional wisdom has it that an incumbent president has overwhelming advantages when running for a second term, so serious challengers are unlikely to spend resources in a futile contest that only saps a party's strength going into the presidential campaign. But in the primaries leading to the nomination of the 1980 candidate, Carter was susceptible: The economy was weak, inflation was high, and the hostage crisis in Iran generated discontent and a perception of weak leadership.

As the first testing ground, New Hampshire has often been a rocky ride for incumbents, but its ability, or willingness, to upset the apple cart should not be overstated. Simply put, Democratic incumbents have always managed to hold off insurgencies and claim an actual victory. In 1968, Lyndon Johnson defeated Eugene McCarthy by more than four thousand votes (and eight percentage points). In 2000, Vice President Al Gore held off a strong challenge from Bill

Bradley to win a four-point victory. The 1980 primary is another example of the staying power of the incumbency, here that of President Jimmy Carter coupled with that of Governor Hugh Gallen, elected in 1978 and the first Democratic governor in a decade.

Carter's main opposition in the Democratic primaries was not a reformer but rather an icon of the liberal Democratic establishment, Senator Edward Kennedy of Massachusetts. Kennedy had flirted with running for his party's presidential nomination in the past but had ultimately declined each time. The third candidate in the race was former California governor Jerry Brown, who had posted a late challenge to Carter from the left wing of the party four years earlier.

The incumbent and the icon both showed a broad base of support among New Hampshire Democrats. (See Table 2.7.) Both performed well in garnering support from both the elite and the working class: Carter's elite score was .91, and Kennedy's was an almost perfectly balanced 1.04. Surviving Kennedy's challenge with his coalition intact, Carter reeled off a series of primary victories and won 24 of the 34 primaries held on his way to the nomination.[56] But Carter's weaknesses on the economy and foreign affairs, which the primary races had illustrated, gave an opening to the winning campaign of Republican candidate Ronald Reagan.

The 1984 Primary: New Ideas for New Hampshire

As the Democrats geared up for the primaries leading to the 1984 elections, they found themselves once again out of power. While the recession of 1981-1982 had revived Democratic hopes of defeating President Ronald Reagan, the subsequent recovery had positioned the Republicans as the party presiding over peace and prosperity. Despite the apparently uphill battle against a popular incumbent, the Democratic field of prospective presidential nominees was crowded.

Everything old was new again in the 1984 Democratic primary season. George McGovern, the 1972 presidential nominee, staged a symbolic run for the nomination. Gary Hart, one of McGovern's main campaign operatives in 1972 and now a senator from Colorado, ran as the candidate of "new ideas" and

TABLE 2.7

1980 New Hampshire Democratic Presidential Primary

Total votes cast: 111,595

Candidate	Total Vote	Total %, all votes cast	Elite Vote	Elite %	Working-class Vote	Working-class %	Elite Score
Jimmy Carter	52,648	47.2	7,482	44.2	18,951	48.4	0.91
Edward Kennedy	41,687	37.4	6,239	36.9	13,951	35.6	1.04
Jerry Brown	10,686	9.6	2,024	12.0	2,874	7.3	1.64

standard-bearer for a new breed of Democrats that were already making their mark in Congress: the neoliberals who took more conservative stances on economic issues than the typical Democrat and more liberal positions on cultural ones. In some ways, however, Hart's candidacy was not new at all but simply the latest model in a line of reform-minded insurgents that dated back to Senator Eugene McCarthy in 1968.

If Hart positioned himself as the reform candidate, Walter Mondale, who had been Carter's vice president, was the establishment's candidate. Mondale was a loyal member of the Minnesota Democratic-Farmer-Labor party, had served as his state's attorney general in the early 1960s, and in 1964 was appointed to fill Hubert Humphrey's seat in the U.S. Senate when Humphrey was elected Lyndon Johnson's vice president. Having been a party loyalist, Mondale was sound, stable, and a bit staid while Hart was young, handsome, and energetic. Hart took advantage of a second-place finish to Mondale in the Iowa caucuses and crafted a message well tuned to New Hampshire's well-heeled Democrats, while his grassroots organization (his campaign team included future governor Jeanne Shaheen) and attention from the media as the New Democrat alternative to the conventional front runner generated interest across the board. Mondale, like other Democratic front runners before him, had hoped that his support among the party elite would propel him through the primaries to the nomination as a candidate of sobriety and moderation.

Mondale's hopes for a smooth trip to the nomination, however, literally disappeared in a New Hampshire blizzard. Hart's nine-point victory in New Hampshire was a textbook example of how an under-the-radar primary campaign can quickly gain that mysterious quality known as momentum. In addition, his support was surprisingly well balanced, as indicated by his elite score of 1.20—a score that indicates far more coalition potential than fellow insurgents who performed well in New Hampshire: McGovern, 1.57; Tsongas, 1.80; Bradley, 1.56. While Hart did extremely well among the New Hampshire elite (defeating Mondale almost two to one), he also defeated Mondale among the former vice president's core constituency, winning more of the working-class vote. As Mondale's elite score of 0.69 indicates, his meltdown in New Hampshire was extreme, leaving him with only a depleted core of working-class support. (See Table 2.8.)

"There was a real distinction between the candidates and what they represented," said Hart delegate Susan Calegari, and "there was almost this battle going on for the soul of the party."[57] Mondale represented the old liberal Democratic Party of the New Deal coalition, whose messages were increasingly losing appeal in a New Hampshire that was deindustrializing and gentrifying. Gary Hart, on the other hand, talked about a "new generation of leadership," attracting people not previously involved in politics. He also called for the Democratic Party to take a more moderate path with policies that did not necessarily take into account the desires of each special-interest group in the party. As campaign operative Susan Casey pointed out, Hart was not a candidate who was easy to pigeonhole ideologically; he was, for example, the first Democrat who stood against the war in Vietnam yet advocated a "responsible stand on national defense" that did not automatically rule out additional spending on such expenditures.[58]

Hart's demonstration in New Hampshire that he could form a coalition among elite and working-class voters boded well for his performance in future primaries. Sure enough, Hart battled with Mondale until the very last days of the primary season, finally losing the nomination to the establishment candidate.

The 1988 Primary:
Not All New England Candidates Are Created Equal

Heading into the primary season for the 1988 presidential elections, the Democrats' prospects might have been promising since Ronald Reagan had

TABLE 2.8

1984 New Hampshire Democratic Presidential Primary

Total votes cast: 101,045

Candidate	Total Vote	Total %, all votes cast	Elite Vote	Elite %	Working-class Vote	Working-class %	Elite Score
Gary Hart	37,702	37.3	6,815	40.6	11,090	33.9	1.20
Walter Mondale	28,173	27.9	3,612	21.5	10,193	31.1	0.69
John Glenn	12,088	12.0	1,981	11.8	3,871	11.8	1.00
Jesse Jackson	5,311	5.3	1,064	6.3	1,113	3.4	1.85
George McGovern	5,217	5.2	1,188	7.1	1,005	3.1	2.29
Ernest Hollings	3,583	3.6	664	4.0	1,204	3.7	1.08

served his two terms. Given past experience, it is not surprising that the New Hampshire primary was crowded with candidates seeking either to make a serious run at the nomination or at least to make a symbolic point by using the platform to raise issues. There were seven candidates, including such national figures as Al Gore, Jesse Jackson, and Gary Hart. One candidate, Governor Michael Dukakis of Massachusetts, had the natural advantage of being the nearest thing to a favorite son, coming from a state adjacent to the one hosting the first-in-the-nation primary.

Being a favorite son is something of a mixed blessing. Certainly, being the boy next door is quite helpful to a New England candidate: Edward Kennedy was the only loser of the four who have run in New Hampshire since 1972 (Muskie in 1972; Kennedy in 1980; Dukakis in 1988; and Paul Tsongas in 1992), and he faced an incumbent president. Put simply, New England candidates are expected to win in New Hampshire simply by virtue of residing in an adjacent state; the only question worthy of speculation (and media handicapping) is the margin of victory. Candidates who do not measure up in the expectations game, like Edmund Muskie, find out that a win is actually a loss. And other candidates who finish second to a New England candidate, such as George McGovern, find that a loss is actually a win.

What distinguished Dukakis from all other New England candidates was his ability to put together a balanced coalition, as his near-perfect elite score of

1.04 indicates. (See Table 2.9.) As governor of Massachusetts, Dukakis had gained a reputation as a liberal who governed in a pragmatic, businesslike fashion; his campaign made much of the so-called Massachusetts miracle, a revitalization of the state's economy that had occurred on his watch.

In contrast, his main competitors were unable to reach voters beyond their core niche of supporters. Illinois senator Paul Simon, who mixed old-fashioned New Deal liberalism with a fiscally conservative call for a balanced budget, attracted reform-minded liberals. Missouri congressman Richard Gephardt's populist message of protecting American companies from foreign trade appealed mainly to working-class voters and resonated in the blue-collar areas of the Granite State, said lobbyist and Gephardt activist James Demers.[59] Given that he was a little-known, underfunded candidate who came out of the House of Representatives, he did very well, Demers said. But Gephardt's appeal did not extend much further than that, with an elite score of 0.69; both Dukakis and Simon polled better among the elite, and Dukakis actually drew more working-class votes than Gephardt in New Hampshire. Simon's appeal was limited to the elite, as shown by a elite score of 1.43.

Dukakis's balanced victory in the New Hampshire primary bolstered his ultimately successful campaign for the nomination. Yet, like so many Democrats before him, he would lose the presidential election, this time to Vice President George H. W. Bush.

The 1992 Primary: Eating Your Spinach

As the Democrats prepared for the 1992 elections, they again faced an incumbent president, one who had led the United States in the highly successful Gulf War that evicted Iraq from Kuwait. The rally-around-the-flag effect that had led to George H. W. Bush's extraordinarily high popularity rankings was flagging, however, given the economic doldrums. Again a large field of candidates entered the Democratic primary in New Hampshire. The early betting was on a heavyweight, such as New York governor Mario Cuomo, to enter the fray, but Democrats waited in vain for him and other luminaries to join the race. Instead, breaking fast and late from the outside was the man from Hope, Arkansas: Bill Clinton.

TABLE 2.9

1988 New Hampshire Democratic Presidential Primary

Total votes cast: 122,913

Candidate	Total Vote	Total %, all votes cast	Elite Vote	Elite %	Working-class Vote	Working-class %	Elite Score
Michael Dukakis	44,112	35.9	12,346	35.5	9,629	34.1	1.04
Richard Gephardt	24,513	19.9	5,810	16.7	6,811	24.1	0.69
Paul Simon	21,094	17.2	6,758	19.4	3,837	13.6	1.43
Jesse Jackson	9,615	7.8	3,034	8.7	1,628	5.8	1.50
Al Gore	8,400	6.8	2,400	6.9	1,997	7.1	0.97
Bruce Babbitt	5,644	4.6	2,091	6.0	840	3.0	2.00
Gary Hart	4,888	4.0	934	2.7	1,669	5.9	0.46

The Arkansas governor's skillfully crafted message, almost Reaganesque in marrying the traditional Democratic base with the more independent, unaffiliated voter, resonated well in New Hampshire, said activist Joe Keefe.[60] It was a period of economic hard times for the state, with the collapse of the housing market, bank closings, high unemployment, and the New England tech boom in the midst of a trough.

The top two candidates in the primary both focused on the faltering economy. Clinton's populist economic message, featuring a tax cut for the middle class, worked especially well in the working-class areas where he outpolled the eventual winner, Paul Tsongas, a former senator from Massachusetts. Clinton's elite score of 0.78 left him well-positioned to establish himself as the coalition candidate in subsequent primaries. (See Table 2.10.)

In contrast, Paul Tsongas abandoned the traditional Democratic economic agenda in favor of a strongly pro-business stance that focused on rebuilding America's industrial base. In 1992, Tsongas's message was that voters would have to bear down in tough times and take responsibility for turning around the economy in a state suffering severely from the recession of the early 1990s. "We were hemorrhaging," said 1992 Democratic gubernatorial nominee Deborah "Arnie" Arnesen. "We knew that change was not going to be easy, that fixing it was not going to be easy."[61] Tsongas's pro-business message of economic austerity was in tune with the attitudes and sensibilities of New Hampshire Democrats, whom Arnesen described as culturally liberal and pro-environment, yet more friendly to business than most in the national party, and fiscally responsible. Arnesen said:

> Democrats in New Hampshire take their job very seriously. We're going to fix it, we're going to pay for it. If it takes taxes, we're going to do it. If you look at the Democrats in New Hampshire, that's exactly how they are: they're "eat your spinach" Democrats. The income tax in New Hampshire is not just about loosey-goosey reform, it's about "let's pay your bills in a legitimate way, and let's be honest about what we have to do."

Tsongas won the primary by appealing mainly to upscale, prosperous Democrats as his score of 1.80 makes clear. But it was Clinton who captured the middle, whose message drew balanced support, a strong indication of his future prospects—winning both the Democratic nomination and then the presidency.

The 2000 Primary: Al Gore, Fighting for the Status Quo

The eight years of Bill Clinton's presidency was marked by many achievements—economic growth most notably, with important effects on New Hampshire, which bounced back from recession and continued on the path of quiet prosperity. In terms of the New Hampshire primary, unlike Lyndon Johnson or Jimmy Carter, Clinton had managed to avoid a primary challenge in 1996, in part because of the diligent attention he paid to the state and the state party.

But however popular Clinton may have been, the last years of his presidency had been marked by scandals that left a stain and a bad taste in the mouths of many voters. His vice president, Al Gore, may not himself have been tarnished by his association with Clinton, but he did seek to separate himself from Clinton's inheritance of personal dubiousness while claiming the benefits of incumbency and economic strength. Whether because of a desire to maintain party unity to keep the White House or the view that Gore was unstoppable,

TABLE 2.10

1992 New Hampshire Democratic Presidential Primary

Total votes cast: 167,624

Candidate	Total Vote	Total %, all votes cast	Elite Vote	Elite %	Working-class Vote	Working-class %	Elite Score
Paul Tsongas	55,663	33.2	19,863	39.9	8,221	22.2	1.80
Bill Clinton	41,540	24.8	11,062	22.2	10,472	28.3	0.78
Bob Kerrey	18,584	11.1	4,532	9.1	4,827	13.1	0.69
Tom Harkin	17,063	10.2	4,169	8.4	4,596	12.4	0.68
Jerry Brown	13,659	8.2	3,789	7.6	2,469	6.7	1.13

most major Democratic politicians bowed out of the primary campaign. Bill Bradley, the former senator from New Jersey, did enter, thus making what had seemed a foregone conclusion into a contest.

Bradley quickly established himself as the insurgent reformer in this contest, promising a new and better kind of politics, obliquely referring to the scandals of the Clinton-Gore administration. As such, he became a magnet for those New Hampshire Democrats discontented with the Clinton legacy. If Gore entered the primary as the establishment candidate, he quickly sought to position himself as the friend of the working people. He portrayed himself as a fighter, identifying himself with the rank-and-file of the Democratic working class. In addition, the Gore campaign portrayed Bradley's proposal on expanding health care as insensitive to the needs of working people.

Bradley, on the other hand, came across as intellectual and showed even less adeptness at connecting to the people than the famously stiff Al Gore. In a closely contested campaign—Gore won with 49.8 percent of the vote to Bradley's 45.7 percent—Bradley sought to identify himself as one in the long line of reformist candidates to jump start a candidacy in New Hampshire. This was done through the endorsement of Niki Tsongas, Paul's widow, who said in a Bradley advertisement that "like my husband, Paul, Bill Bradley is a passionate supporter of working people, and he, too, is challenging us with a bold vision for America. . . . On Feb. 1, let's tell the rest of the nation it's time for truth, it's time for courage, it's time for Bill Bradley."[62]

Such a claim did Bradley little good. Like Tsongas, his support came heavily from elite areas of New Hampshire Democrats—his elite score was 1.56, slightly lower than Tsongas's 1.80 but hardly indicative of a campaign that could weld together a coalition. (See Table 2.11.) In contrast, Gore ran a more balanced campaign, yielding an elite score of 0.76. This strong base among the working class positioned Gore well to win his party's nomination, and Bradley effectively conceded in early March. But strategists questioned the viability of Gore's populist message, which he extended through the general election campaign.

The Changing Ideology of the New Hampshire Primary Electorate

New Hampshire's place at the beginning of the presidential primary calendar has long been criticized because of the state's presumed idiosyncrasies as an unfortunate eccentricity of the nomination process. One such piece of conventional wisdom on New Hampshire is that voters in both parties are more conservative than their national counterparts. Manchester, the largest city in the state and host of long-closed textile mills, was acknowledged to be the center of working-class conservatism. Its newspaper, the *Union Leader,* was notorious for the blistering editorials of its publisher, William Loeb; in 1972, negative stories on the wife of Edmund Muskie during the primary season drove the senator to a fiery (some say teary) defense of his spouse in front of the newspaper's offices.[63] As late as 1984, Democratic candidates were sizing up the state's electorate as moderate to conservative.[64]

Recent exit polls of New Hampshire Democrats, however, prompt a significant correction to their conservative image. According to a comprehensive review of primary exit polling by Emmett Buell,[65] only 17 percent of New Hampshire voters in the 1984 Democratic primary described themselves as conservatives, a smaller percentage than was found in Massachusetts, Illinois, Maryland, Ohio, or New Jersey, for instance. Self-described moderates were a majority of the primary vote that year. In 1992, only 14 percent of all voters casting ballots in the Democratic primary described themselves as conservatives; that figure dropped to 7 percent among strong party identifiers. In contrast, six

TABLE 2.11

2000 New Hampshire Democratic Presidential Primary

Total votes cast: 154,290

Candidate	Total Vote	Total %, all votes cast	Elite Vote	Elite %	Working-class Vote	Working-class %	Elite Score
Al Gore	76,897	49.8	24,226	43.6	13,805	57.4	0.76
Bill Bradley	70,502	45.7	29,083	52.4	8,084	33.6	1.56

of ten strong party identifiers described themselves as liberal, and that label was adopted by 43 percent of all Democratic primary voters. Moderates were also quite prominent, representing 32 percent of strong party identifiers, 50 percent of independents, and 42 percent of all primary voters.

Exit polling from the 2000 Democratic primary reinforced the profile of New Hampshire Democratic voters as liberal to moderate. An outright majority of Democratic primary voters, 54 percent, identified themselves as liberals, 38 percent as moderates, and just 8 percent as conservative. The primary electorate is also noteworthy for its large number of upscale voters, both well educated and well off financially. About six of ten voters reported making $50,000 or more a year; 16 percent more than $100,000. Twenty-five percent held a bachelor's degree, and 29 percent had gone on for advanced graduate studies.[66]

The ideological movement of New Hampshire Democrats has corresponded with an equally significant geographic movement: The balance of power within the New Hampshire Democratic Party (and thus within the New Hampshire Democratic presidential primary), firmly ensconced in the cities for most of the twentieth century, now has moved back toward the once-rural towns where the party started back in the nineteenth century.

Examining the number of votes cast in New Hampshire's urban areas provides confirmation of the declining influence of the cities and the working-class voters who inhabit them. Back in 1976, the year Carter ran a campaign explicitly targeting the working-class vote, the state's nine cities with a significant manufacturing base[67] produced 48.5 percent of the Democratic primary vote. By 1984, the year Hart defeated Mondale, voters in these cities cast just 38 percent of the total vote. Eight years later, when Tsongas defeated Clinton, voters in the cities cast 31.5 percent of the vote. And in the latest primary, fewer than three of ten Democratic primary votes (28.4 percent) came from these nine cities—all told, a drop in voting power of 20 percent in a quarter-century.

In contrast, consider Bill Bradley's top twenty-five areas, in each of which Bradley carried 60 percent or more of the primary vote.[68] All of Bradley's best performances were in towns; none took place in any of the cities. (Compare this to Al Gore's best performances, which included wards in Somersworth, Manchester, Laconia, Berlin, and Nashua.) Bradley's top twenty-five towns combined produced just under 4,500 votes back in 1976. Twenty-four years later, that number had more than doubled to just under 11,000 votes—growth that exceeded the increase in the total number of ballots cast in the Democratic primary.

The mill towns and the Democrats who inhabited them are relics of the past, said Arnesen, now a host of political talk-radio and of a public affairs show on WNDS-TV in Derry. The vestiges of blue-collar Manchester, which traditionally had supported establishment candidates, will not exist five years from now, and Manchester will go the way of surrounding towns, such as Bedford, Goffstown, and Merrimack. The process of gentrification is, Arnesen suggested, ineluctable: "We're going to turn into yuppies, all of us." With the rapidly expanding airport as its engine of economic change, Manchester and its environs have become places where traditional appeals by Democratic primary candidates are unlikely to remain effective. "And if Manchester was the place that a lot of Democrats had to go because they thought that this was the traditional base, they're going to have to play a different song," Arnesen said.

Rural areas of New Hampshire are becoming increasingly important to the state Democratic Party and to candidates seeking votes in the presidential primary. Rural areas used to be bastions of Republicanism, said activist Jeff Woodburn,[69] and the rule used to be that the greater the population in a town or city, the better Democrats did in that area. Migration patterns are undermining that formula, however, as people pursuing a different quality of life are choosing to relocate into rural areas: western Hillsborough County, Cheshire County, and northern New Hampshire. A town like Randolph, in northernmost Coos County, that "used to be just a place where you'd have a cabin in the woods," Woodburn recalls, has now become a place for full-time residents. As a result, Democratic strength there has increased.

The movement of votes away from cities and dispersed among the towns means that candidates must change the way they allocate a scarce commodity: campaign time in New Hampshire, said Gephardt activist James Demers. Once, candidates could focus a large portion of time on activities based in large cities like Manchester, sending volunteers door-to-door, for example. Now campaigns have to reach into the towns, and the geographical scope of a campaign has to broaden accordingly, said Demers:

> It used to be that the candidates would come in and they would spend their time in Manchester and Nashua, Dover, Portsmouth, and many times some of these small towns would never see a candidate. And now, when those neighborhood house parties are being held, you see that there are parties in Amherst and Goffstown, and that's a clear indication that the vote has spread out, and . . . the candidate's time and resources have to spread out too.

In a crowded race, Demers said, hundreds of votes could make the difference between victory and defeat. Even in the two-person race of the 2000 primary, only a few thousand votes separated Gore and Bradley; this is why both candidates spent time in towns known as Republican strongholds, in the hope of capturing whatever Democrats were there. Furthermore, those towns have a large number of independent or "undeclared" voters, who can vote in either of the party primaries. "It used to be primary elections were for the most loyal of the party; that tended to be the people who came out to vote," Demers said. "And, while that's still a factor, it's changed because of the independents, and the independents could very easily walk in and take either ballot on Election Day. So, there's a new fight for those more undecided, open-minded independents. And that's why, I think, at the end of campaigns, that's where a tremendous amount of a campaign's focus and effort goes."

New Hampshire's open primary is a raucous affair, like a college party open to all, said advertising executive Pat Griffin. A closed primary (open only to registered party members), in comparison, is like having a quiet keg in one's dorm—"the right people know, the right people are invited," and no one gets in trouble. In an open primary, where people are invited indiscriminately to participate, "not only are the regulars showing up, we got some townies coming to the party, we got some people we've never seen before." The result is that things get out of hand, Griffin said. No one is quite sure who is going to show up, and the people never seen before are not controlled by traditional partisan behavior. "It's the latecomers, it's the intensity you can't measure, a year, or six months, or three months before the vote takes place, that is really, really hard to control."[70]

CHAPTER THREE

Storms from the Left: Gene McCarthy and George McGovern

The first storms of the modern New Hampshire Democratic primary arrived from the Left. Galvanized and united by their opposition to the Vietnam War, the liberal wing of the state's Democratic Party marshaled their forces behind a single candidate promising change in the party and in the nation: Eugene McCarthy in 1968, and George McGovern in 1972. In each case, they faced a party establishment riddled with cracks and divisions, struggling to maintain unity behind a mainstream candidate: President Lyndon Johnson in 1968, and Senator Edmund Muskie in 1972. In both cases, the party establishment managed to win the battle of New Hampshire, but the reform-minded insurgents won the war. Neither McCarthy nor McGovern managed to defeat their opponent at the ballot box, but both candidates dented their opponents severely, sending their campaign vehicles reeling off the road soon after leaving New Hampshire.

Clean for Gene: The 1968 New Hampshire Primary

New Hampshire has long enjoyed a reputation as a send-a-message primary. Voters here take an "almost in-your-face" attitude toward the primary, observed local political advertising executive Pat Griffin, as if they are saying, "Don't tell me he's going to win. . . .That's got nothing to do with this. I don't care. I have an opportunity in the next couple weeks to make up my mind about how I'm going to vote."[1] New Hampshire voters have a general sense that they see politicians differently from voters in other parts of the country, and therefore they feel no compulsion to go in the direction dictated by conventional wisdom, said former Democratic state party chair Ned Helms.[2] New Hampshire voters are surrogates, Helms said, for all the people who cannot sit down and meet with a person who wants to be president.

Perhaps the most famous send-a-message primary was the 1968 Democratic contest with campaigns that did not begin until just weeks before the election. The intensity of the battle did not stem from the charisma of the candidates themselves. One of the main combatants, President Lyndon Johnson, did not even show up in New Hampshire; the other, Senator Eugene McCarthy of Minnesota, looked like "a gray, tired, old college professor," according to one potential supporter.[3] McCarthy, however, was armed with a message that split his party in two and rallied legions of young men and women to trek north on his behalf: End the war in Vietnam.

Eugene McCarthy's campaign is often identified as part and parcel of the flower-power revolution of the late 1960s. Its most ardent ground troops were college students who famously tidied up their appearance to go "clean for Gene" and campaigned door-to-door for their candidate. Less famous, but perhaps even more important, were a small corps of activists who did not appear at first glance the least countercultural: They included lawyers, professors, and an advertising executive.

McCarthy's core in New Hampshire was a group of liberal activists in the Democratic Party, as few as a dozen. During the 1960s, racism, poverty, and the Vietnam War were the wedge issues that divided liberals and conservatives within the party. Johnson did have the support of the party regulars, but the establishment was largely passive during the primary campaign. The party regulars led by Governor John King and Senator Thomas MacIntyre were part of what longtime activist Jean Wallin called the Jacksonian wing of the party—Jacksonian as in Andrew Jackson, with an emphasis on conservative values such as limited government.[4] Some thought that Johnson would win the primary easily and so did not bother to make much of an effort on his part. In addition, a number of high-profile New Hampshire Democrats had "quietly refused to serve" on Johnson's state reelection committee. Johnson himself decided not to begin to campaign so early in the election year nor did he make any personal appearances in the state; instead, he had his campaign team stage a write-in campaign as had been done in the 1964 primary.[5]

At the time, liberals controlled the primary since the activist base came mainly from them. They tended to be well-educated professionals, such as lawyers and professors, with advanced degrees.

Two such professionals were Merv Weston and William Farrell, who lived in the Manchester area.[6] They were among the founders of the state chapter of the NAACP in 1964, which grew to become the largest white chapter in the country, with 500 whites and just over 200 blacks as members. (The establishment of the chapter provoked the ire of *Manchester Union Leader* editor and publisher William Loeb, who opposed President Johnson's civil rights legislation, declaring it unconstitutional. He penned a 1964 editorial questioning the need for such an "activist political organization" in New Hampshire, where there were few African Americans and "fewer instances of discrimination." He dismissed the chapter as "a 'liberal'—dominated . . . political movement motivated more by political than moral considerations."[7])Weston was an advertising executive who had started his own firm in 1950, the largest agency north of Boston. Weston, a Democrat, found little competition in picking up candidates as clients; his first was John F. Kennedy's 1960 campaign. In all, he participated in nine presidential campaigns and about forty gubernatorial and senate campaigns.

Farrell, who eventually was elected a member of Eugene McCarthy's slate of convention delegates in New Hampshire, was a sociology professor at Saint Anselm College in Goffstown when he signed on with McCarthy for his first presidential primary campaign in New Hampshire. His principal motivation for joining the campaign was his opposition to the war in Vietnam. He and like-minded individuals had been looking to Robert Kennedy to lead such an antiwar campaign in 1967, but Kennedy decided against challenging President Johnson for the 1968 nomination. Indeed, for much of 1967 liberal antiwar activists in New Hampshire and nationwide were without a candidate. Two progressives, activist Allard Lowenstein and Curtis Gans of Americans for Democratic Action, took it upon themselves to find a candidate for the antiwar movement. With Robert Kennedy still refusing to enter, McCarthy announced his challenge to Johnson on November 30, 1967.[8]

Even with the pending clash between McCarthy and Johnson, no one expected New Hampshire to be the site of a decisive battle in 1968 presidential politics. At the end of November 1967, McCarthy stepped forward from a list of potential challengers to oppose Johnson and end American military involvement in Vietnam. Like Estes Kefauver before him, McCarthy aimed to show strength among the Democratic Party by entering selected primaries in specific states; unlike Kefauver, New Hampshire was not on the initial target list. For McCarthy, Massachusetts, Wisconsin, Nebraska, Oregon, and California all appeared to be better opportunities than the Granite State. As historian Charles Brereton put it:

> McCarthy's avoidance of New Hampshire was not difficult to understand. It was considered territory too hawkish and conservative for his dovish crusade. . . . The Portsmouth Naval Shipyard, the Pease Air Base near Portsmouth and Sanders Associates pumped tens of millions of dollars into the New Hampshire economy. Any anti-Vietnam crusade could be construed by many of the state's workers as a threat to job security.[9]

Two members of the N.H. McCarthy for President Steering Committee, David Hoeh (who eventually led McCarthy's New Hampshire campaign) and Gerry Studds, were still trying to persuade McCarthy to enter the state primary as late as December 1967, just three months before the primary. "There is nothing to be lost—and a great deal to be gained—by coming into New Hampshire," they wrote in a memo to McCarthy.[10]

An important part of the upside for McCarthy, they argued, was in playing the expectations game. In particular, they stressed that expectations would be so low for McCarthy in New Hampshire, which was regarded as pro-war and conservative, that even a halfway decent showing would be "hailed as a stunning performance."[11] (One of Johnson's most prominent supporters, Senator Thomas McIntyre, had already predicted that McCarthy would receive no more than five thousand votes if he entered the primary.) In addition, McCarthy would prove that he was a serious, national candidate by willingly entering the New Hampshire contest against the odds—much like John F. Kennedy did in 1960 by competing in (and winning) the Democratic primary in West Virginia, a Protestant-dominated state that was not expected to be friendly to a Catholic candidate. Finally, they argued that New Hampshire was, quite simply, *the* place for an underdog candidate to make a big splash:

> Every minute spent in New Hampshire in January, February and March will bring massive, national exposure for Sen. McCarthy; New Hampshire is the principal focus of the national media during this period; the troops in Wisconsin, Massachusetts, California, Oregon, etc. will read of, see, and hear the Senator every day he spends in New Hampshire.[12]

McCarthy eventually agreed to compete in New Hampshire, on January 2, just weeks before the March 12 primary date. A flurry of activity on behalf of the candidate proceeded, not always with much coordination but with a vitality that caught the attention of the national press.

One of the ways the McCarthy campaign tried to attract attention about its candidate was house parties, which began in earnest just a couple of months before the primary. Celebrities such as Paul Newman were sometimes the featured attraction, warming up the crowd for the candidate. The press would call, ask if they were serving food and liquor, and show up as well, Farrell said. Farrell recalled arranging for Newman to visit various ethnic social clubs, then popular in Manchester.

Eugene McCarthy was not well known nationwide, but he was recognized within Catholic intellectual circles, said Pat Morris, who also was active in the civil rights and peace movements in New Hampshire during the 1960s.[13] McCarthy was "probably the first idealistic candidate since Adlai Stevenson," said Morris; he was "the kind of intellectual you love, and nobody knows what he's saying." The candidate himself was an "enigma to everybody," Weston said. "A total enigma. We couldn't quite figure him out."[14] He was shy and aloof, said Jean Wallin, and while she adored the man, he was nonetheless a lazy campaigner. As has been the case for several insurgent campaigns over the years, the candidate's supporters often displayed much more enthusiasm than the candidate himself. "My campaign may not be organized at the top," McCarthy said, "but it is certainly tightly organized at the bottom."[15]

One of the defining characteristics of the McCarthy campaign was the presence of "incredible young people," Morris said. College students spent their winter recess working in New Hampshire for McCarthy. The leaders of the New Hampshire campaign, wary that the youths' appearance might repel some voters, insisted that those who wanted an outside job contacting voters had to dress "Neat and Clean for Gene"—that is, trim their hair and wear conservative clothing.[16] The young volunteers were "so hopeful," Morris said, "Everything's possible at that age." In the evenings, the campaign would "throw them into storefronts" to spend the night. "Everybody had kids in the house," Morris recalled. The "young army" caught the eye of *Washington Post* columnist Mary McGrory, who wrote a piece a week before the primary that put them in the spotlight.[17] The young volunteers even received the grudging approval of New Hampshire's governor John King, a leading supporter of Johnson; when asked why McCarthy was gaining on Johnson, he blamed (or praised) "those damned kids."[18]

Grassroots politics were certainly important to McCarthy's success, but the campaign also possessed a sophisticated media strategy, led by Weston, that aimed to blanket the state. In the late 1960s, the cornerstone of such a mass-media strategy was radio. There was no television "worth a damn" in New Hampshire, Weston said. WMUR-TV, now the premier station in New Hampshire, at the time possessed only a small staff, a very weak signal, and poor reception. Advertising on Boston television, which had some penetration in New Hampshire, was quite expensive. Instead, the McCarthy campaign turned to radio, an inexpensive mass medium that was easy to program; last-minute changes were easy to make with a simple phone call, allowing McCarthy's operatives great flexibility in what message they delivered.[19] For McCarthy, Weston ran a radio blitz that inundated the whole state in the weeks before the primary, spending $23,000 on advertising time, at three to five dollars for a sixty-second spot with twenty to thirty spots a day on each local station.[20]

The number-one issue was Vietnam, and its gravity only deepened with the onset of the Tet Offensive, during which the North Vietnamese attacked major cities in South Vietnam. Morris recalled the aftermath in New Hampshire: "Four bodies came home to New Hampshire, and they rolled into the airport here. . . . Four bodies lined up. You couldn't take that away." The war was front and center in McCarthy's advertising, as in this thirty-second ad:

> *Senator McCarthy speaking:* . . . we are involved, this nation, in what has become a major war, and most of you know what the cost of that war has been and know that those costs are continuing.[21] (*Announcer: voice over:* There is an honorable alternative to the continuing drain of men and materials that endless escalation has imposed upon us in Vietnam. Senator McCarthy will not turn away from our responsibilities in Asia but he will explore every avenue to begin meaningful negotiations for peace. There is an alternative. McCarthy for President.)

The McCarthy campaign's ability to improvise on the ground in New Hampshire gave the challenger a clear advantage over the incumbent president. Assuming the presidency in 1963 after John F. Kennedy's assassination, Johnson had no opposition for the nomination in 1964 and did not bother to visit New Hampshire for the primary. Four years later, with his public approval ratings below 50 percent, "Johnson could not call upon past personal contact to halt the drift of eroding fortunes," historian Charles Brereton observed. "He had never spent a winter's morning standing outside the Brown Paper Company in Berlin greeting workers arriving for their shift."[22] All in all, the president "was at the mercy of his surrogates," Brereton wrote, "a captive of his post."[23] State party leaders sent out pledge cards to New Hampshire Democrats and undeclared voters, asking them to fill out the card and return it if they planned to write in the president's name on primary day.[24] McCarthy's supporters leaped on this, accusing Johnson and his New Hampshire supporters of intimidation tactics; McCarthy's team put ads on the air stating, "You don't have to sign anything to vote for McCarthy," and asking, "Whatever happened to the secret ballot?"[25] Governor King countered by declaring days before the election that a significant turnout for McCarthy would be "greeted with great cheers" by the North Vietnamese Communists.[26]

On primary day, March 12, McCarthy was unable to pull off a victory, yet his eight-point loss to the incumbent president nonetheless had the impact that New Hampshire activists had desired. McCarthy's strong showing was trumpeted nationally as a severe blow to Johnson. By the end of March, Johnson announced that he would not seek a second term.

In retrospect, New Hampshire succeeded in making a name for McCarthy and in making a name for itself as a giant killer, a reputation that inflated over time and subsequent primaries. Clearly, McCarthy's performance in New Hampshire succeeded in establishing him as the alternative to the incumbent—at least for a short time. In some ways, McCarthy succeeded too well in New Hampshire: Johnson's surprise departure was an earthquake that radically reshaped the contours of the race for the Democratic nomination, and McCarthy's campaign was not the better for it. Johnson's vice president, Hubert Humphrey, entered the race for the nomination as the new candidate of the party establishment. And McCarthy found his insurgent mantle contested by New York senator Robert Kennedy, the assassinated president's brother, who had initially passed on challenging Johnson. Senator Kennedy was also assassinated after winning the California primary. Humphrey did not run in any contested primaries; instead, he relied successfully on the power of party bosses to get him enough delegates to win the nomination. Like Kefauver before him, McCarthy found that his primary victories ultimately held little value when it came to the prize of the nomination. Humphrey accepted the nomination in Chicago in the summer of 1968 while police battles with antiwar demonstrators outside the convention hall were broadcast around the country.

1972

Senator George McGovern of South Dakota had few amenities as he began his campaign for the Democratic presidential nomination. He did not enjoy the backing of the Democratic Party's leaders who had flocked to the man from

Maine, Senator Edmund Muskie, Hubert Humphrey's running mate four years earlier. Not coincidentally, McGovern struggled to raise money while his main opponent was awash in cash. Last but not least, McGovern did not appear all that presidential as he began a lonely quest in New Hampshire. Journalist Hunter Thompson recalled bumping into McGovern, at first not recognizing him, at a motel lounge in Portsmouth:

> I had never seen a presidential candidate moving around in public without at least ten speedy "aides" surrounding him at all times. So I watched him for a while, expecting to see his aides flocking in from the lobby at any moment . . . but it slowly dawned on me that The Candidate was by *himself*: there were no aides, no entourage, and nobody else in the room had even noticed his arrival.[27]

McGovern did enjoy one luxury, however: the luxury of time, said Joseph Grandmaison, one of the candidate's key staffers in New Hampshire.[28] Specifically, McGovern enjoyed the luxury of months and months to build a campaign that would make a splash in the New Hampshire primary—and then the luxury of time to capitalize on his better-than-expected showing and catapult his candidacy to the party's nomination.

McGovern announced his candidacy for the 1972 Democratic nomination on January 18, *1971*—539 days before the party convention. The timing of McGovern's announcement was a stark departure from the norm. In 1952, the eventual Republican candidate, Dwight Eisenhower, announced his candidacy June 4, just 33 days before the start of the convention; the Democratic nominee, Adlai Stevenson, never made a formal announcement of his candidacy. In 1960, eventual Democratic nominee John F. Kennedy announced his candidacy on January 2, 191 days before the convention; his rival Hubert Humphrey announced three days before him. In 1964, eventual GOP nominee Barry Goldwater announced January 3, 192 days before the convention; his chief rival, Nelson Rockefeller, announced roughly two months earlier. Eugene McCarthy announced his candidacy 270 days prior to the convention during the 1968 nomination season; Richard Nixon, the eventual Republican nominee, announced 186 days prior to the GOP convention.[29] Since McGovern, early announcements have become the norm for those aspiring to the nomination;

over the last three decades, the politician who decides to run for the presidency must be prepared for a long-distance race. It is becoming the norm for would-be contenders to announce their candidacies more than a year before their party's national convention and a year and a half before the November general election. In the 2000 election season, Bill Bradley spent many months in 1999 cultivating the grass roots in New Hampshire, in hopes of pulling an upset there against Vice President Al Gore in the first-in-the-nation Democratic primary.

Although McGovern's campaign in New Hampshire was considerably more lengthy and more systematic than McCarthy's improvisational effort four years earlier, the goal was the same. McGovern sought to establish himself as the principal liberal alternative to Muskie, the moderate front runner. With the United States still engaged in the apparently futile war in Vietnam, divisions among Americans were deep and volatile, and they were especially sharp among Democrats. Although Muskie did say he would end the war in Vietnam, it was McGovern who declared the war "a moral and political disaster—a terrible cancer eating away the soul of the nation," adding that "the Establishment Center," to which Muskie belonged, had built a "vast military colossus based on the paychecks of the American worker."[30] McGovern also advocated amnesty for those who avoided the draft; took a pro-choice position on abortion (though he argued that the issue was best left to the states); and favored moderating state penalties for the use of marijuana. Timing is "only everything" in New Hampshire, said Grandmaison. A candidate and his positions on issues some-times "catch a wave," and the candidate "clicks into the psyche" of the voters. Such was the case of McGovern in 1972. Four years after Senator Eugene McCarthy's liberal challenge to President Lyndon B. Johnson, the continuing rift between elites and traditional working-class constituencies again caused an unexpected winter storm in the New Hampshire primary.

This time the candidate engulfed by the storm was a New England native son. In the months before the New Hampshire primary, Muskie, promoted as the "Man from Maine," enjoyed all the advantages of a front runner: a large lead in the polls, heavy press coverage, and the blessing of the party bosses. To top it off, he was literally the boy next door, born in the mill town of Rumford, near the border of New Hampshire. Other major Democratic politicians—Edward Kennedy, Hubert Humphrey, Senator William Proxmire of Wisconsin, Senator

Henry "Scoop" Jackson of Washington state, and Mayor John Lindsay of New York City—passed on running for the nomination.[31]

Muskie fashioned a mainstream campaign focused on his ability to defeat President Richard Nixon and lead the Democrats back to the White House. Confident and perhaps complacent, "Muskie had every expectation," wrote primary historian Charles Brereton, "that New Hampshire would do for him what it did for another Catholic Democratic senator from New England: provide the presidential launching pad as it had done for John Kennedy just over a decade before."[32] In the end, New Hampshire did indeed jump start a campaign, but it was McGovern's that got the boost.

McGovern was the only major challenger to Muskie in New Hampshire. (Other challengers included Indiana senator Vance Hartke; Arkansas congressman Wilbur Mills, who ran a write-in campaign; and Los Angeles mayor Sam Yorty, who received the vociferous support of the *Manchester Union Leader* and its publisher, William Loeb.[33])

In the classic fashion of the reformist candidate, McGovern conducted a rigorous regimen of grassroots politicking, led by Denver lawyer Gary Hart, who would run and win the New Hampshire primary twelve years later as the U.S. senator from Colorado.[34] Grandmaison, whose involvement in New Hampshire politics spans four decades, said that when campaigning here, a candidate must revert back to the techniques he used when he started his political career in a race for the city council or for a seat in Congress.[35] McGovern's warm and engaging personality along with his sense of humor served him well here, he said. He recalled a reception for McGovern in Nashua; the candidate was running late and Grandmaison was trying to hurry him out the door. "You know, Joe," McGovern said, "in South Dakota we never leave without saying good-by."

McGovern's campaign also was proof that for a national campaign to be successful in New Hampshire, people from New Hampshire should be in charge of scheduling, allocation of resources within the state, and the face of the campaign, Grandmaison said. The McGovern campaign was successful in recruiting talented New Hampshire people in every city and town. Nowadays, presidential primary campaigns are often "vendorized," hiring professionals to handle direct mail and phone banks rather than developing a corps of volunteers to handle such tasks. Often a campaign's idea of a model volunteer is someone who writes a check to the campaign, Grandmaison said. Without the grassroots efforts of volunteers, however, and the cumulative effect of neighbors talking to neighbors, groundswells of support for a candidate do not build as they once did. A campaign should strive to come as close as possible to the candidate knocking on the door and asking for a citizen's vote.

In September 1971, a Muskie campaign poll put the candidate at 42 percent.[36] Five months later, nothing—and everything—had changed for Muskie. On the one hand, Muskie managed to maintain his strength in New Hampshire despite a barrage of attacks from the left and right. In particular, conservative *Manchester Union Leader* publisher William Loeb launched a series of attacks on Muskie. Loeb's harsh criticism of the candidate was not in itself unusual. As the Democrats moved leftward in the 1960s and 1970s, Loeb regularly pounded the candidates in his newspaper, said current *Union Leader* publisher Joseph McQuaid.[37] In 1968 he criticized Johnson for not prosecuting the Vietnam War strongly enough, but had no love for McCarthy or the anti-war movement, calling McCarthy a "skunk." In 1972, Loeb thought that both McGovern and Muskie would pull the United States out of Vietnam, but he concentrated his fire on Muskie. After the 1972 election, Loeb washed his hands of the Democrats and concentrated on Republican primaries, where he perceived he had more influence.

Loeb ran a letter of dubious authenticity (and an accompanying front page editorial) claiming that Muskie had laughed at an aide's use of the word "Canucks," a derogatory slang term for French Canadian immigrants.[38] Loeb also reprinted a *Newsweek* article that portrayed Muskie's wife in an unflattering light.[39] The publisher's attacks provoked the candidate to launch a fiery riposte from a flatbed truck in front of the *Union Leader* building, just before the primary. Muskie appeared to lose his composure on more than one occasion, and some media reported that he had begun to cry. (Other reporters stated that Muskie's face was wet from falling snowflakes.)[40] Loeb responded that anyone who would get so upset about what a newspaper publisher in New Hampshire said should not have his finger on the nuclear button, McQuaid recalled.

Notwithstanding the roughness of the campaign, Muskie finished first in New Hampshire, and his showing on the day of the primary—at 46.4 percent, the best showing by any candidate in an open Democratic primary—was actually slightly better than the polls of the previous autumn. Muskie learned the hard way, though, that to stamp out an insurgency, front runners must do better in New Hampshire than simply run in place. Although he won New Hampshire, he was unable to use the primary to stop his insurgent challenger in his tracks, perhaps in part because one of his New Hampshire operatives, Maria Carrier, predicted he would at least get 50 percent of the vote.[41] But Muskie's loss was not merely a failure to meet expectations. More important, the New Hampshire contest pointed out glaring signs of weakness in Muskie's strategy as an establishment candidate, as his campaign was marked by "ineptness, misman-agement and over-confidence" that led to an attempt "to win without a message, plan or program."[42]

And again, as in 1968, McGovern's 37 percent showing, a strong second in New Hampshire, was enough to accomplish the task of vaulting a long shot into the limelight. McGovern also enjoyed the luxury of time after the primary, Grandmaison said. After McGovern's better-than-expected showing in New Hampshire, he had the time to send out letters to raise additional funds for the campaign. In today's front-loaded presidential nomination season, candidates no longer have time to reap the benefits of a surprise New Hampshire finish.

George McGovern's most unlikely nomination as the standard-bearer of the Democratic Party was the pinnacle of New Hampshire liberals' influence in presidential nomination politics. Reform-minded elites, of course, would play an important role in subsequent primaries. Never again, however, would they be the sole catalyst for such important events in their party. In 1968, they aided in the political demise of a president whose war they detested. And in 1972, they succeeded in knocking a front runner off his perch and launching an obscure liberal senator into the national political spotlight. George McGovern, however, turned out to be an anomaly in New Hampshire presidential politics: A candidate supported mainly by the state's Democratic elite who eventually managed to capture the party's nomination. Four years after McGovern, the New Hampshire primary belonged to a candidate with quite different ideological stripes: Jimmy Carter.

CHAPTER FOUR

Storm from the Right: The Rise of Jimmy Carter

The triumphs of the liberal wing of the Democratic Party in the 1968 and 1972 New Hampshire primaries held important lessons for candidates of various ideologies. In both 1968 and 1972, a candidate who mustered the support of just one faction of the party in New Hampshire was richly rewarded in subsequent contests. Both Gene McCarthy and George McGovern rode a wave of media-generated momentum through the rest of the nomination season, attracting like-minded Democrats to their campaigns. Even after 1972, however, the importance of New Hampshire to any candidate seeking his party's nomination was still not clear to all. It was apparent, though, to a politician from the "New South" who sought to steer the party back toward the center. In 1976, it was former Georgia governor Jimmy Carter who unified working-class voters behind his candidacy in New Hampshire, frustrating liberals who split their votes among several candidates. And once again, a New Hampshire victory was key to a relative unknown's successful quest for his party's nomination.

1976

You can't beat something with nothing, according to the old adage, but Jimmy Carter's campaign proved you can beat somebodies with nobodies.

Buckley, Rogers, Shaheen: These names are well known today among New Hampshire Democratic Party activists, and voters statewide have cast ballots for Shaheen. But back in 1974, when a former governor from Georgia began to visit New Hampshire as part of his apparently quixotic quest for the presidency, all these people enjoyed relative anonymity in political circles. Established party activists in the state tended to flock to other, more liberal candidates, with the exception of prominent liberal Jean Wallin. The presence of name activists, however, was not enough to offset a campaign with a candidate who wore the mantle of change, a clear knowledge of where to find votes in the small universe of the state Democratic electorate, and the dogged determination of a bunch of nobodies to get those voters to the polls.

A basic strategy for candidates is that "in every campaign you look for new blood," Bill Shaheen said. "New blood works like you'd never believe. If they believe in you, they'll go through walls for you, they'll work their heart out for you." Shaheen worked for Carter in 1975 and 1976, and "it's because I was new blood that I was willing to make those sacrifices, that I believed so passionately in him that I didn't care if I won or lost, I just had to do it."[1]

While Carter was still governor of Georgia, he attracted the attention of Bill Shaheen and his wife, Jeanne. Bill, born and raised on the seacoast in Dover, was attending University of Mississippi Law School; Jeanne, a schoolteacher, worked in one of the first integrated schools in the South. Bill Shaheen recalled his first favorable impression of Carter: The governor put up a picture of Martin Luther King in Georgia's state capitol and declared that segregation was over in Georgia. "We thought that was such a courageous thing to do that we thought we'd pay attention to this guy, because he was really a breath of fresh air for the South," Bill Shaheen said. At a time when the Watergate scandal had tarnished the political process, Bill Shaheen "was struck by Carter's honesty and his integrity . . . that's what the American people wanted . . . they were tired of the typical politicians, they needed what I believed to be a true leader." Bill Shaheen had reached the conclusion that voters were tired of lawyer-politicians and wanted a candidate who was a departure from the norm; Carter, who worked as a physicist and a peanut farmer before entering politics, was an attractive alternative.

The Shaheens returned to New Hampshire in 1973. When Carter began making the rounds in the state the following year, Bill Shaheen was one of the first to get on board the campaign, taking half-time off from his job practicing law. He became the Carter campaign's New Hampshire cochair by default; the campaign had sent out 500 letters to Democrats whom they thought were potential recruits. Of those 500, 8 showed up for a meeting, and "we started around this table, the first seven all had excuses not to be the chair, so they all looked at me and said, 'OK, Shaheen, you're it.'"

Bill Shaheen recalled a conversation with one of Carter's campaign workers, who asked how they could win with such a small number. Shaheen replied to her, "don't think about winning and losing. The only question you've got to ask yourself is 'Are you with the right man? Would this man ever embarrass you?' That's all you have to think about, you can't think about winning and losing. If that's what you're going to handicap, then you'll never make a decision based upon your heart and your mind." Bill Shaheen recalled telling Carter he had better keep up his end of the bargain: "If I ever catch you lying to me, I'll turn on you." (He put it more colorfully to *Time* magazine, warning that he would figuratively cut Carter's throat in New Hampshire.)

Another Carter recruit, Katherine Rogers, now a lawyer and member of the Concord city council, has nearly thirty years of experience in New Hampshire politics. But she still remembers vividly the first time a presidential candidate came courting. In 1974, at the age of eighteen, Rogers was the youngest person ever elected to New Hampshire's constitutional convention. Rogers later was invited to meet Carter in Bedford at the Wayfarer Inn—then, as today, the most famous watering hole in New Hampshire during primary season. She was one of six who showed up to meet Carter. An African studies and economic development major in college, Rogers came armed with questions on the Third World, thinking she would stump the southern politician with a question on the Great World Grain Bank. Carter surprised her with a ten-to-fifteen minute disquisition on the institution. After the meeting, Rogers and another activist headed to the bar with Carter and his son, Chip, and spent the rest of the evening in conversation. She recalled, "I was nineteen, it was the first time I'd ever been 'courted' in a presidential race, and I thought this was amazing. I also thought he was . . . an exceptional gentleman, a lot more conservative than I am, in hindsight, but just the way he was, very straight-arrow, never-questioned integrity, and so forth. And the fact that he spent that amount of time talking to me kind of overwhelmed me."[2] Two days later, Rogers received a call from Carter's staff, which then consisted of two people, asking if she would like to volunteer, and she actually felt "somewhat obliged" to do so. Rogers eventually became an intern for the Carter campaign, earning $27.50 a month, and worked for him from the fall of 1975 until the presidential election, campaigning in some fifteen different states in the primary season.

Gradually building a band of newcomers, Carter began to reach out to voters in New Hampshire. For presidential candidates, campaigning here months and months before the primary requires dogged determination in an atmosphere of equal parts uncertainty and tedium, especially for a candidate whom voters do not recognize. Bill Shaheen recalled a day with Carter and his aide Jody Powell, meeting voters at the Portsmouth Naval Shipyard and handing out "greenies," green cards with information on the candidate, including information on his naval service. "It was him, me and Jody Powell handing out these greenies. And guys would say, 'Oh, no, I'm from Maine, I don't count,' and . . . throw it on the ground, and Carter and I would go pick it up. . . . I would be in front of Carter, saying, 'Meet Jimmy Carter, the next president,' and they'd say, 'No, I'm from Maine,' and I'd say, 'Well, he's going to run in Maine, too.'" Through it all, a campaign must maintain its focus on the things it can actually affect, Bill Shaheen said: "You don't worry about other people. . . . You have to think about who it is you're representing, and what is their commitment. And that's what you have to worry about. You'll go crazy if you worry about somebody else, because those are the things you can't control."

In the early days, the Carter campaign lived off the land, and relied on people's hospitality in lieu of campaign funding. Carter would go anywhere there was a crowd, Bill Shaheen said, and take any opportunity to further the campaign. If people expressed interest in holding a coffee in their home, the campaign would not hesitate to take them up on their offer. The candidate slept over in people's homes because it saved money on the campaign.

Day after day, the candidate would get up and do it all over again—give speeches, shake hands, and travel the state. Campaigning in the early stages, months and months before the primary registers in voters' minds, is one tedious day after another, with no clear signs of whether all the work is making an impact. Campaigning, after all, is nothing so much as saying the same thing to as many different people as possible, going to bed, getting up, and doing the same thing all over again. Carter was a tireless campaigner; he "wouldn't leave you alone, so you had to listen to him," Rogers said. The first slot on Carter's daily campaign schedule was at 6 A.M., and it did not conclude until 11 at night. Bill Shaheen recalled the "doldrums" of the summer of 1975 as seemingly "endless." By the fall, "I could literally give a speech for [Carter]. I could sit back and lip-synch it. And if he was asked a question, I could give the answer by lip-synching, I knew exactly what he was going to say every time he said it."

What was Carter saying in speech after speech? This was often open to interpretation and dispute because Carter was not ideologically consistent from issue to issue. On economic issues, he tended toward conservative stances, yet he was firmly liberal on matters of civil rights. On the issue of abortion, he was accused of wanting to be on both sides—against a constitutional amendment banning the practice yet voicing his personal opposition to it and his willingness to impose other types of restrictions.[3] Like other insurgents, however, Carter's most consistent message was a call for change and reform. Again and again he told audiences, "I want a government that is as good, and honest, and decent, and truthful, and fair, and competent, and idealistic, and compassionate, and as filled with love as are the American people."[4]

In the wake of the Watergate scandals of Richard Nixon's administration, Carter's message and style had a unique resonance with voters, said Rogers. A candidate's charisma can never be discounted in New Hampshire, she added, but what counts as charisma varies from election to election. Any other year Carter's idealistic, straight-arrow persona might not have played as well, but in 1975 and 1976, when the candidate said in his stump speech that if he ever told a lie or an untruth, people should not vote for him, "you believed him . . . that, at that time, was very charismatic."

Carter hated to be late for any event, Rogers recalled, but at the same time he also talked to everybody, never leaving an event without shaking every person's hand and making some kind of personal impression. The personal connection was the hallmark of Carter's field operation in New Hampshire. The strategy in the field in a state where no one knew the candidate was for Carter, or someone who knew him, "to talk to everybody in the state a few times," Rogers said. The Carter campaign was not only about quantity of contacts, Rogers said, but quality of contacts as well. Voters were contacted by someone "that knew who they were talking about."

The strategic environment dictated such a strategy. Throughout the campaign, the number of candidates shapes each campaign's determination of how a candidate focuses on "where and what kind of votes they need in order to win," said activist Jim Demers. As a rule, the more crowded the race, the more important it is to make a targeted effort. For instance, in an eight-person race, a candidate might decide to focus on a particular demographic, such as the senior citizen vote, or a candidate could focus on a specific region, such as the vote-rich southern third of the state, in the hopes that directing efforts toward that area could yield more votes than a statewide effort. In 1976, Carter was one candidate in a crowded field, but he had the right wing of the field all to himself since the other moderate to conservative in the race, Senator Henry "Scoop" Jackson of Washington state, had decided to skip New Hampshire. Carter reached out to blue-collar workers, said Bill Shaheen, and appealed to traditional New Deal Democrats who wanted the country to settle back into a normal routine after the Watergate trauma. The campaign studied the 1972 primary vote, recalled Jeanne Shaheen, and targeted towns that Muskie had carried, reasoning that these areas would be more open to a moderate-to-conservative Democrat.[5]

The Carter campaign's chief operatives, Hamilton Jordan and Chris Brown, also incorporated into their strategy the fact that their campaign teams were small but fiercely dedicated to their candidate, said Rogers. In executing that voter outreach strategy, having a crew of green recruits had its advantages. Rogers recalled standing on Elm Street in Manchester at one o'clock in the morning on a Saturday night, collecting signatures on a petition to get Carter on the primary ballot. "Anybody that would stand on Elm Street in Manchester in the middle of the night on a Saturday is either crazy, or committed, or should be committed," Rogers said. But this sort of dedication pays off by demonstrating to potential voters the resolve of those working with the candidate.

A small campaign also gave new political talent room to flourish. Jeanne Shaheen, the woman who would become New Hampshire's first female governor, began her political career by organizing Strafford County for Carter. Shaheen found the challenges of starting up a political organization to her liking. One of the first challenges was to find out where the voters were, not an inconsiderable task in the days before computerized voter files. To get the voter file for the town of Rollinsford, Shaheen had to peruse index cards kept in shoe boxes (one for men and another for women) with no addresses or phone numbers attached to the names. A good organizer is also up to the challenge of asking people to do things and avoiding discouragement when they say no. During the Carter campaign, Shaheen contacted "everybody I had ever met" in New Hampshire. Her rule of thumb was that twenty calls might muster only two or three volunteers. If someone turned her down to do one thing, Shaheen would not hesitate to call them again to ask them to do something else. "I like to call it the guilt factor," she joked. "By the time you call them three or four times, they're feeling like they have to do something to help you."

Keeping the operation small had other advantages as well. The Carter campaign was free of much of the organizational bloat that often puts a drag on the campaigns of front runners. In particular, the Carter campaign was, for the most part, free of what they called clutchers, people who just wanted to come along for the winning ride, Rogers recalled. Clutchers tend to grasp onto a front-running campaign or well-known candidate in order to be seen with the candidate as much as possible. In the Carter campaign, the clutchers did not emerge until the last couple of weeks before the primary. "They were never there when you needed somebody to go do door-to-door on a [cold] day . . . or drive somebody . . . ," Rogers said, "but when it was someplace where they were going to stand next to the candidate and look important, they were always available." At Carter's inauguration ceremony, clutchers were prominent, she said.

When asked what were the main lessons from that campaign, Rogers's first memory is of little bags of peanuts. Each bag had a seal with Carter's picture, and the words "Jimmy Carter for President." Carter volunteers would hand out the bags of peanuts with brochures, reasoning that while voters might throw away the piece of paper, most would keep the free food. The volunteers even gave away the peanuts to tollbooth attendants as they drove through.

The Carter campaign also was well known for its Peanut Brigade, a group of Georgians who came up to New Hampshire to campaign for Carter. The members of the Peanut Brigade disembarked from their plane on a cold, snowy day in Manchester, the women dressed in mink coats and open-toed heels. Rogers recalled that one Georgian claimed that if they could drive in the Georgia mud, they certainly could handle the New Hampshire snow; about half an hour after they got on their way, the campaign office received the first distress call from a Georgian stuck in a snowbank. Out-of-staters had crossed into New Hampshire in previous campaigns, but they mainly were college students, such as those working for the McCarthy campaign in 1968. What was unique about Carter's Peanut Brigade, Rogers recalled, was that its members were a varied group—professional people, lawyers, doctors, and housewives—and that helped them to get a fair hearing when they knocked on people's doors. The best campaigner was Carter's Aunt Sissy, who came up to New Hampshire one week a month. A volunteer would drive her from town to town with a simple directive: go to the town and meet everybody. "It's crazy when you think about it," Rogers said.

> But you'd send her to a town like Hooksett. She might well come into this Dunkin' Donuts, spend an hour, and have a conversation with everybody in here. And it might have been part of [being] Southern, they were more used to people just being more open and friendly. But they would literally come and talk to everybody in the place. And you're going to remember, a little later on, that you talked to this crazy little old woman that was really sweet, but her favorite nephew was running for president.

Candidates in subsequent primaries copied Carter's methods: Walter Mondale had his "Fritz Blitz" from Minnesota; Michael Dukakis sent cabinet and elected officials from Massachusetts to go door-to-door; Clinton imported fellow citizens from Arkansas.

All in all, the Carter field strategy was not based on volume but on both precision targeting of voters and quality of voter contact. The campaign placed its resources in the more conservative areas of the state. On the Carter campaign, volunteers would go door-to-door to talk with voters and then go back to headquarters and write a note that would go in the mail to the voter. Another example was the single Carter volunteer who visited each voter at least three times as she canvassed the working-class towns of Allenstown and Pembroke and was later at the polls on election day.

Nowadays making personal connections still matters in New Hampshire, but campaigns increasingly forgo taking on those types of sustained efforts. For a campaign with more resources, Rogers said, it is important to have as many contacts as possible with people, at least three. The telephone is increasingly difficult to use because people do not respond well to being called at home. Instead, campaigns pursue a blanket approach, sending large groups of volunteers into one area on one weekend, a second area on the next weekend, and so forth, trying to cover all voters. This fieldwork method overlooks a basic principle that the Carter campaign understood, said Rogers: "It's not just the quantity, it's the quality." In an ideal field operation, the campaign sends people out into the field who have a personal connection with the candidate, Rogers said. Or, if you visit the same voter several times over the course of a campaign and then see that voter outside the polls, a campaign volunteer and a voter can cement a relationship.

The Carter campaign's efforts in New Hampshire received a boost in January 1976 when he finished first in the Iowa caucuses. The victory was less than overwhelming—Carter carried 27.6 percent of the vote while the uncommitteds totaled 37 percent—but it significantly upgraded the candidate's perceived potential, said Bill Shaheen. Before Iowa, Carter was considered at best the candidate of the South, a potential deal maker, but once he won Iowa, he became a national candidate. "What gave us the push was Iowa," Bill Shaheen said, ". . . it was like the wave was breaking. Carter was telling us how good he felt about Iowa, that Iowa would really help us out a lot, and boy, it sure did."

Gaining momentum was especially important to the Carter campaign because it compensated for one of its chief defects, a lack of funds. The Carter campaign spent almost all its money in early primaries in the hopes of cashing in on early success. Right before the primary, the New Hampshire campaign needed $15,000 to send voter guides to likely voters. Bill Shaheen went down to Atlanta for a meeting of the various state financial chairs of the Carter campaign with Hamilton Jordan. Each of the chairs reported to Jordan on how much money they had raised. Then, Shaheen recalled, they reached New Hampshire:

> I said, "I'm not bringing in any money, and I need $15,000 that you won't give me, and I need it now."
>
> And he got pissed at me, he really got pissed at me. He said, "What?"
>
> I said, "I told you, I need the fifteen thousand bucks to do the sample ballot, because if we win New Hampshire, all this money is not going to mean anything, because it's going to just start pouring in, once you win New Hampshire."

Next up was the finance chair from Texas, who informed the group that he had $75,000, but the campaign was only getting $60,000; the rest was going directly to New Hampshire. Shaheen got the money and had his sample ballots published.

Rogers, now a veteran of several New Hampshire primaries, said that superior field organizations can get a candidate two or three percentage points on election day but not a "home run." Carter did not hit a home run on primary day in New Hampshire, carrying just under 29 percent of the vote. But in a crowded field of candidates, 29 percent was enough to eke out a five-point victory over his nearest competitor, Arizona congressman Morris Udall. After Carter's success in New Hampshire, fund-raising concerns eased as "all that publicity, all that momentum, plus all that money" came "pouring in," Bill Shaheen said.

1980

How do you run a campaign without a candidate? That was one of Jeanne Shaheen's dilemmas in the run-up to the 1980 New Hampshire primary. Jimmy Carter, who spent so many days in New Hampshire during the 1976 primary season, hardly set foot in the state during the 1980 campaign.[6] Carter ran a Rose Garden campaign, at least in part because he decided he could not go on the campaign trail during a time of foreign crisis. In November 1979, Iranian students had seized the U.S. Embassy in Tehran, and fifty-two Americans were held hostage. A month later, the Soviet Union invaded Afghanistan.

The second dilemma for Shaheen was her candidate's lack of popularity. At a time when the country's "misery index" (the unemployment rate combined with the rate of inflation) was approaching 20 percent, Carter's popularity, even within his own party, was cratering. In May 1979, a *Boston Globe* poll of New Hampshire Democrats indicated that Carter would lose a challenge by Senator Edward Kennedy of Massachusetts by more than 20 percentage points.[7]

Liberal Democrats had waited for years for the youngest Kennedy to pick up the flame dropped by his slain brothers, even after the scandal of Chappaquiddick. Kennedy had passed on running in 1972 and 1976. But after four years of Carter's conservative brand of Democratic politics, Kennedy seemed serious about challenging the incumbent, addressing New Hampshire Democrats at their state convention in September 1978. Kennedy, according to activist Jeff Woodburn, "had a draw" in New Hampshire: "I mean, there was the Irish, the Catholic, the idealism of Robert and John Kennedy, the deep history that some people had, or felt they had, or wanted to have, with that family [that] played itself out."[8] In 1980, there were still people in New Hampshire who had worked on John Kennedy's campaign twenty years earlier and were connected with Bobby Kennedy "and the whole Kennedy apparatus," said activist Dayton Duncan, who was then working as chief of staff and press secretary for Democratic Governor Hugh Gallen.[9] In spring 1979, Executive Councilor Dudley Dudley and former Democratic state chair Joanne Symons began a campaign to draft Kennedy to run against the president. Kennedy formally announced his candidacy in November, declaring, "For many months, we have been sinking into crisis. . . . Government falters. Fear spreads that our leaders have resigned themselves to retreat."[10]

Twelve years earlier, a liberal senator had done great damage to an incumbent Democratic president who had campaigned via his New Hampshire surrogates. This time, however, Carter was far more effective at using the tools of incumbency than Johnson had been in 1968. First lady Rosalynn Carter made appearances in New Hampshire, as did Vice President Walter Mondale and other members of the Carter administration, Jeanne Shaheen said. In addition, Governor Gallen, whom Carter had helped in his 1978 election campaign, returned the favor by getting on board the president's campaign early in 1979.[11] Gallen's support was not enough to prevent Kennedy or California governor Jerry Brown from entering the race. But the governor's expressed support for a primary candidate swayed other state Democrats to get on board and made others pause before jumping ship. For candidates, "if you want to really help yourself in a state . . . the one you want to bag is the governor," Duncan said. "The fact that [Gallen] came out for Carter," he said, "gave pause to a lot of Democrats who were getting ready to jump onto the Kennedy bandwagon." Without the governor's presence in an already bruising primary, the contest might have broken wide open, Duncan said. In addition, Gallen's political organization was put to work for Carter's efforts in New Hampshire, Jeanne Shaheen said. Finally, the Carter administration ensured that tens of millions of federal dollars would find its way to New Hampshire to fund various and sundry projects in the months before the primary.[12]

In retrospect, Kennedy's best day of his New Hampshire campaign was his first day, recalled Jeanne Shaheen. Kennedy stumbled almost immediately after he left the gate, giving an interview to CBS reporter Roger Mudd in which he was unable to explain why he was running for the presidency. Carter defeated Kennedy by ten percentage points, approximately 47 percent to 37 percent, with Jerry Brown carrying just under 10 percent of the vote. Just as in 1968, however, a Republican victory followed Democratic in-fighting during the primary season, and many New Hampshire Democrats blamed Kennedy for Carter's loss, Jeanne Shaheen said. The ill feelings were the catalyst for an enduring split between liberals and moderate-to-conservatives within the state Democratic Party.

CHAPTER FIVE

The Center Holds: 1984 to 1992

Jimmy Carter's defeat of Ted Kennedy in 1980 was the last New Hampshire Democratic primary to feature an incumbent for sixteen years. Republicans Ronald Reagan and George H. W. Bush occupied the Oval Office from 1980 to 1992, leaving Democrats to conduct the equivalent of open auditions for their presidential nomination. In such an uncertain environment, one might have expected the unexpected in the New Hampshire primary—and those expectations were fulfilled. In 1984, Colorado senator Gary Hart revived the Granite State's reputation as a giant-killer, handing former vice president Walter Mondale a lopsided defeat. And in 1992, an obscure former U.S. senator from Massachusetts, Paul Tsongas, carried the primary and became Bill Clinton's most unlikely challenger for the nomination.

Surprises aside, however, these primaries all produced a common result: the triumph of centrist candidates over those who represented one faction or another in the Democratic Party. In 1984, Hart succeeded in gaining both elite and working-class votes in New Hampshire, and came agonizingly close to the nomination. Massachusetts governor Michael Dukakis methodically stuck to the center in 1988, and succeeded in deflecting all challenges from the wings of the party. And in 1992, Arkansas governor Bill Clinton failed to win New Hampshire, but displayed an ability there to build coalitions of voters that eventually carried him to the nomination.

1984

Presidential primaries in New Hampshire, said activist and author Dayton Duncan, can be divided into two separate contests: the campaign for activists and the campaign for votes.[1] From winter to early fall of the year before the primary, candidates earnestly pursue the support and endorsement of local and state politicians and activists. Getting local names on board is trumpeted as an early sign of momentum and perhaps even as a sign of inevitability of victory.[2]

Throughout this part of the invisible primary, one of the assumed rules of the game is that more is better: Better to have more local politicians on board than fewer, better to have a long list of names to print in the newspaper advertisement than a short list. While winning the campaign for activists has some influence over the final outcome, it is not necessary for winning the primary itself, Duncan said. Indeed, a candidate who wins the campaign for activists and gets established as the front runner sometimes falls victim to an insurgent backlash during the second (and obviously more important) campaign for votes. For example, during the run-up to the 1984 primary, the rush of activists to front runner Walter Mondale only hardened the resolve of activists to support the upstart Colorado senator Gary Hart, to "beat the giant" and "take on all these forces, all these important people that say they can do everything," said Mondale operative Katherine Rogers.[3]

Mondale, Jimmy Carter's vice president, was the presumptive front runner during the run-up to the 1984 primaries, especially after Massachusetts senator Edward Kennedy announced that he would not run for the nomination. Mondale Inc., as political insiders called the campaign, led all other contenders in both fund-raising and endorsements from the party elite, including the support of the AFL-CIO, the National Education Association, and the National Organization for Women.[4] As a result, Mondale began the race with a "target on his back," said Dayton Duncan, who served as deputy press secretary for

Mondale's campaign. "If you're the presumed front runner," Duncan said, "everything's important."

Mondale's overall strategy, then, was to take the fight to his opponents for the nomination at every opportunity.[5] In this national full-court press, no contest was too small for the front runner to enter in the hope of proving his opponents unworthy. During the year before primaries actually started, for instance, Mondale entered straw polls held by various state parties; his opponents would follow him, hoping to impress party elites and increase their fund-raising with an unexpectedly strong showing. Mondale's national campaign, which would fight for every delegate to the convention in every state, was not only designed to win his party's nomination, but also to serve notice that he was better poised to compete against the popular incumbent president, Ronald Reagan, than any other Democrat, Duncan said.

Mondale's main challenger was presumed to be Ohio senator John Glenn, the astronaut hero of the 1960s turned politician. On paper, at least, Glenn was a model candidate for the New Hampshire Democratic primary, being more moderate than Mondale and thus more appealing to the Democrats' moderate-to-conservative bloc of voters.

In 1983, the year before the primaries began, Gary Hart was squarely in the second tier of candidates for the nomination, joining liberals such as the nuclear-freeze advocate, Senator Alan Cranston of California, 1972 presidential nominee George McGovern, and Jesse Jackson; among the conservatives were Senator Ernest Hollings of South Carolina and Florida's former governor Reubin Askew. Throughout the year before the primaries began, Hart's campaign was periodically reported to be on life support—short of cash and short of any kind of breakouts from the pack of candidates following Mondale.

What Hart did seem to have, even early on, was that most intangible of assets—a message for the times. Months and months before the primary, a good candidate is developing a message, "something to hang their hat on . . . what is this guy about? Does he or she have a handle on what our concerns are?" said Merrimack County activist Rob Werner, whose first experience with the primary was on the Hart campaign.[6] Iowa and New Hampshire give politicians the ability to test market their ideas, Werner said, as well as the ways they convey those ideas to ordinary voters: After a campaign event, for instance, a candidate might step back and think, "Maybe I still think I have a good idea, but for whatever reason, I'm not communicating it well, or I'm not clear enough, or I'm not saying it in a way that is compelling."

A candidate needs a core message that tells voters why they should vote for him, Werner said, but the message does not necessarily need to be a laundry list of policy prescriptions. In Hart's New Hampshire kickoff speech in Manchester in February 1983, for instance, the candidate focused on themes larger than his own candidacy: "We are facing the greatest challenges ever in our nation in the mid-1980s, and we must meet those challenges with unity and determination. This coming election is not for a candidate, but rather it's an election to recapture the vision for the future."[7] Throughout the campaign, Hart presented a range of new ideas, Werner said. They all supported a common theme of the need to retool the Democratic Party, to keep core values while taking a different approach to issues in response to new realities, such as changes in the economy and the need to prepare people for those changes. Hart was one of a new wave of Democrats who argued that while the party did not need to cast aside its principles, slavish obedience to every old government program the party had started was misplaced, said Hart activist Ned Helms.[8] To Helms, Hart conveyed the sense of certainty of a man who knew what he was about.

Hart spoke to a crowded hall on that February day in Manchester, but for many of the following weeks, the candidate's New Hampshire team often found itself operating in isolation. "We assumed that if someone was running for president of the United States, there was a plan, there was money, there was national staff to implement the plan," recalled campaign operative Susan Berry Casey in her memoir of Hart's New Hampshire campaign. "We could not, however, have been further from the truth."[9]

Hart deliberately left campaign management in the hands of state organizations, rather than allow a national office in Washington, D.C., to call the shots.[10] Casey and campaign director Jeanne Shaheen were largely left to their own devices to build the organization. Shaheen was pleased with this arrangement, she said, recalling that she would not have joined the New Hampshire campaign if she had not been promised control over the operation.[11] Then as now, Shaheen believed that a New Hampshire campaign is successful when people on the ground in the state have real influence over its activities and its allocation of resources, especially how much time the candidate spends in the state and what the candidate does on campaign trips. When Hart gave his kickoff speech in Manchester that February, Shaheen and Casey had succeeded in forming that "first circle" of activists that would provide the core for future expansion of the campaign.[12] Indeed, as Hart struggled to gain some footing for most of 1983, it often appeared his New Hampshire organization was carrying the national campaign, rather than the other way around.

Mondale operative Katherine Rogers experienced none of the struggles of Hart's start-up organization. When the candidate is a virtual unknown, it is more important to get activists on board early because they lend the campaign credibility and offer the candidate access, Rogers said. In contrast, people rushed to sign on for Mondale's New Hampshire campaign very early, both because of the candidate's prestige as the former vice president and because of his status as the acknowledged front runner. But when it came to building the legs of the campaign—establishing the door-to-door canvass, getting people to make phone calls, recruiting the personnel needed for setting up an effective Election Day operation—the presence of so many activists tended to be more of a hindrance.

For example, a front runner's ability to attract a Who's Who list of prominent New Hampshire activists often stunts the campaign's ability to attract new young activists, Rogers said. In 1984, Mondale's campaign did have a lot of volunteers, but those volunteers did not perceive that they had the ability to make a difference in the campaign in the way that Hart's volunteers did. This inability to make a difference was perceived in a number of ways, including the seemingly most mundane task of who got to drive around the candidate. Whenever Walter Mondale was someplace in New Hampshire, Secret Service agents were his drivers. Back in the Carter campaign, volunteers like Rogers had driven the candidate and his wife around the state. "If you ended up spending a couple hours driving the candidate or a family member," she remembered, "you were kind of personally vested then, and that made your commitment really strong."

Rogers recalled one small success in this regard: a group of students from Memorial High School in Manchester who became enthusiastic volunteers and had the chance to hang out with Mondale on one occasion. One of Mondale's sons, Teddy, came to a volunteer party and talked to them, treating them as if they were friends. Because the commitment had become personal, the high school students came to work every night and on weekends, Rogers said.

The personal connection is especially important for cementing the relationship between the candidate and new rookie volunteers, whose enthusiasm for the campaign borders on the "rabid," Rogers said. Candidates who sign up lots of established activists inadvertently stymie that connection for the new volunteer since the established activists tend to monopolize the personal space around the candidate.

Walter Mondale's campaign, for instance, found itself in a Catch-22 when it came to the recruitment of activists. On one hand, Mondale's operatives considered it vital to get as many top-tier activists as possible on board to bring credibility to the campaign. Mondale's front-runner status meant that any top-tier activist he did not get on board was considered a loss for the campaign. Rogers recalled betting a bottle of Dom Perignon that she could get two thousand names for Mondale's New Hampshire steering committee before the formal announcement of his candidacy. Perhaps it would have been better, Rogers mused, to have spent that time building personal connections between Mondale and new volunteers.

In contrast, the Hart campaign was free of crowds of activists, so newcomers had access to the inner circles of the campaign. Debbie Butler, a lawyer who works in the state capital of Concord, still has fond memories of working for Hart's New Hampshire campaign—the most fun campaign she has ever worked on, she said.[13] Single at the time, Butler would volunteer for the campaign when not working at her job. She recalled going to the airport in her diesel Volkswagen to pick up the candidate. Hart traveled without an entourage, Butler said, which put the candidate in close contact with his grassroots supporters. Volunteers like Butler would take him to one destination, take his bags out of the car, and pass him off to the next person.

A hallmark of the Hart campaign was very early voter contact, Shaheen said. Cheshire County activist Andi Johnson recalled learning much on the importance of early campaign work from Shaheen.[14] Johnson met Gary Hart with ten other people in a living room in Lebanon, where she was then living. Hart told the assembled group that he was going to finish second in Iowa and then win New Hampshire. ("And we're going, 'Yeah, right,'" Johnson recalled with a laugh.) Hart was talking about "working in concentric circles" and going door-to-door in order to raise his name recognition: "You tell this person, and this person will tell this person, and this person will tell this person, who'll tell this person, who'll tell this person, and so on." Hart and his New Hampshire team astutely recognized that the first stage of a campaign is important for generating word of mouth. The hope, at this point, is not necessarily to win over large numbers of voters, but simply to get the candidate's name out there in a positive way, in the hopes that the first mention would make the voter more receptive to more information about the candidate in the future. The next stage is doing the door-to-door work, using "walk lists," lists of frequent voters by order of street address which are supplied by the party. Successful door-to-door work requires the personal touch, Johnson said, someone to "knock and talk," to engage in a conversation with the resident or leave a signed note if the person is not at home. Volunteers had a plethora of their candidate's position papers, said Butler, and were walking encyclopedias of the candidate's views in their own right. All in all, the Hart campaign knocked on tens of thousands of doors in the fall of 1983, Shaheen said, while other campaigns spent time trying to win straw polls in other states in order to gain media attention and prove their candidates had momentum.

Very little good news filtered in from Hart's national campaign during the year preceding the primary. From early March to mid-June of that year, the candidate only visited New Hampshire twice.[15] Morale was a key challenge for the insurgent campaign, Helms said. During the Hart campaign, there were continual reports that it was light on money and could not possibly win. "When you can't pay the bills" and people working for the campaign are not getting paychecks, and the national media are reporting that the candidate will drop out in a couple weeks, "that weighs on the morale," Helms said.

Hart's campaign remained buoyant, however, because of its "home-grown understanding and excitement," Shaheen said. During that campaign, as in Jimmy Carter's eight years earlier, people had reached out to their friends and acquaintances in the state—and as a result, the sometimes dreary day-to-day activities of campaigning became less of a chore and more of a crusade. Brainstorming sessions on ways to reach voters were part of the campaign's routine, Shaheen said. "That keeps people interested because when they feel like they have input into what happens, they're a lot more excited." Volunteers sometimes paid out of their own pocket for local campaign efforts when Shaheen refused to use scarce funds for them, Butler recalled; for instance, a Hart volunteer in a particular town might take it upon herself to write postcards to all of the town's registered Democrats. "The Hart campaign had all the people that took the Kool-Aid," Butler said. "They just completely believed in what they were doing," as opposed to just going with the likely winner.

When times were tough, the Hart campaign stuck with their mantra: The candidate would not drop out, and in fact the base for victory already had been laid on the ground.

The campaign's boasts were met with some skepticism. Hart hardly had any name supporters, and his campaign "was so subterranean, that for many of us, we just didn't see anything happening through the whole fall," recalled Mondale activist Ray Buckley.[16] At the time, it was an open question whether Hart was just staying in the race long enough to collect his federal matching funds and pay off his campaign debts. Hart's concentric-circle organizing "was all quiet. None of us who were involved in the party saw any of this stuff going on because it wasn't among the average party activists," Buckley said.

To this day, Mondale operative Katherine Rogers describes Hart's organization as just a well-executed example of a "blue smoke and mirrors" operation, a campaign that succeeded in looking much larger than it actually was. "They were at the right place, at the right time, doing the right things, so people talked," Rogers said, and the positive word of mouth helped to move voters their way. When a candidate has a small but dedicated core of volunteers, his campaign will try to create a field operation that is "smoke and mirrors," Rogers said. The goal for such an operation is to create good buzz for the campaign, to get word out on the street that the candidate has lots of good organization working for him. In any neighborhood, the campaign should have a map with the houses of opinion makers highlighted: members of the media, elected officials, and known activists. The campaign makes sure that each of those movers and shakers is visited by campaign personnel; that each is included on the literature drops; that yard signs are placed on nearby properties. "You want them thinking that you're everywhere and you're doing everything," Rogers said, "because they'll talk about it." People like to think they are voting for a winner, so providing them with some prima facie evidence of a winning campaign makes them more inclined to vote for your candidate.

Shaheen maintains that Hart's field organization in New Hampshire was vital to his victory there, but agrees with Rogers that the campaign played the media game as well in order to make its limited resources look as robust as possible. At the state party convention in October 1983, for instance, Mondale delegates outnumbered Hart delegates, and Hart's campaign had no money to buy space at the convention to place signs. So instead, the campaign borrowed an RV and placed it in the parking lot outside the convention for free, and put signs on the roof of the building where the convention was held (also for free).[17]

In addition, the Hart campaign made the decision early on to cultivate New Hampshire reporters, reasoning that New Hampshire voters would get more information on the campaign from local newspapers and television than national media, Shaheen recalled. The campaign made sure that local reporters would have time with the candidate and were persistent in keeping reporters in the loop on campaign activities. Hart's operatives also made note of times when prominent national reporters would be in the state and which local political "regulars" they would habitually contact. People on the Hart campaign who knew these activists personally would contact them and offer information on the campaign, in the hope that they would pass it on to the national media.

During the month before the primary, Hart's goal—to separate himself from the rest of the field challenging Mondale and to become the alternative to the front runner—began to be realized. The national media began to tout Hart as the candidate who could replace Glenn as Mondale's main challenger.[18] The media's new conventional wisdom about the Democratic race crystallized the night of the Iowa caucuses, the week before the New Hampshire primary. Hart finished second in Iowa—a weak second place, but one that vaulted him ahead of John Glenn to the status of lead challenger to Mondale.

The voter volatility in the 1984 New Hampshire primary was not atypical, said political advertising executive Pat Griffin.[19] To explain, Griffin divided the primary voting audience into three parts. The first part is the local community of political activists, those who are engaged in political matters to the highest degree. At the other end of the spectrum are those voters who are not particularly engaged and make up their minds very late in the game. They tend to be uninformed followers, most prone to vote for the candidate who seems to be the inevitable winner. In between these two relatively small groups, Griffin said, is the "great middle," a large group of voters with an intermediate level of attention and interest, who may support one candidate for awhile, then shift its support to another. Candidates must make appeals to all three groups, but the "great middle" are the most coveted:

> [It's] like working a lounge act in Vegas. It's tough. There's the drunks, who laugh at anything. And then there's the people who basically say, "Yeah, everyone else is laughing, so I better laugh, too." But there's the people who show up sober and say, "OK, forty-two bucks for this ticket, this guy better be funny." And that's the toughest part of the room to work.

In a primary, when perhaps a third of the electorate is new, it is difficult to do traditional voter contact, and it is also difficult to come up with hard numbers of candidate support, Griffin said. Even if the voter came to a coffee with the candidate, even if the voter has been sent mail and contacted by the campaign multiple times, the voter should not be counted as committed unless she has been spoken to the previous night, Griffin said. Too many things happen over the months before the primary to be able to identify voters weeks or months in advance. Griffin concluded, "In New Hampshire, we get to dance with a lot of people before it's time to go home."[20]

The week between the Iowa caucuses and New Hampshire, no one seemed to want to dance with front runner Walter Mondale. It was a week Katherine Rogers would just as soon forget: She had developed pneumonia, had no voice left, and she had to wake up Mondale, the former vice president of the United States, not once but twice to tell him he was losing New Hampshire.

New Hampshire had become the right place at the right time for Hart, in part because the challenge from Mondale's supposed chief rival, John Glenn, simply evaporated, much to the frustration of the Mondale campaign. Going into the last month and a half before Iowa and New Hampshire, Mondale's campaign felt confident that he would defeat Glenn in New Hampshire, Duncan said. "We hadn't anticipated . . . that [Glenn's] whole campaign would implode after Iowa."

Glenn's collapse changed the dynamics of the multicandidate field in New Hampshire in subtle, unpredictable ways. Most Democratic voters had made one basic decision: whether they were with Mondale the front runner or against him. The Mondale campaign estimated that they had secured not a majority but perhaps just under 40 percent of New Hampshire voters. Mondale's standing in New Hampshire had been consistent throughout the months preceding the primary, enjoying a 35 to 40 percent standing in the polls. In a multicandidate field, the Mondale campaign estimated that this probably would be enough to win, with each of the other candidates carrying various shares of the remaining 60 percent of the vote.

But with Glenn's collapse and the slow fade of most of the remainder of the field, what the Mondale campaign got instead in New Hampshire was a two-man race between the front runner and Hart. Duncan recalled: "If you'd already said you weren't voting for Mondale, you were pretty much told if you were watching the news, 'Don't waste your vote on this pathetic guy from Ohio, because that campaign's gone nowhere. Your choice, if you decide you're not voting for Mondale, is this exciting new product: His name is Gary Hart.'"

The Hart campaign, said Duncan, had worked on the grassroots level in order to capitalize on this wave of media-generated momentum. Hart activist Andi Johnson recalled that about three weeks before the primary, the campaign began to see voters breaking toward Hart in their canvassing. Hart was not the status quo, Johnson said, and generated more excitement than Mondale. Duncan maintains, however, that Hart's grass-roots organizing was not what ultimately created his victory in New Hampshire. He pointed out, for instance, that Hart also succeeded in places where he had no organization set up. A week after New Hampshire, Hart manhandled Mondale in the Maine caucuses, despite the fact that Mondale had made a significant grassroots effort there and the insurgent had spent virtually no time and developed no organization.

In the reconstruction of [the 1984 New Hampshire primary], it's that they [Hart] had this very good local organization, where the Mondale [campaign], the Cadillac Imperial campaign, didn't. Well, that's not true. We might have been the Cadillac Imperial candidacy in some people's eyes, but the grassroots campaign—getting out the vote, talking to people, walking the walk—was just as much ours as it was theirs. It's just that when the bolt of media lightning hit, they were fully prepared to take advantage of it. And they gave Mondale and our campaign a good pasting here.

When the media lightning hit right after Iowa, "by the time it was clear what was happening, it was almost too late to do anything about it," said Duncan. While Mondale had done "beyond overwhelming" in Iowa, Duncan said, Hart had finished second, exceeding expectations and thus gaining momentum that his campaign in New Hampshire exploited. When Hart took Glenn's place as the alternative to Mondale, he benefited from the subsequent media glare on Mondale and alleged mishaps in the front runner's campaign. "Hart was viewed as storming" toward the stumbling front runner, Duncan said, and the perception helped to create the reality.

Meanwhile, Mondale's front runner status only seemed to hurt him by making his campaign simultaneously cautious and arrogant.[21] Fresh off his victory in the Iowa caucuses, Mondale's national campaign directors decided that the candidate should enter New Hampshire "as a conquering hero, kind of like [General Douglas] MacArthur . . . because he kicked ass in Iowa," Rogers said. At the time, Rogers objected that such a display would not go over well with voters in New Hampshire, who did not want to be told who the nominee should be, and she quit briefly in protest. After that, "everybody said, 'oh, well, Mondale's coming in like he owns the place,'" Rogers recalled, acting as if he were the self-declared winner who did not seem to need anybody's vote.

Mondale's victory lap in New Hampshire was short-lived. On the Thursday or Friday before the primary, the Mondale campaign received reports that the undecideds, rather than dispersing among several different candidates as would normally be the case, were all breaking to Gary Hart. Rogers remembered calling Mondale's national campaign director in Manchester and the two of them going to the Wayfarer in Bedford to wake up Mondale and deliver the bad news.

The Mondale campaign decided the way to stem the Hart wave was to increase turnout because the more passive voters (those less likely to vote) were more likely to favor Mondale. Attempts to increase turnout, however, were hampered by the fact that the campaign was up against the federal spending cap in New Hampshire. And when Hart received his matching funds, he had invested it in commercials on New Hampshire television and actually had put more ads on the air in the last two weeks than Mondale.

By the weekend before the primary, all signs pointed to a disaster for the front runner, both from the polling data and from the Mondale campaign's nightly calls and canvassing results. It was a "tidal wave," Rogers said, and riding the top of the wave was Gary Hart. Mondale's ground organization was well prepared to deliver the vote, given its excellent get-out-the-vote organization in terms of people, targeting, and canvassing. On election day, Mondale had door-to-door canvassing in every city and many towns, as well as phone canvasses. The problem, Rogers recalled, was that "we didn't have enough people to pull out." As she summarized, the voters "had shifted . . . people liked Gary Hart, but I think they were angry at Mondale. . . . He came into the state and said, 'I won. I'm coronated. I'm going to be the nominee.' Gary Hart was out throwing the axe, being young, being vital. The press thing . . . had more to do with it than the organization."[22]

Shaheen contended that it was voters' lack of emotion toward Mondale's candidacy that hurt him in New Hampshire. Voters simply were not excited about Mondale. The former vice president's campaign compounded the problem, she said, by running a traditional campaign, highlighting his status as the former vice president.

The Mondale disaster culminated on primary day. "If anything could go wrong for Walter Mondale that day, it went wrong," Rogers said. In the early morning hours, the snow began to fall and the sleet followed, "the worst weather I've ever seen in New Hampshire," she recalled. For a campaign depending on high turnout for a victory, the game was already over before it had hardly begun, despite the campaign's door-to-door canvassing. The passive voters Mondale was counting on did not come to the polls. To cap off the day, the tires on the airplane scheduled to take Mondale out of New Hampshire went flat, so the candidate had to ride in a hastily assembled motorcade to Boston.

For Gary Hart, primary night confirmed his never-wavering belief that he would win New Hampshire, Helms said. Hart always felt that "the media wants a race, and the people want a race, and all you had to do was to make it to that next stage so you can make it a race, and then all of a sudden you had a race," Helms said. And so it was, all the way to the last primaries in California and

New Jersey months later. Although Hart fell short of the nomination, he proved what it took to win New Hampshire, said Butler: smart people who understand the local landscape, a good chunk of money, and believers.

1988

In contrast to 1984, the 1988 Democratic primary season had no front runner. Despite this absence, the New Hampshire Democratic primary turned out to be a relatively quiet, uneventful affair because one of the candidates, Governor Michael Dukakis of Massachusetts, exploited his home court advantage to the fullest.

Gary Hart, the insurgent who had nearly won the nomination four years earlier, was cast this time around as the front runner during the invisible primary season in the year prior to the actual electoral contests, although he continued to lack support from party regulars. Hart's operatives did not think that their candidate would necessarily score an early knockout in Iowa and New Hampshire. They realized that Missouri congressman Richard Gephardt would likely do well in the Iowa caucuses and that Dukakis would have the backyard advantage in New Hampshire. Nonetheless, as long as Hart finished in one of the "money positions" in those early states—first, second, or third—the candidate had the financial wherewithal to make it through the Super Tuesday southern primaries and then triumph over any surviving contenders in the remaining contests.[23]

In New Hampshire, Susan Calegari was a lead operative on Hart's campaign. She recalled that Hart's front runner status was a hindrance as the campaign tried to re-create the magic of 1984.[24] The candidate no longer enjoyed the possibility of coming from nowhere; Calegari recalled a political cartoon of the 1988 candidates, modeled after "Snow White and the Seven Dwarfs," with Hart as Snow White. The presence of the media, sparse in 1984, was now a constant, Calegari said. "We were worried that we would be perceived as the establishment campaign, and we were doing our darndest to have these little house parties and have the intimacy" that had characterized the 1984 campaign. The Hart campaign was trying to reach out to the supporters of 1984 rivals such as

Mondale as well as bring new people into the process. "We actually were looking forward to Dukakis getting into the race," Calegari said, so that the Massachusetts governor could be pinned as the front runner, the candidate most likely to win New Hampshire. "Strategically, we were ready to position ourselves to make it look like we might not win."

All the strategizing and campaigning came to an abrupt halt in May 1987 when Hart left the race amid allegations of an extramarital affair. Suddenly the race for the nomination was left to much lower-profile candidates such as Dukakis and Gephardt, who had based their strategies on becoming the alternative to Hart during the course of the primaries.[25] The Massachusetts governor wasted no time asserting the seriousness of his candidacy, raising $4.2 million in his first quarter as a candidate, more than double the amount of his nearest competitor. Dukakis continued to put up impressive fund-raising numbers throughout the rest of 1987, consistently raising at least $1 million a month, while Gephardt borrowed against his federal matching funds in order to keep his campaign in operation.[26]

At the time, not a lot of people knew Gephardt; he did not have the stature or connections he has today after serving as House Democratic Leader, said New Hampshire activist James Demers, whose relationship with Richard Gephardt dates back to 1985.[27] Gephardt's preliminary strategy, Demers said, was to put a tremendous focus on Iowa, in the hopes that an Iowa win would give a bump into New Hampshire and that the domino effect would kick in as a result.

Dukakis and his operatives, however, considered New Hampshire a must-win and took nothing for granted in the months before the primary.[28] In New Hampshire, Dukakis did not so much overwhelm the field; he simply squeezed the air out of the primary, leaving competitors little oxygen with which to spark a surge against him.

Dukakis had been an innovative governor in Massachusetts and had built and maintained a formidable organization there, including captains in towns and city wards whose job it was to get out the vote for the candidate, said Katherine Rogers, who became a lead operative on his campaign. In general, governors have stronger organizations than senators, she said, because of the number of jobs a governor controls. More people owe personal allegiance to a governor than a senator. Each of those ward and town captains was assigned a town in New Hampshire and established personal contacts with residents. At every event Dukakis did in New Hampshire, names of those who attended would be collected on sign-in sheets and sent down to Dukakis's base in Massachusetts. There, Dukakis operatives would enter the names into his database, which was already set up for his gubernatorial campaigns. Letters were generated and sent out within the week to each person who had attended the event. Thus, a voter attending a house party in Goffstown would shortly thereafter receive what appeared to be a handwritten note from the candidate. In this way, technology helped to improve personal contact with primary voters.

Dukakis's fellow Greek Americans were another key to his victory, spearheaded by Chris Spirou, who later was head of the state Democratic Party, Rogers said. (Dukakis was the first Greek American to run for the presidency.) Spirou knew every Greek in the state, Rogers said, and every pizza parlor, every restaurant, every convenience store owned by someone of Greek ethnicity had a Dukakis poster or yard sign displayed.

A second key, said Rogers, was the presence of expatriate Massachusetts residents who had moved north across the border into New Hampshire but remained liberal Democrats. Furthermore, if the expatriates still read the Boston newspapers or got their nightly news from one of the city's three major television stations, they could hardly avoid news of Dukakis's exploits on the presidential campaign trail. "He was getting an excessive amount of television coverage that no other candidate was getting," said Demers.

In addition to importing his organization from south of the New Hampshire border, Dukakis himself was able to make frequent appearances by taking a short trip north after work to Manchester, Nashua, or Portsmouth.[29] Working for Dukakis in the border city of Nashua was Jane Clemons, who now represents the city's Fourth and Sixth wards in the state legislature. "You name it, I did it," Clemons recalled: making phone calls, walking the wards, providing street maps or food, attending events, "whatever they needed me to do."[30]

Clemons's fifteen years of experience in New Hampshire politics has taught her that there is no substitute for the candidate's physical presence. Big events are one thing, Clemons said, but what wins campaigns is

Walking the wards, going door-to-door, going to the businesses. When they say to me, "So-and-so's coming to town, and we're going to do these events," my first thing is, "OK, let's walk downtown." . . . we go door to door to door to door, to businesses, introduce the candidates, have them find out how their businesses are doing, what changes they'd like to see, talk about issues that are personally affecting them.

Outdoor cafés, fire stations, the dump—all these places have voters who have things to say, "and they want to say them" to the candidate. A New Hampshire campaign requires the candidate's physical presence, Clemons said: "You be here, and you be where you need to be. You need to go into those wards and meet people."

As Dukakis gained a hammerlock on New Hampshire, lesser-known candidates found it difficult to even find a toehold. After Hart dropped out of the race (temporarily, as it turned out), Susan Calegari joined the campaign of Bruce Babbitt, the former governor of Arizona. Babbitt, like Hart, was a candidate of "new ideas," calling attention to the yawning federal deficit, advocating a national "consumption tax" and means-testing for entitlement programs, including Social Security.[31] On the ground in New Hampshire, however, the Babbitt campaign was the exact opposite of Hart's 1984 campaign. The circle never expanded. House parties never attracted more than small groups of people. Absent crowded houses, Calegari recalled, the campaign tried to attract whoever they could with the line, You want to meet a presidential candidate? Babbitt had an awful debate performance in July 1987, and "it was really the end of the campaign at that point."

Babbitt had campaign operations in Iowa and New Hampshire only, and the campaign made a decision to send most of the money to Iowa because Babbitt seemed to have more appeal to midwestern voters. With funds dried up, Babbitt's campaign in New Hampshire tried to organize for the state party convention in the fall of 1987 but was outshone by Gephardt's and Dukakis's efforts. Babbitt's small core of diehard supporters loved him for his integrity and honesty, his emphasis on children's issues, and the unconventional nature of his candidacy. But for Babbitt, the core was the end of the line: "he was a lot of people's second choice . . . it was hard to get people paying attention,"

Calegari said. Babbitt's poor showing in Iowa was the death knell, and the week between Iowa and New Hampshire was a tough one for the candidate and the campaign, knowing that nothing would change Babbitt's fortunes. "It's like getting ready for a war, and you're training, and you're really ready," said Babbitt supporter Jeff Woodburn, but in the end, "we weren't picked. Nothing we could do about it."[32]

Iowa was kinder to Richard Gephardt who succeeded in winning the caucuses, earning just over 31 percent of the precinct delegates elected.[33] Gephardt had succeeded in the farm belt state with a protectionist stance on international trade. His campaign ran a very successful ad highlighting how much a South Korean-made Hyundai would retail for in the United States if Korean tariffs were applied to it.[34] The congressman, however, was unable to shake off Senator Paul Simon of Illinois (who finished at almost 27 percent in Iowa) and to establish himself as the primary challenger to Dukakis in New Hampshire.[35] Dukakis finished third with 22 percent.

Gephardt arrived in New Hampshire not especially well suited for a late surge. The pro-labor, anti-free trade message used in Iowa, for example, was seen as a hindrance to the candidate's prospects in New Hampshire, said campaign operative Mark Longabaugh.[36] Gephardt's New Hampshire campaign was so low on funds by that time, however, that they never filmed a single ad for New Hampshire, and instead, after cutting out the farm scenes, reran the ads shown in Iowa. In addition, Gephardt operatives were concerned about changing the message of the campaign in midstream, so they reran the Hyundai ad in a state prospering via free trade. The only alternatives were either to try and discredit Dukakis's record as governor of Massachusetts in an effort to attract southern-tier New Hampshire residents who allegedly fled north to escape "Taxachusetts"; or, to allow Gephardt to move completely on the strength of momentum from the Iowa victory. "We were counting on the Iowa win to do everything," Longabaugh said, "and it just couldn't do that."

In addition, while Gephardt was concentrating on the New Hampshire front runner, Dukakis, other candidates were pursuing Gephardt. Candidates had learned from the sudden momentum that Gary Hart gained in 1984, and they aimed to stop Gephardt before he was able to start converting his Iowa win into New Hampshire momentum, said Longabaugh. During the eight days between Iowa and New Hampshire, Paul Simon directed his attacks not at Dukakis, but at Gephardt in order to stop his momentum in its tracks. Simon felt the fight was for second place. During debates just before the primary, Simon attacked Gephardt, Gephardt had to defend against attack, and Dukakis was allowed to walk away "feeling like he never had a glove laid on him, because all the rest of the candidates were waging a war for second place," Demers said. That was a strategic error, because none of those candidates were in a position to capitalize on a second-place finish.

The infighting among the second tier of candidates only aided Dukakis, who had succeeded in raising more funds than his rivals for the Democratic presidential nomination. Despite his status as the governor next door, Dukakis found, just as Mondale had, there was a ceiling to his support. The campaign realized that Dukakis could not get above 40 percent of the vote in New Hampshire. Therefore, the key to winning New Hampshire was to keep all his competitors under 30 percent in order to be able to make a convincing claim of victory. And in order to keep all competitors under 30 percent, it was important that all the other campaigns stay vital enough to hold onto the votes they had. If one candidate surged and others collapsed in the week before New Hampshire, then New Hampshire might become a one-on-one race, and Dukakis's 40 percent would not be enough to win. Michael Dukakis's campaign learned from the disaster that befell Mondale four years earlier, said Ray Buckley, a Dukakis supporter.

In order to do their part in keeping all his rivals going, Dukakis campaign operatives paid close attention to daily polling and canvassing to judge which of his rivals was up and which was down, Buckley said. The last weeks of the campaign resembled the carnival game of Whack-a-Mole: "You lay off that person that's collapsing, and you go after the person that's building up some support, so you're constantly shifting who you're going after."

Dukakis carried New Hampshire by 16 points—the first time a contested New Hampshire Democratic primary had been won by more than 10 percentage points.[37] Gephardt finished just ahead of Simon with nearly 20 percent of the vote, failing to get the bump he hoped for; when he went into later primary states, more resources did not materialize. Meanwhile, the Dukakis campaign continued to gather momentum toward the Democratic nomination.

1992

Even for New Hampshire, 1992 was a wildly unsettled year. To get a sense of what was in the air, consider the top two finishers in the Democratic presidential primary that year. In first place was yet another Greek from Massachusetts, Paul Tsongas, a retired U.S. senator and cancer sufferer whose campaign centered around a book on economic policy. In second place was Bill Clinton, a governor from a small southern state who entered the field late, quickly became the front runner, was bombarded by personal revelations, nearly crashed and burned— and wound up spinning an 8-point loss in New Hampshire into a comeback. It was that kind of year.

In 1991, quietly prosperous New Hampshire, over the previous two decades the fastest-growing state in New England, was on its heels economically. Its unemployment rate had more than doubled over the past four years; 10 percent of the state's nonfarm jobs, 50,000 in all, had disappeared. The state's five biggest banks had closed. Bankruptcy rates and those qualified for welfare and food stamps were both sharply increasing. Fewer than one in five voters in a *Boston Globe* poll approved of how President George H. W. Bush was handling the economy.[38]

As electoral storms go, the 1992 New Hampshire Democratic primary was the slowest to develop since 1968, when Gene McCarthy stepped in three months before ballots were cast to challenge a sitting president. The chattering class of American politics waited, and waited, for a formidable Democrat to challenge President George H. W. Bush, who was riding a sky-high approval rating nationally after a quick and successful war against Iraq in the winter of 1991. It waited for Mario Cuomo, the governor of New York and eloquent defender of the liberal faith. It waited for Senator Al Gore of Tennessee to try again, or if not him, another southerner such as Senator Sam Nunn of Georgia, or Senator Jay Rockefeller of West Virginia, or Senator Lloyd Bentsen of Texas, the 1988 vice presidential nominee. It waited for a leader of the party's congressional delegation, such as House Majority leader Richard Gephardt of Missouri, or Senate Majority leader George Mitchell of Maine. It waited for Jesse Jackson to build on his better-than-expected performance in 1988. It waited for a neoliberal, such as Senator Bill Bradley of New Jersey, to take up the cause of moving the party toward the center.[39] The Democrats waited and waited for the first team to take the field. In the end, however, even the star player, Mario Cuomo, never got off the bus, leaving longtime New Hampshire activist Joseph Grandmaison and a team of supporters literally waiting on the phone until the afternoon of the filing deadline for the primary.[40]

Although the Democrats did not get the specific candidates they expected, they did get representatives of almost all the important factions in their party. Instead of Cuomo, they got Senator Tom Harkin of Iowa, a fiery defender of traditional liberal values. Instead of the neoliberal Bradley, they got Senator Bob Kerrey of Nebraska, a former governor and Vietnam War veteran who had earned a reputation as an unorthodox liberal who was impervious to accusations of being soft on national defense.[41] In place of Jackson, they got the maverick progressive Jerry Brown, former governor of California, now in his third decade of attempts to win his party's nomination.

And, instead of Gore or Nunn, the Democrats got Governor Bill Clinton of Arkansas, a moderate and former chair of the Democratic Leadership Council (DLC), an organization formed in 1985 with the express purpose of moving the party back toward the center after Mondale's crushing defeat in 1984.[42] In announcing his candidacy in his state's capital of Little Rock, Clinton wove a message directed at the middle class into the time-honored Democratic platform, advocating a tax cut for middle-class taxpayers and stating that he expected welfare recipients to take on more personal responsibility for their plight:

> Middle-class people are spending more hours on the job, spending less time with their children, bringing home a smaller paycheck to pay more for health care and housing and education. Our streets are meaner, our families are broke, our health care is the costliest in the world and we get less for it. The country is headed in the wrong direction fast, slipping behind, losing our way, and all we have out of Washington is status quo paralysis.[43]

In the fall of 1991, in the absence of so many Democratic heavyweights who took a pass, Clinton took his place at the head of the first tier of candidates, along with Harkin and Kerrey.

And finally, the Democrats got someone whom no one expected and no one especially wanted after Michael Dukakis's general election debacle. Paul Tsongas, the two-term congressman and one-term senator from Massachusetts, had been out of politics for seven years, retiring from the Senate because of cancer.[44] Declared cancer-free by his physician,[45] Tsongas was reentering national politics at, of all places, the level of the presidential primary. He was the first to enter the contest in May 1991, "and the one who was last to be taken seriously," said his campaign manager, Dennis Kanin. "We had a few weaknesses . . . Greek, Massachusetts . . . out of office for seven years, no name recognition, unusual speech pattern, [and] a perceived charisma deficit."[46]

But Tsongas, like Clinton, had his finger on the issue that would move voters nationwide in that presidential year: the tailspinning national economy and the rising insecurity this spawned among Americans. Tsongas was first belittled for his focus on the economy, "but Tsongas got it," said Kevin Landrigan of the *Nashua Telegraph,* "which was, there's a chord up here, people are hurting, and the national media isn't tuned into it because of the war clouding everything else out."[47] James Carville of Bill Clinton's campaign came up with his mantra, "it's the economy, stupid," in Manchester, four or five months before it became a national story, Landrigan recalled. In February 1992, it was the no-nonsense technocrat from Lowell, Massachusetts, and the middle-class populist[48] from Arkansas who caught the attention of a state besieged with bad times. In 1992, it was the candidates with the most substance who fared the best in the primary, said New Hampshire activist Rob Werner. In economic hard times, voters wanted to know what, specifically, candidates were going to do to get the country out of the doldrums. As Clinton pollster Stan Greenberg put it, the voters of New Hampshire "said to us . . . that they wanted a plan, they wanted specifics. . . . We want to know what you're going to do to change America and get this economy moving."[49]

If there was ever a candidate who fit the part of a middle-class populist, it was Bill Clinton. He was the very model of a crossover candidate, a politician who could appeal to elites and working-class voters alike. On one hand, to working-class Democrats like Coos County chairman Paul Robitaille, Clinton was "a trailer-park guy from down the street who made good."[50] During his campaigning in New Hampshire, Clinton was known for his late-night stops at bowling alleys and doughnut shops. On the other hand, accompanying Clinton on his jaunts were a trio of lawyers, including a future state Supreme Court justice who described him years later as "one of the most unusual people I have ever met."

The future justice, Manchester lawyer John Broderick, was part of the early core of Clinton supporters in New Hampshire.[51] During the 1988 presidential season, Broderick had been cochair of the short-lived campaign of Senator Joseph Biden of Delaware. (Biden left the race before the primaries began after allegations that, on one occasion, he borrowed passages of a speech by British Labor politician Neil Kinnock without attribution.[52]) After the 1988 election, Broderick and others started the New Hampshire Democratic Forum in an attempt to moderate the message of the state Democratic Party and move it away from "social extremism," he said, in order to be palatable to middle-class voters in New Hampshire; Michael Dukakis and Walter Mondale, they felt, had both been too far left for the good of the party. "We thought the Democratic Party had become so liberalized, it had become elitist," Broderick said. "There was kind of a laundry list of things you had to subscribe to or you couldn't be a Democrat." While party regulars were not happy with the goals of the new group, the forum did attract moderates such as Dick Swett, who later became the congressman from New Hampshire's western Second Congressional District.

In 1990, members of the forum formed a state chapter of the Democratic Leadership Council and invited Clinton to speak at the kickoff meeting in Concord in August 1991. The state party leadership boycotted the meeting and considered the attendees Republicans in Democratic clothing, Broderick said. The Democrats even objected to the DLC using "Democratic" in the organization's name, recalled fellow founder Terry Shumaker,[53] and the group incorporated as the "New Hampshire DLC." Given that Clinton had already been mentioned as a possible candidate for president, Broderick admired the fact that the governor had the courage to show up for the event. Clinton's message at the DLC event seemed different from Dukakis's in 1988, Broderick said, more concerned with ordinary, middle-class folks, with a toned-down social agenda and a mainstream economic agenda.

After the meeting, Broderick recalled, Clinton walked to the state Democratic headquarters, on Main Street in Concord, a large group of press in tow. The group jammed into the small party offices with Clinton and Chris Spirou, the state party chair who had refused to attend the speech. All in all, the press conference went well, Broderick said, although Spirou "basically trashed" the DLC; Clinton offered a glib comment in response.[54] Reflecting on the day afterward, Broderick recalled,

> I thought, that's an unusual guy. He makes friends with all those people with the DLC, but he didn't shy away from going over to the lion's den, and meeting the people who didn't even come to his event. . . . He could have said, "I'm not going across the street, that could get embarrassing." And I thought to myself at the time, "Wow, this guy can play without practice. He's ready for primetime without practice."

The next month, Clinton called to tell Broderick he was going to run for president, and Broderick signed up before Clinton even asked. Broderick then met with another early supporter, fellow Manchester lawyer and former state party chair George Bruno, who had known Hillary Clinton for two decades. The two promptly moved on to sign up Terry Shumaker, a Concord lawyer and another founder of the New Hampshire chapter of the DLC, and another prominent New Hampshire lawyer and DLC member, Steve McAuliffe. By the time Clinton returned to New Hampshire in October, he had a core of half a dozen activists waiting for him.

At this early stage, the people of New Hampshire had virtually no knowledge of Clinton, whose name recognition was at a lowly 3 percent. Shumaker recalled walking with Clinton to early events in New Hampshire "and people knew he was somebody, because he was tall and he was handsome and he was well dressed, but nobody had a clue who he was." On his trip to New Hampshire in October, Clinton walked back and forth through a craft fair at the Center of New Hampshire Holiday Inn in Manchester without a single one of the fairgoers taking heed of him. "Not one head turned," said Broderick, and he recalled thinking that his candidate did not have "a chance in the world." Later during the trip, Broderick asked Clinton if he thought he was starting too late in the process, and Clinton responded calmly that he thought when he had a chance to meet the people, they would like his message and that things would be fine.

Over the years, a good number of candidates for the presidential nomination have lost their way in the political wilds of the Granite State. Politicians of national renown have traveled north with considerable fanfare and vanished after the primary, leaving little impression on the native population. "The fact is that a lot of these senators and governors are driven around, they're treated like royalty" in their home states and in Washington, D.C., said Jeff Woodburn, an activist and former chair of the state Democratic Party. In New Hampshire, however, the royalty are treated more rudely. Woodburn recalled a trip with Governor Doug Wilder of Virginia, who was contemplating a run for the 1992 Democratic nomination, to meet workers at the mills up north in Gorham and Berlin. "Every third person is telling him to go to hell," he recalled. "They're just getting up in the morning, they're getting to work, and somebody's bothering them, trying to stick their hand out." All the while, a television camera crew was capturing the scene.

Faced with this kind of test of his campaigning skills, Clinton had some advantages including, surprisingly enough, the fact that New Hampshire did not seem all that much different from his home state of Arkansas. Clinton had visited New Hampshire prior to his presidential run, Shumaker pointed out, and Clinton and former New Hampshire governor Hugh Gallen had been friends. In addition, both New Hampshire and Arkansas are fairly small states, both count tourism as a major industry, and both states had been dominated by one political party (New Hampshire by Republicans, Arkansas by Democrats then). Both states at that time made their governors run for reelection every two years. Both have relatively small state governments; it was common in Arkansas, as it was in New Hampshire, for citizens to walk up and speak to the governor as he walked along the streets of the state capital.

In addition, as a governor, Clinton was closer to the people, unlike a senator who is used to being placed on a pedestal and having people take care of things and who, as Shumaker put it, "really gets thrown for a loop here when some shopkeeper asks a really difficult question about foreign policy or [her] children's education." Clinton also was very adept at picking up an issue at the spur of the moment and making it newsworthy, Bruno said. One of the lasting issues of the 1992 campaign, for instance, was President George Bush's apparent disconnect with the concerns of ordinary Americans, brought to life when he entered a store and did not know the price of a gallon of milk. Shortly after, Clinton went into a grocery store off Elm Street in Manchester, Bruno recalled, and bought milk and bread.[55]

Despite the abbreviated campaign season, Clinton's organization in New Hampshire followed the same path as previous primary campaigns: have the candidate meet as many activists as possible and build from the initial core outward. Clinton's core group was supremely confident in their candidate's ability to win people over, said Shumaker, and they joked that if Clinton could talk to every Democratic voter in the state, he would get every vote. At the state party convention in November, the Clinton campaign rented an RV trailer, and the New Hampshire core brought prominent fellow Democrats to the trailer for some one-on-one time with the candidate. Shumaker recalled one such meeting with a county commissioner who was considering a run for higher office; the commissioner asked if Clinton would be willing to support him in turn down the road. The two were sitting side by side, and the candidate "gave him that Clinton look . . . [and] he's talking to you like you're the only person on the planet." Clinton put his hand on the commissioner's knee and vowed, "I'll be with you 'til the last dog dies." (Clinton would repeat those words a few months later in Dover, while he was fighting to bounce back in the last days of the campaign.) The commissioner joined on the spot.

Not all of Clinton's one-on-one encounters were so successful. "He made my skin crawl," Concord lawyer and political activist Debbie Butler recalled saying about the candidate after meeting him. During their meeting, Clinton had empathized with her about the economy and said that he knew just how she felt. "It just absolutely rubbed me the wrong way, that I could walk into a meeting, and somebody could tell me that he knew how I felt, and he knew everything about me," Butler said. "He didn't ask me anything, he hadn't been so well prepped that he knew my whole life's story . . . I just thought he was fake."

On other occasions, though, Clinton showed ability to win over those with whom he disagreed on matters of public policy. Former state representative Jane Wood, a self-described "pro-life Democrat" opposed to abortion, asked Clinton about the issue in 1991 when he visited the lakes region of New Hampshire where she lived. Clinton's pro-choice position conflicted with Wood's, but Wood believed that Clinton was sincere when he said that simply banning abortion was the wrong answer to the problem, but that a host of other issues had to be addressed in order to minimize the demand for abortion.

Wood and her husband Patrick eventually became the go-to people for Clinton in Laconia during the general election.[56]

All in all, Clinton succeeded in putting together a broad coalition of high-profile activists, including not only moderates like Broderick and Shumaker but liberals such as former gubernatorial candidate Paul McEachern and former state party executive director Ricia McMahon, who became Clinton's New Hampshire political director.[57] In those early months of the campaign, recalled longtime New Hampshire activist Joseph Grandmaison, Clinton showed the ability to reach beyond the core of the Democratic Leadership Council and attract liberals to his campaign as well.[58]

In that particular primary cycle, Shumaker recalled, groups of New Hampshire activists who had worked together on previous campaigns tended to stay together. Activists who had supported Dukakis in 1988, for instance, tended to sign up with Harkin, the most liberal of the candidates. Hart activists from his 1984 campaign, including Jeanne Shaheen, moved to Kerrey. Paul Tsongas did not draw from any group of activists in particular and had very little institutional support, said Peter Sullivan, a Tsongas field organizer on the seacoast who now is a lawyer and state representative from Manchester.[59] A few political pros were involved in the campaign, mainly old Tsongas hands from the politician's days in Massachusetts. Generally, though, nobody had his career riding on Tsongas's success, and no one was hoping to work for the DLC when the campaign was over, Sullivan recalled. For a large percentage of the Tsongas activists, it was their very first campaign. That meant that the campaign's energy level was high—and its "clueless level" was as well, Sullivan said; at the ripe old age of twenty-five, Sullivan found he had more experience than most. Currently most Tsongas activists are not involved in state Democratic party activities although some went on to work for the Concord Coalition, a public interest group that advocated fiscal conservatism and balanced budgets.

Not only did Tsongas have few experienced activists in his organization, he lacked funds as well. In the preseason to the primary, Tsongas was consigned to the unelectable second tier of candidates, along with Jerry Brown and Douglas Wilder. "A projection was made that Tsongas had absolutely no chance to win, that his ideas were respectable, that he was contributing to the Democratic debate and all of that, but that he could not win," said Tsongas's campaign manager Dennis Kanin.[60] To make matters worse, the 14,000 Greek contributors to Michael Dukakis's campaign in 1988 showed little interest in supporting another Greek for president so soon after Dukakis's humiliation in the general election. As a result, Tsongas's campaign managed to raise only about $19,000 a week in the year before the primary, $1 million in all by the end of 1991—a paltry amount that Clinton, Harkin, and Kerrey far outraised after only three months in the race.[61]

With no money to carry it out, Tsongas's national campaign had no choice but to focus all its efforts on New Hampshire. Kanin described how they hoped that a strong New Hampshire campaign would have national repercussions and boomerang back to Granite State voters:

> The dilemma for us . . . was how to convince people in New Hampshire that Paul Tsongas was a national candidate, because as long as they thought he was a regional candidate, we had no chance. What we did was to make a virtue out of necessity. We decided to use events in New Hampshire to impress the national press and generate some national publicity so, in turn, we could convince people in New Hampshire that we were a national candidate.[62]

On the ground in New Hampshire, Tsongas's operatives in the field resorted to guerrilla tactics to make the candidate's feeble resources look formidable, Sullivan said. The goal was to create as many high-visibility moments as possible for the campaign, to get Tsongas's name in front of as many voters' eyeballs as possible. The campaign put up signs and banners in high-traffic areas, such as traffic circles and main streets in city downtowns. When Tom Harkin's organization ran a campaign event on a cruise ship in the Lakes region, intrepid Tsongas volunteers trailed the ship in a rowboat; when the media turned on their camera lights, they unveiled banners for their candidate. The goal, said Sullivan, was to make the media believe that the campaign was everywhere because if they thought so, their readers and viewers would also think so.

The candidate, at first glance at least, seemed to need all the hype he could get. Tsongas seemed unlikely to be able to re-create himself as an insurgent who could catch fire in New Hampshire and parlay that into national momentum. He was a soft-spoken, reserved man, recalled Peter Sullivan, the kind of person you would be surprised to see with a beer in his hand; his wife, Niki, was much more of a dynamo on the campaign trail than her husband. The candidate was, however, willing to have the one-on-one conversations with voters at the heart of a New Hampshire grassroots campaign. His tendency to stay extra time at events to conduct such conversations sometimes made him an advance man's nightmare.

In addition, despite doubts about Tsongas's electability, no one denied that he was a candidate of substance, integrity, and intellect—a politician who always erred on the side of offering too much detail, Sullivan said. The symbol of that substance was an eighty-six-page book titled *Call to Economic Arms,* in which Tsongas described his plan to reverse the country's economic decline in the face of international competition. In the face of severe economic pain, Tsongas called not for economic relief but for belt-tightening in order to reform the economy for the long term. He denounced "old Democrats who are into giveaway, giveaway, giveaway, antibusiness corporate-bashing." He was unabashedly pro-business, pro–nuclear power, and pro–free trade (only he and Clinton supported the proposed North American Free Trade Agreement). He opposed a tax cut for the middle class, proposed by Clinton, deriding it as "generationally irresponsible" because it would increase the federal deficit. He alone defied labor by opposing "strikebreaker replacement" legislation.[63]

In essence, Tsongas brought an eat-your-spinach message to a state that was suffering severely from economic recession, said Deborah "Arnie" Arnesen, the Democrats' 1992 gubernatorial nominee who ran on a pro–income tax platform in a notoriously antitax state. At such a time, Tsongas's tough message resonated. Bill Clinton's message, in contrast, was a sugar-coated "mush," Arnesen said, featuring a middle-class tax cut.[64]

Tsongas drew together an unlikely coalition of various constituencies, Sullivan recalled. Moderates supported his economic plan. People active in the gay and lesbian community supported him because of the candidate's socially progressive, pro-homosexual rights stance. Many environmentalists backed him, deciding that, given his legislative track record on such issues, despite his support of nuclear power, he was the best option available. Then there were the independents who, surprisingly enough, seemed to be choosing late in the campaign between Tsongas and Patrick Buchanan, the fire-breathing conservative challenger to President Bush in the Republican primary. Tsongas and Buchanan agreed on virtually nothing, Sullivan said, "but there were a lot of people who, I think . . . were looking to throw the finger at the political powers-that-be that year. And they had two options: they could throw the finger at the Democrats or at the Republicans."

Such voters were looking for a "straight shooter," Sullivan said. Thus, unlikely as it would have seemed months earlier, the candidate brandishing a book was paired up in some voters' minds with Buchanan, a candidate who proclaimed he was leading peasants brandishing pitchforks. Both Tsongas and Buchanan had, at their core, the message of an insurgent candidate: "no more bullshit," Arnesen said. Both Patrick Buchanan and Tsongas were "talking to the fear, and they were both addressing the fear. [Buchanan] builds walls, and Tsongas builds futures," Arnesen said. Sullivan speculated that Tsongas picked up voters who would later cast votes in the general election for Ross Perot, the self-financed independent candidate who won 19 percent of the vote on an agenda of reforming the political system.

Slowly but surely, Tsongas's campaign gained traction in New Hampshire. "We had a very incremental program here," said campaign manager Dennis Kanin. "We were doing it step by step, trying to build one thing on another, and it was all kind of an illusion."[65] In December, the campaign borrowed against its federal campaign matching funds to saturate the airwaves with its first commercial, an ad displaying Tsongas swimming to prove his physical fitness for the office. The ad was timed with an impending *Boston Globe* poll that showed Tsongas tied for first place in New Hampshire with the still-undecided Cuomo. As the new year began, the candidate at the back of the second tier had vaulted to the top shelf, crowding out Harkin and Kerrey to become Clinton's main challenger.[66]

While Tsongas was surviving on a diet of grass roots in New Hampshire, Bill Clinton was flourishing as the de facto national front runner in the continued absence of Mario Cuomo. The Arkansas governor had quickly become the perceived front runner among political pundits—in part by largely ignoring New Hampshire. The national campaign, for instance, chose to have the candidate do twenty fund-raisers in the first half of December—a decision that "drove our New Hampshire supporters absolutely crazy," recalled Clinton operative David

Wilhelm, because the candidate stayed out of the state for so long as a result.[67] Clinton succeeded in raising $2 million in December 1991, twice as much as Tsongas had succeeded in gathering during the entire year. In addition, Clinton's organization succeeded in pulling off a symbolic victory that month at the Florida state Democratic convention, where Clinton trounced Harkin in a straw poll, 54 percent to 31 percent, despite Harkin's backing by organized labor. The straw poll meant nothing in terms of future convention delegates, but it served to buttress the emerging conventional wisdom that Clinton was the man to beat.[68] Unlike Tsongas, for whom all hope rested on New Hampshire, Clinton strategists did not view the first-in-the-nation primary as a make-or-break contest. "From the beginning, we were running a national, general election campaign," said Clinton polling consultant Stan Greenberg. "We decided that the best strategy for winning the Democratic nomination was being a candidate who could capture America and not necessarily a candidate who could win specific primaries."[69]

In New Hampshire, the Clinton team anticipated that their candidate would run behind Tsongas and Bob Kerrey until close to the primary. If there was a win to be had in New Hampshire, it would come as the result of a late surge. These projections turned out to be excessively conservative, as the candidate burst out in New Hampshire ahead of schedule. On January 15, a month before voters went to the polls, Clinton was in the lead, catching other first-tier candidates like Kerrey flatfooted.[70] John Broderick recalled that when Clinton returned to New Hampshire in January and did an event in Merrimack, people were spilling out of the building. It was clear at that point, Broderick said, that his candidate had strength at the grass roots, with "real people" organizing for him with a personal investment in an unusually intense campaign. "I thought to myself, maybe my mother felt this way about John F. Kennedy," Broderick said. With Cuomo finally out of the running, the contest in New Hampshire suddenly appeared to be a two-man race between "Mr. Inside Tsongas and Mr. Outside Clinton," as national political reporters Jack Germond and Jules Witcover described them.[71]

Then, in the final four weeks leading to the primary, Clinton suffered a one-two punch that left him struggling to get off the ropes. First, on January 17, tabloids reported that Clinton had been accused of several affairs, according to a lawsuit filed by a fired former Arkansas state employee. Clinton denied these allegations, but a week later an Arkansas state employee, Gennifer Flowers, declared that she had had an affair with the governor. Flowers added that she possessed audiotapes of conversations with him and later played portions of these tapes at a news conference. In response to the furor, Clinton and his wife, Hillary, appeared together on the television program *60 Minutes* on Super Bowl Sunday.[72]

A week and a half later, on February 6, just twelve days before the primary, the *Wall Street Journal* ran a story quoting a former draft board official and a former ROTC recruiter who claimed that Clinton had improperly avoided being drafted for military service during the Vietnam War. Clinton, who had opposed the war, denied attempts to manipulate the process in order to dodge the draft.[73] John Broderick recalled that, upon hearing the Flowers story, he first thought perhaps those who had been cautious about joining Clinton's campaign had known more about the candidate than he had known when he first got on board. But Broderick had come to know and like Clinton, and he stuck with him, even appearing on WMUR-TV after the *60 Minutes* interview to support the candidate.

The first time Broderick saw Clinton after the media furor was in a van in Nashua; Broderick was to accompany the candidate to his next campaign stop. When Clinton arrived in Nashua that day, he was confronted by a copy of a letter he had written in 1969 to the head of the University of Arkansas ROTC, thanking him for "saving me from the draft" and explaining his conflicted feelings about the war. The combination of the Flowers story and the draft story, coupled with the candidate's absence from New Hampshire, had reversed the campaign's momentum. Clinton's internal polling showed that he had dropped in New Hampshire from 37 percent in the polls to 17 percent in just a few days.[74] Activists were growing concerned, and Broderick and Shumaker had written a memo to the campaign, urging the candidate to get out and meet the voters.

When Broderick first caught sight of Clinton in Nashua, he "looked so defeated, I had never seen him look like that." Clinton was besieged by hordes of media people and had resorted to reading prepared statements, something Broderick had never seen the candidate do. The statement was well done, but the candidate "had no spirit" in delivering it, Broderick said. On the way north on Interstate 93 to a campaign stop at Stonyfield Yogurt in Londonderry, Broderick asked Clinton point-blank, "Do you want to be president of the United States or not? Because this campaign is going in the tank. . . . Are you going to let some guy with a pocket protector become president . . . ?" he asked, referring to Tsongas. Both Broderick and Shumaker recalled feelings of dread, reminiscent of the disaster that befell Joe Biden's campaign four years earlier. A cloud of gloom descended on the campaign, Bruno said, and it took hard work to make sure that Clinton's New Hampshire supporters did not break ranks.

In the last days before the primary, Clinton's New Hampshire advisors and his national campaign staff concurred that the candidate had to get out in front of voters at every opportunity in order to salvage what he could. Rather than shrinking from exposure to the voters, Clinton seemed to gain a second wind from such encounters, such as a visit to the Burger King at the Mall of New Hampshire. In addition, Clinton's core supporters stayed true to their candidate, said Bruno, even though they were in the uncomfortable position of lending their reputations to a candidate who had been called into question. They continued to vouch for the candidate to fellow New Hampshire residents. Supporters from Clinton's home state also arrived to campaign, reminiscent of Jimmy Carter's Peanut Brigade of Georgians in 1976. "The word-of-mouth thing matters," Shumaker said.

What also helped Clinton in that difficult period, said Shumaker, was that he had already experienced political defeat more than once in his career. Back in Arkansas, Clinton had run for Congress and lost, but came back to win elections for state attorney general and for governor. Most significantly, Clinton had been defeated in his bid for a second term as governor of Arkansas, a loss that shaped the rest of his political career. "Here he was, the wonder boy, and after one term, he was turned out of office," Shumaker said. Clinton returned two years later to recapture the governor's office. "And I think that was something that, when it really got hot and ugly here . . . that was something that really served him well. He never gave up, he never backed down, he never in any way threw in the towel."

Indeed, Clinton's engine simply refused to quit, and that refusal distinguished him from other candidates who may have looked better on paper. On the night before the primary, Broderick recalled, the candidate simply refused to let him go home, working tables at the Puritan Backroom restaurant in Manchester then talking with people at a nearby bowling alley. What makes a candidate viable in New Hampshire, said state party chair Kathy Sullivan, is the willingness to work, to shake every hand in the place, and to talk to every last person who wants to talk to them.[75] "It's a brutal process," she said, and not every candidate is up to the challenge. In 1992, Nebraska senator Bob Kerrey, a Vietnam War veteran with an independent streak, appeared to be a good fit for a strong performance in New Hampshire. However, "it seemed for a long time that those of us who supported him wanted it more than he did," recalled Sullivan. "The weekend before the primary, I ran into him on Elm Street, and he just had this fiery look in his eyes, and he was pumped up, and I said, 'My God, where has this been?' If he had been like this for the last four months, maybe he could have won this thing." Another Kerrey supporter, Mary Rauh, echoed Sullivan's sentiments:

> Kerrey was inconsistent in campaigning. There would be days when he would have an audience, and he would just be really turned on, and he would turn the audience on. . . . Then, there would be times when you didn't know what happened—nice big audience, but nothing there. . . . We were just disappointed that he wasn't able always to really communicate to voters.[76]

Kerrey finished a poor third in New Hampshire with just 11 percent of the vote.

On primary night, both Tsongas and Clinton claimed victory, and both had good reason to do so. Tsongas won the primary with 33 percent of the vote, a tribute to an unorthodox candidate and an equally unorthodox strategy that targeted Democrats in towns that were Republican strongholds, said Sullivan. The candidate considered least likely to make an impact was now one of the few remaining survivors. Clinton, who finished in second place with about a quarter of the vote, won by assuring that his national strategy would not be upended by a New Hampshire disaster. Even in defeat, he displayed a broad base of support in New Hampshire, drawing from working-class city wards and from suburban elites. Why the broad appeal? In part because Clinton was as much of an intellectual as Michael Dukakis, said state senator Lou D'Allesandro, but he did not intellectualize his campaign as Dukakis did in 1988. Unlike Dukakis, Clinton was a flesh-and-blood politician who excelled at connecting with people, D'Allesandro said; he was "a people-hugger and a people-grabber."[77]

Clinton's personal connections with New Hampshire lasted well beyond the primary. Longtime observer Dayton Duncan said this was not unusual: Once the personal connection happens, he said, it has a great effect on activists, and they are bonded to "their" candidates for years to come. For an activist, when "the person that you worked so hard for when they were a nobody, and they became president of the United States, that's a euphoric thing to happen. You're going to stick with them through thick or thin, barring I don't know what." Moreover, stories abound of how Clinton kept in close contact with New Hampshire Democrats, especially those who had worked with him in the 1992 campaign. One of Clinton's core supporters, Portsmouth activist Anita Freedman, recalled that when her husband, Norman, became ill and died in 1995, Clinton had staffers call the Freedmans' house frequently to check on his progress.[78] The morning after her husband died, Clinton was on the phone, asking Freedman what he and his wife could do to help her through this and inviting her to the White House for a visit soon afterward. Freedman speaks of the Clintons as if they were members of her extended family: "When I hear anybody bad-mouth Bill Clinton, they don't get away with it if I'm sitting there." When the Monica Lewinsky scandal broke, Freedman refused to listen or read about it, and maintains that she did not know or care about his private life: "All I know is he's a wonderful friend, he's a very, very capable person."

Clinton's ability to keep New Hampshire activists engaged in his presidency was one key factor, said Jeanne Shaheen, in avoiding a fate that befell the two preceding Democratic incumbents: a primary challenge prior to running for a second term in office. Clinton, for instance, hosted a New Hampshire Day in the White House during his first term, inviting several hundred local Democratic elites down to Washington, D.C., to discuss state politics and the upcoming race. Keeping tight connections with activists made it more difficult for potential rivals to gain a foothold in the Granite State, Shaheen said. In addition, the Clinton-Gore reelection campaign ran an aggressive campaign to turn out primary voters in 1996, despite the apparent lack of opposition.

CHAPTER SIX

The Storm Last Time

In the spring and summer of 1999, two campaign vehicles started down the road during the mud season of the New Hampshire primary: a dreary time in New Hampshire when thick mud has replaced the pristine snow and all one can do is trudge through it in the hope of firmer ground ahead. These two particular vehicles appeared to be mismatched, both in terms of resources and strategy. In one lane stood Vice President Al Gore's sports utility vehicle, loaded with all the bells and whistles a presidential campaign could possibly want. It was an automobile that had been custom-built over more than a decade, dating back to Gore's first failed bid for the presidency in 1988. This time around, Gore's vehicle was filled to capacity—perhaps excess capacity—with passengers from both the national and local party establishment. It was a vehicle designed to comfortably carry the vice president to the Democratic presidential nomination.

In the adjoining lane was an unassuming vehicle—a used Honda Civic—carrying an equally unassuming passenger, retired New Jersey senator Bill Bradley, and very little else. What happened when both vehicles started their engines, however, was remarkable. The Bradleymobile, built for speed, shot down the road, fueled by what campaign manager Mark Longabaugh called the four key ingredients of insurgency: attitude, message, persona, and organization.[1] The Goremobile, in contrast, spun its wheels in the mud, to the consternation of the drivers and the frustration of its many passengers. So began the months of preparation leading up to the 2000 New Hampshire Democratic primary.

The Early Bradley Campaign: Creating a Conversation

In May 1999, the Bradley campaign in New Hampshire resembled a start-up company working out of a garage. It had exactly two organizers on the ground, managing the campaign by cell phone. Longabaugh, a Democratic consultant who was still in Maryland at the time, had recruited Susan Calegari to be Bradley's deputy campaign director in New Hampshire. Calegari's story of her first exposure to presidential politics is too good to be manufactured: Woman minding her own business meets presidential candidate. Calegari recalled Christmas shopping in downtown Laconia in 1975: "it was one of those days there was nobody on the street. And as I was walking down the street, this tall man in a trench coat came walking across the street, and he looked at me and said, 'Hi, I'm Mo Udall, and I'm running for president, and I'd like your vote.'"[2] That encounter with the Arizona congressman (who finished second in the 1976 primary to Jimmy Carter) is what the New Hampshire primary is all about, Calegari said: "Anybody can play." Time and again, Calegari has been on the side of the unknown, underdog insurgent who takes on the front runner who enjoys the backing of the state and national political parties. Calegari had worked on two such New Hampshire campaigns: Gary Hart's in 1984, Bruce Babbitt's in 1988, and now she was on board with a third.

Bill Bradley once was on the short list of Democratic presidential candidates. A Princeton graduate and basketball star of the New York Knickerbockers in the 1970s, Bradley succeeded in his first run for public office, winning a U.S. Senate seat in New Jersey in 1978. During his time in the Senate, he developed a reputation as a thinking man's moderate, supporting international free trade and helping to design a tax-reform bill signed by President Ronald Reagan in 1986. Bradley survived a much closer than expected race for reelection in 1990 and was one of the several top-flight Democratic candidates who opted out of a challenge against President Bush. He surprised observers by refusing to run for a fourth term in the Senate, declaring that "politics were broken."

Bradley's intellectual reserve was not a novelty to Calegari. Her candidates—Babbitt, Hart, and Bradley—have all been "a little removed," she said. Each had special talents: Hart shone in his command of issues, Babbitt in his intellect and integrity, Bradley in his notoriety as a sports hero. Throughout the campaign, Bradley was "on and off on the stump." When he was on, he was terrific, but when he was off, he was just going through his talking points and did not connect with an audience. Many candidates have their good and bad days, Calegari noted, but what was different about Bradley was that "he didn't like being a candidate." As politically savvy as he was about modern campaigns, he did not like to use people as props. "There was a piece of him that just didn't want to play the candidate game."

After Longabaugh and Calegari, one of the first people on the ground for Bradley in New Hampshire was Matt Rodriguez, who joined in spring 1999 and became the campaign coordinator for the Second Congressional District, covering western New Hampshire. In the early stages, Rodriguez said, the fledgling Bradley organization had to quickly develop an ability to multitask and operate on several fronts.[3] Quite simply, lots of things need to be done: phone calls need to be made, envelopes stuffed, letters written, signs held. Initially, a couple of people are hired early to work at building volunteers and generating buzz for the candidate.

All of these mundane tasks, Rodriguez said, are directed toward the key goal in field operations in New Hampshire: "moving message early." What a campaign does early plays a large role in what happens later, especially in the case of an underdog candidate who might be way down in the polls. For such a candidate, getting even twenty to thirty people to a house party a year before the primary is a significant accomplishment. A multiplier effect takes place: 20 or 30 people at a February house party may lead to a rally of 80 in the summertime, which may in turn lead to a town meeting of 200 in the fall, just a few months before ballots are cast.

Building a crowd is one of the most stressful jobs for field organizers because one never knows whether a crowd will turn out, said former state party official Nicole Rizzo.[4] For some events, people arrive spontaneously without calls; at other times, despite repeated invitations, the field operatives cannot pull people out for the event. A less than full room is an embarrassment for the candidate, who may proceed to turn in a subpar performance, Rizzo said. And even if the candidate turns in a good performance nonetheless, "Who cares? Because there's nobody there." In the presence of the media, "it's mortifying to have a small crowd . . . it's definitely cause for a panic attack for whoever organized the event," especially if the candidate arrives with staff. For this reason, campaigns habitually make sure the candidate arrives late in order to ensure the largest crowd possible.

Numbers alone, though, do not tell the story, Rodriguez said. Another key question in crowds of people is whether they are the same old political junkies and activist faithful or new faces drawn to the candidate. In February or April, familiar faces are all right. But as the year progresses, field operatives hope to see a sea of unfamiliar faces, as Rodriguez did in a Bradley event in Concord in December, just weeks before the primary. All in all, the initial field operatives need to grow a campaign from generating 40-person crowds in the early stages to 400-person crowds as the election draws closer. As a rule, a campaign may depend on a 10 to 20 percent success rate for its phone calls: To get 20 people out to an event, it might take 100 calls or more; to get 200 people out, it might well take more than 1,000 calls.

Among the early tasks were putting together events for Bradley's visits, such as house parties. The house party, a traditional format for candidates to meet voters and activists that dates back to the days of Eugene McCarthy, still is employed today. Typically, Calegari says, there are a lot of familiar faces at such parties: one's neighbors, for instance, or political or issue activists of long standing. In the old days, locals heard about house parties by word of mouth, but the media now show up at these events, placing greater emphasis on looking good early. In 1984, Calegari recalled, media attention on the Hart campaign was sparse, and it was rare to see a reporter at these events; usually, they were not even invited. In recent years, the media are much more likely to show up because they follow the campaigns so much earlier. Still, house parties are the opportunity for the campaign to create a "smaller, more intimate environment" where activists actually can meet the candidate, shake hands, and say a few words, Calegari said.

Randy Benthien of Goffstown was an early Bradley supporter. He got on board with Bradley, he recalled, because the candidate seemed to be a "thinking person" who had pondered in-depth answers to issues of the day.[5] Bradley also impressed Benthien as more forthcoming and less political—that is, more transparent in what he thought and believed. Bradley was more apt to use persuasion than Gore, who seemed much more willing to pander to voters. All in all, Bradley's appeal was not so much about his issue positions, Benthien said, as how he approached issues: "He didn't seem glib, he wasn't blow-dry pretty . . . he seemed like a thinking person's politician."

The Bradley campaign quickly spilled out of the house parties into events in larger venues such as restaurants and halls to accommodate the large number of people interested. At their first early summer meetings, the Bradley campaign was expecting ten, perhaps fifteen people, Calegari said, and instead they were getting, twenty, thirty, forty, fifty people attending, "which was shocking for us." What was more surprising, Calegari said, was that many of the attendees had never been involved in politics. Some were attracted by Bradley's celebrity status as a sports star, Calegari said, but others were simply shopping for an alternative to the vice president. "We didn't have to orchestrate these meetings," Calegari said. More people than expected were showing up at these initial meetings seemingly spontaneously, and this outpouring was the first sign that the Bradley campaign might catch fire.

While the Gore campaign had its candidate doing photo-ops, the Bradley campaign was running town meetings—a venue to reach voters that the Gore campaign eventually imitated, said Longabaugh. The town meeting, he said, was just one component of a plan aimed at "creating a conversation" between Bradley and New Hampshire voters—a conversation that was possible because of the small size of the electorate. Before holding a town meeting, the campaign would call hundreds of Democratic and independent voters in order to build crowds. The campaign also would follow up early canvassing with phone calls to tell voters of the opportunity to meet the candidate and then have Bradley "close the sale" at the town meeting.

Longabaugh recalled explaining the process to Bradley just before a town meeting in Nashua. Minutes later, Bradley proceeded to ask the crowd to raise their hands if they had had a canvasser come by their home; 40 percent of the crowd raised their hands, Longabaugh said. The show of hands was an early sign to Longabaugh and Calegari that they were moving the Bradley message. "If you can get in there and hustle enough, the universe is small enough that you really can meet voters, and you can get into the race," said Longabaugh. It works, Calegari said: "You invite them to something to meet the candidate, they meet him, they like him, they sign up to help," and the circle expands. "We shocked ourselves. . . . Whoa! What do we have here?"

During the summer of 1999, the Bradley campaign brought in about ten interns. From that core of volunteers, "stars arise," people who graduate from volunteer status and take on full-time paid jobs in the organization, Calegari said. "You just have to be able to assess how far you can push them." Six or seven of the summer interns became field organizers in various parts of the state. Young activists (such as Alex Grodd, a student who deferred admission to Harvard to work on the Bradley campaign) add an element of excitement to the campaign and act as magnets, drawing additional volunteers by the force of their own energies and personalities.

Without the muscle power of volunteers directed by field organizers, a campaign can easily come undone. Even the best-run campaign is always behind, Rodriguez said. There is never as much time in the day as needed, even when the day stretches to midnight. In order to keep up with the never-ending work flow, a campaign must be able to attract, keep, and maintain a solid base of volunteers. A volunteer who will come in regularly to make the phone calls, stuff the envelopes, and perform the myriad of other mundane tasks is worth the person's proverbial weight in gold. The thing about volunteers, of course, is that they can come and go as they please. If people come in ready to help, but a campaign fails to have tasks ready for them, that failure can be the "kiss of death" for a campaign, he said, as can a phone call from a volunteer that is not returned. Thus, a good field organizer with an appealing personality who is good at getting volunteers into the office to work is invaluable, Rodriguez said. Often the volunteer will not return for the sake of the candidate alone but because of the organizer. Conversely, volunteers will not come in to the office to work for somebody who is unorganized and personally unappealing.

During the summertime, "we kept raising the bar" for ourselves, Calegari said, in order to keep "pushing the campaign organization along." In July, for instance, the campaign conducted a large-scale canvass of voters, a task that gave the Bradley operation a chance to cut its teeth on a complex logistical challenge.

Mica Stark began working on the Bradley campaign in the summer of 1999 and later became one of his field directors, working on the seacoast.[6] At the end of August, he recalled, each of the half-dozen field directors was given a box filled with paper and informed that each was responsible for calling and identifying each of the several hundred names of likely primary voters in the box—and each had one week to do it. All the field directors were looking at each other, wondering who exactly was going to get all this done, Stark said.

From August to November, Bradley was on a hot streak, Rodriguez said. Lots of people were committing to him, and he was doing very well among independents. Much of Bradley's success seemed to stem from the fact that the campaign was playing an aggressive, run-and-gun game in an attempt to set its larger opponent on his heels. Early on, the Bradley campaign was aggressive in going after the undecided voters, Rodriguez said, knocking on doors, doing literature drops, and paying attention to person-to-person encounters with voters. The key to these efforts was to make Bradley viable early. The Gore campaign, in contrast, was more focused on casting a broad net for New Hampshire voters and emphasized the phone banks. By moving message early and creating and maintaining an aggressive field operation, the Bradley campaign also succeeded in earning stature for its candidate at a time when he was an underdog, Rodriguez said. When people see movement and activity in a campaign, their curiosity is aroused. Aggressive activity in the field also creates the appearance of an organized campaign, one with energy emanating from the candidate as well as the base, he said.

Bradley's early success, however, could not be chalked up simply to hustle and attitude. In some ways, Gore and his national campaign did too good a job of scaring people out of the race for the 2000 nomination, said Gore's New Hampshire director, Nick Baldick.[7] Because no other candidates entered the field to challenge Gore, Bradley automatically assumed the role of the alternative to the vice president. Given that Gore was the favorite and had a lock on about 42 percent of the vote (as Muskie had in 1972, Mondale in 1984, and Dukakis in 1988), it would have been to his advantage to have three people in the race. If, for instance, Richard Gephardt had decided to enter the race, his votes would have largely come at the expense of Bradley, and New Hampshire would have become a single-elimination tournament for Gore's two challengers. New

Hampshire would have become a race for second, a race for who would be the alternative to Al Gore.

As it was, in a two-man race, most of the state's party activists quickly chose Gore. But the activists' rush to Gore caused an equal and opposite reaction: The Bradley campaign attracted people who had never been involved in politics—a phenomenon that had occurred in previous campaigns. In every political party, there is always a set of ins and outs, the establishment and the outsiders, said activist Jeff Woodburn.[8] That pattern of ins and outs is often replicated in presidential primaries, as it was in 2000 with Al Gore and the state Democratic Party. The very fact that Gore courted activists so avidly, however, only emphasized the distance between the ins and the outs of the party. In addition, the absence of party activists on the Bradley campaign "opened the doors" for new people to get involved, Calegari said, just as it had for Gary Hart in 1984.

The new kids on the block developed an in-your-face attitude toward their establishment opponents. As a U.S. Senator from New Jersey, Bill Bradley made one of his traditional campaign events a meet-and-greet with voters on the beaches of the Jersey shore. In June 1999, the Bradley campaign decided to duplicate the event on the beaches of New Hampshire. It was a big success, Longabaugh recalled, with national media coverage. A few weeks later, the Gore campaign scheduled a beach event. There were only two roads into the site of the event, and on both Bradley interns stood with large painted plywood signs. Longabaugh recalled that the signs said "Been There" and "Done That," and a third, "Bradley Beach Walk" with the date of the event, and a fourth, "Bill Bradley for President." One of the Bradley interns, Longabaugh said, even hired a plane to fly over the Gore event with a banner saying "Bill Bradley for President" and an American flag trailing it. The Gore people were outraged, Longabaugh said, and accused the Bradley people of ambushing the event.

Gore's Early Campaign

Unfortunately for Al Gore, mockery of his campaign became all too typical in 1999. It is difficult to think of a campaign so successful in achieving its ultimate goals and so maligned for its efforts as Gore's campaign in New Hampshire.

From the beginning Gore had put his eggs in two baskets, said his deputy field director Judithanne Scourfield McLauchlan: Iowa and New Hampshire. The strategy was to "crush Bradley," she said, with big wins in both of the first two contests on the primary calendar.[9] While Bradley supporters might argue that Gore's four-point victory in New Hampshire was hardly much of a triumph for a sitting vice president, a win was, in this case, still a win. Unlike other candidates who lost but whose better-than-expectations performance propelled them to future successes (Gene McCarthy in 1968, George McGovern in 1972, Bill Clinton in 1992), Bill Bradley emerged from New Hampshire to go absolutely nowhere. Five weeks later, after being swept in a series of primaries from coast to coast, Bradley's insurgent campaign was over.

However, back in the early days of the New Hampshire primary season, it was the Gore campaign that appeared to be headed nowhere fast. In each of the three components of the vice president's strategy—image, message, and grass roots—glaring problems were apparent. The problems varied, but they always seemed to boil down to a common question in the Gore campaign: Who decides? If politics at its most basic is about who gets what, the internal politics of a presidential campaign are all about who gets to decide what. And on the Gore campaign, a common complaint among activists was that the people with the most power over his campaign in New Hampshire had the least knowledge about the state. Inside Gore's luxury vehicle, a lot of people were fighting over the map and shouting directions.

The fact that almost all of the state's activist elite had climbed on board the Gore bandwagon was supposed to be one of the campaign's main assets. The vice president had succeeded in winning over a tough audience. New Hampshire activists like access at least as much as and often more than ordinary primary voters do, and they are much more accustomed to the candidate's undivided attention than ordinary voters. Their ease of access makes them notoriously difficult to impress. As Nashua Democrat Jane Clemons pointed out, when prospective 2004 candidates Richard Gephardt and Joseph Lieberman each attended fund-raisers for Nashua Democrats, this was par for the course and "nobody's impressed." If a house is full of people and the phone rings, and a voice at the other end says Vice President Gore is going to call in fifteen minutes, will you be available?—"nobody's impressed." When your walls are decorated with hand-signed Christmas cards from the Clinton White House, as Clemons's walls are, to have a candidate make an impression can be a tall order. Smart candidates get started early, she said: They get out and meet the locals, help Democrats get elected, and support candidates with their money and their presence.[10]

The shower of attention from the presidential primary has tended to make the state Democratic Party lazy, said activist Katherine Rogers.[11] New Hampshire Democrats expect prospective candidates and their money men to raise money for the state party and its candidates. As a result, state Democrats have not done a good job of cultivating small donations, which often are signs of commitment to the party. "It's easy to just call up every presidential campaign and say, 'Oh, send me money, maybe I'll support you next time.'" No other state party in the country operates that way, Rogers said. "When you go into other states, people are just amazed when you say that Walter Mondale was in your living room, or Bill Clinton came to your high school. They're just like, 'God, you mean you actually touched them.'"

Al Gore had been working on making an impression on New Hampshire activists for years and years—sometimes one activist at a time. Anna Tilton, a leading Democratic activist in Cheshire County, remembers the call she received from the vice president.[12] "I would have supported Gore in any case," said Tilton, a self-described centrist who supported Clinton in 1992. "But he called me personally and asked me to work for him. Bradley . . . never made that call. I don't have a huge ego, but if he's interested in getting my work and my support, he could make the call."

After paying his dues for years, Gore was in with the ins of the state Democratic Party. He had his own political action committee, Leadership '98, designed to give money to potential Democratic candidates and foster goodwill in key states. Gore was working New Hampshire as early as 1994 and 1995, said Baldick, and already had secured most of the party establishment. If one was very active in the party, "chances are you spent a long time with Al Gore over the course of four, eight, twelve years," said former state party chair Jeff Woodburn. When Woodburn was chair of the party, Al Gore "did anything we wanted, anything we asked him for, paid attention, called, built that relationship." For party insiders, the principle of one hand washing the other is honored, said Woodburn: "You're much more attuned to loyalty, relationships, you're not a maverick." And so, when Al Gore was seeking Woodburn's support for his 2000 run, "for me, it wasn't a choice."

For Gore, the campaign organization had a ready-made structure because the party establishment people were already behind him, Calegari said. For instance, county party organizations would check with Gore when planning events, she said, while the Bradley campaign was considered only as an afterthought. But having the backing of the party establishment had its downside, too: With the support of the party establishment came "certain obligations to people in the party that actually tied his hands a bit," Calegari argued. For Bradley, "the disadvantage to not having a party establishment is you have to create it yourself. The advantage to that is that you don't have to play games with some people."

In 1999, for instance, the locals and the Beltway boys were playing the time-honored game of tug of war in New Hampshire, said Joe Keefe.[13] New Hampshire activists like to say the campaign is not running perfectly because the Washington people screwed it up, while the Washington pros tend to think the New Hampshire locals "fell off a turnip truck." During the Gore campaign, New Hampshire activists complained early and often that their candidate was not accessible to the voters in their grassroots tradition and that the campaign was ignoring their advice. Washington consultants, not people on the ground in New Hampshire, were making too many of the campaign's decisions, said activist Jim Demers:

> Campaigns sometimes fail to establish a procedure for local input. It appeared that the folks in Washington knew more about New Hampshire than the folks in New Hampshire.... The orders were coming down, and that's the way the campaign was going to be run, and it was turning into a very frustrating situation for people here, who knew that many of the things they were doing just weren't the right approach for New Hampshire.[14]

Stuck in the middle between Gore's national campaign operatives and the New Hampshire activists was Gore's New Hampshire campaign team. Leading the Gore effort in New Hampshire was the state director, Nick Baldick, a consultant for the Dewey Square Group of Boston and Washington, an organization that had been involved in both the Dukakis and Clinton campaigns. Baldick's job was to oversee and manage the operations of the Gore campaign within New Hampshire. Second in command was the field director, Craig Schirmer, whose job was to handle voter files, lists, accounts, literature pieces, and vendors for mail and phones. The highest-ranking local activist was political director Caroline McCarley, at the time a state senator from the seacoast. Scourfield McLauchlan was Gore's state deputy field director; New Hampshire was the first stop on an eighteen-month journey that took her coast to coast on behalf of the vice president. Her job in New Hampshire was to manage field staff, specifically, to supervise the eleven regional field offices in the state and a total field staff of twenty-five.

Gore's New Hampshire campaign team emphasized that they were sensitive to the role and importance of the local activists. "If anybody was not happy, we were quick to know about it from them," Scourfield McLauchlan said. In fact, when activists wanted to express their opinions, they would often go above the heads of the field staff. Activists had access all the way up to the White House, and used it. "We had all of the establishment types," Scourfield McLauchlan said. And while it is excellent to have those people on board who lend credibility to a campaign, they are not necessarily interested in doing the mundane tasks of fieldwork. When Richard Gephardt is "calling them on the phone for their birthday, why would they need to come and schlepp from door to door?" she asked. Activists sometimes do these menial tasks, but more often "they're interested in strategizing, in talking about issues, when the bottom line is, all you're trying to do is crack through your phone banks, you're trying to crack through your canvasses, actually talk to voters, convince them to vote for Al Gore," she said.

To make matters worse, activists' egos sometimes clash with one another to the overall detriment of the campaign, Woodburn said.

> You're infighting, you're wondering who gets to introduce [the candidate], you're fighting over it, only one person can introduce [the candidate], and the seven who don't introduce him are pissed off, and they're not going to work, and then it will be backing up into the press, and to other activists . . . one may

leave the campaign and support another candidate, because they felt they were slighted. Then a supporter can be something that's a liability, because you have to constantly be managing them.

Having so many activists on board created tensions and challenges, said McCarley, whose job it was to keep the campaign aware of the local political dynamics of the state.[15] All elected officials, from time to time, let their position go to their heads, she explained; therefore questions of who was invited when, and who was standing where at an event, are important in any political campaign. These issues of status are magnified in a place like New Hampshire, where local politicians and activists get the chance to see candidates more often and come to feel as if they know them better than their counterparts in other states. It was not uncommon, McCarley said, to field calls from New Hampshire Democrats who wanted to know why the vice president of the United States could not stay overnight at their home, as Bill Clinton had done back in 1991.

As chair of the Gore campaign in New Hampshire, Bill Shaheen said part of his job was "to keep everybody focused and put out fires."[16] The sources of those fires were often internal; one member of the campaign would become angry at another member for an offense or perceived slight. Shaheen saw his job as providing perspective; "sometimes you get so close to it, you get bent out of shape," he said. In such situations, Shaheen would get on the phone and talk to the aggrieved party, reminding them, "We're not doing it for ourselves, *so relax.*"

The challenge for any New Hampshire presidential campaign, Woodburn said, is to try to find people who can "actually bring things to the table, who will work, and will give you good advice." Locals know the lay of the land in their communities, said activist Bill Stetson, and can provide local knowledge essential to a grassroots campaign that hired guns from out of state cannot.[17] Activists love to claim that they were the ones who gave the candidate good campaign advice, but Woodburn pointed out that no one who has decided to run for president shows up in New Hampshire and blindly follows the advice of local activists. "When it comes to big issues and directions," he said, "they hold the cards close to the vest and they make the decisions based upon their inner circle."

One of the main tasks of Nick Baldick, as state director of the Gore campaign, was communicating with activists. Baldick spoke with activists in order to get their advice and to plan and set up events for Gore around the state. Maintaining that network among the hundreds of activists signed up for the Gore campaign presented a challenge in management that was worth it in the end.

Tensions did exist between the local activists and the staffers from out of state, Baldick said, about as much as in any other campaign. An out-of-state operative running the campaign often prompts complaints from locals that the operative is not listening to them. Hiring a local activist to run the show, however, does not necessarily lead to a reduction in tension among those on board the campaign. Sometimes "the other activists don't want to hear" orders from an in-state person whom they know, Baldick said.

The best activists made two important contributions to the campaign, as field workers and as "opinion leaders [who] would talk to their friends . . . the kind of people that people look up to," Baldick said. When asked what his most valuable activists provided for the campaign, Baldick responded, they "put up staff, put up volunteers in their homes, organized lit drops, brought food and coffee for the poor people walking out in the cold, hosted house parties, called their neighbors, called their friends. We had a lot of people who did a lot of that, and they were great."

In contrast to Calegari's experience with Bradley, Scourfield McLauchlan found it difficult to get new faces as opposed to political insiders involved in the campaign. "It was hard being the establishment, yet trying to run a grassroots campaign," she said. Bill Bradley, she conceded, did a great job of getting new people involved in politics, especially young people and college students. The Gore campaign had both a college coordinator and a student coordinator who concentrated on Boston-area schools, but it was "very hard to get college students to want to throw themselves into Al Gore." For whatever reason, Gore did not have the intangibles—the "panache," she called it—that attracted college students, and Bradley did.

Gore's campaign had such difficulties because it did not convey that ordinary people could make much of a difference with their personal involvement, Woodburn said. While he had a good experience with the Gore campaign, he wants to support a candidate in 2004 who is "more of a long shot . . . not an incumbent type of a candidate like Al Gore was, but somebody where I could have an impact." He added:

Al Gore wasn't my friend. Al Gore was vice president when I met him, and he's not my friend, he's not anybody's friend. He's the vice president of the United States. But if you were . . . driving Bill Clinton around, who was the governor of some small state . . . he's a person, and he's not president of the United States, and then it's a totally different kind of a relationship. That's appealing, that's the great story of the New Hampshire primary, that Jimmy Carter stayed at my house . . . nobody drove around Al Gore.

Another motive for activist unrest was that the locals were starting to smell a loser in Gore. The New Hampshire activists may have been contentious and demanding at times, but they also put their finger on a problem in the Gore campaign that the candidate's Washington operatives seemed to have trouble grasping: Gore's lack of accessibility. The issue eventually moved from being a point of complaint among the party elite to a problem hampering his campaign. In part this occurred because Gore and Bradley appeared, on paper, to be rather similar; both had developed reputations as moderate-to-conservative Democrats during their political careers. As is often the case, the difference between candidates' issue positions in presidential primaries often pales in comparison to the difference between rival candidates in a general election. In the absence of issue contrasts between Bradley and Gore in the early going, other factors rushed in to fill the vacuum and provided the contrast between the two.

In New Hampshire, to borrow a line from Marshall McLuhan, the medium became the message: The ways that the two candidates campaigned became issues in and of themselves and symbolized the candidates. Bradley quickly put on the garb of the populist insurgent, easily accessible to the people, while Gore wore the robe of the incumbent like a tight suit that sometimes seemed closer to a straitjacket.

"The one thing that New Hampshire voters like about the process more than anything is access, and we've always had it," said Gore supporter Jim Demers. Bill Bradley could give the voters what they wanted because he could go anywhere he wanted at the spur of the moment: If Bradley wanted "to walk into a Dunkin' Donuts at ten at night, he could just tell the driver, 'Pull over and let's go talk to them,'" Demers said. But for Al Gore, "everything had to be prearranged, prescreened, the Secret Service had to go in and check out the building, and that made campaigning in New Hampshire, I think, more difficult. I'm not saying it wasn't necessary, but it cramped the ability to connect with people the way that people here expect."

Gore's staffers agreed that the campaign was handicapped by the candidate being the vice president, likening it to wearing handcuffs. "We were cursed the entire campaign by the fact that we had to travel in huge motorcades that blocked traffic," Scourfield McLauchlan said. She added that Baldick was in an ongoing fight with the Secret Service to try to pare down the motorcade, "so Al Gore could be an average guy, talking to voters in New Hampshire at the coffee shop" and doing retail politics without his entourage. "Our activists were saying for six months, you've got to get closer to the ground. . . . And they were absolutely right," Baldick said. "But trying to break down the routine, and the barriers of motorcades and staff, and this and that, it's very tough." If Gore ventured into a coffee shop to speak one-on-one with voters, the quiet eatery was transformed into a minispectacle. Baldick said, "When he walked into a coffee shop, it was like a zoo. He'd walk in, and there'd be eight Service people, and press corps, and someone advancing the press corps, and four staff, and four people at the coffee bar . . . that wasn't Al Gore's fault."

That insulation hurt Al Gore in New Hampshire, and it eventually damaged him in the general election, Woodburn argued: "If Al Gore had run for president the way Jimmy Carter did, he wouldn't have been huffing and puffing during that debate with George W. Bush, because he would have had a better feel for how to come across. I really believe that the process does more to improve them than it does to give us some great exposure."

Furthermore, the Gore campaign was acting as if it were running for a third term in the White House—not for the first term of a new candidate, Demers said:

I felt that they were waging a campaign from the beginning that was a continuation of the Clinton reelection effort—but it was no longer a reelection effort. The ideas that were coming out looked like Al Gore was already the president and he was running for reelection. People in New Hampshire don't look at it that way. He was the vice president, and he needed to wage a campaign, just like everybody else, where he went through the same kind of grind that any candidate would to become the nominee. And it didn't resemble that kind of campaign.

As a result, too many candidate events did not have the personal touch, but rather were orchestrated shows with fancy backdrops and individuals specially selected to be on stage to participate in discussions. Many New Hampshire advisors argued that this would not sell in their state.

The emphasis on orchestration and control also backfired by inadvertently highlighting the candidate's weaknesses. The media had reported for years that Al Gore was stiff and rigid and did not connect with people. When the Gore campaign began arranging events in New Hampshire, this image was reinforced. Because New Hampshire is known for one-on-one, grassroots politicking, it "should have been an ideal venue for Al Gore to overcome some of the perceptions that were out there," Demers said. "It's a style of campaigning where, if you do it the way New Hampshire people expect it, you can't help but come away looking very relaxed and very engaging." But Gore's campaign techniques that kept him separated from the public by rope lines sent the wrong message.

Gore's New Hampshire chair Bill Shaheen was just one of many local activists who warned the Gore campaign of its missteps. He recalled listening on his speakerphone to the planning of a visit by the vice president:

> I can remember in this office, on this phone, listening for *hours,* and I mean literally *hours,* of laying out the format of what was going to happen: The Vice President is going to get out of the car. He's going to walk fifty paces. He's going to open the door. He's going to turn to the left. He's going to walk down the hallway . . . I'm going, *Jesus Christ.* I said, "Stop it!" They said, "No, no, no, we've got to go through this. And then he'll sit on a brown stool. . . ." The minutiae! It was unbelievable! And I said, "You guys are crazy! We're in New Hampshire here!"

Over the summer and early fall of 1999, Gore's standing in the polls dropped precipitously. At a meeting called by Gore's national campaign, Shaheen recalled being asked, What's the problem? He replied:

The problem is, people in New Hampshire don't give a shit that he's the vice president. Got it? . . . He's a man like everybody else. And he's got to come up here and he's got to campaign like everybody else. And he's got to ask for their vote just like everybody else. And he's got to sit there and answer questions just like everybody else. There are no free rides in New Hampshire. And until you guys learn that in Washington, you are going to continue to lose this election.

Gore's early campaign events, Shaheen recalled, were always scripted and packaged with an eye toward television. "You come here with these goddamn props," he said at one troubleshooting meeting in Manchester. Gore, for example, would have cards waiting for him with the names of people who had submitted questions in advance. Shaheen recalls telling Gore, "Throw the goddamn cards away! Sit there and ask this person if they have any questions. You're smart enough to handle it . . . all you have to do is sit there and listen to their questions and answer them. They'll judge whether you're good or bad, or whether you're full of crap or not."

New Hampshire voters do not want a flashy, glitzy campaign, but do want the opportunity to hear the candidates' stands on the issues and personal access to the candidate, Demers said. The polls proved this, and it was not until Al Gore personally intervened that the format of the campaign changed, he observed.

The vice president, for instance, made it his business to field any and all questions at a series of town hall meetings. These meetings, Shaheen contends, were key to Gore's rebound in New Hampshire. Another of Shaheen's recommendations was that Gore "get out there and look people in the eye and ask them for their vote"; every time Gore stopped somewhere, he should factor in ten to fifteen minutes to shake hands with bystanders. "Billy was very good at making our trips more—how do I put it—real," said Baldick. "All of a sudden, you started seeing Al Gore walking the streets, walking up to strangers and chatting with them," said Demers. "And rather than having fancy issue programs, he had a stool in the middle of a gymnasium, and he had actual town meetings where the people there could engage him, [and only then] did he start to swing the numbers back where they belonged."

After struggling to find a format that gave Gore the best opportunity to communicate with New Hampshire voters, the campaign finally settled on the town hall meeting as a showcase for its candidate. On one hand, Gore was "totally overqualified to be president," Baldick said. "He knew everything. He was on top of the issues . . . he understood the ins and outs of these issues." The problem for the campaign in New Hampshire, however, was how best to convey the candidate and his qualifications to the voters. Traditional house parties, Baldick said, were not Gore's element. While the candidate was able to field questions well at a party, Gore would get off on the wrong foot because of his necessary entourage.

The campaign decided the best way for Gore to display these abilities was to place the candidate in the middle of a hundred people, let him talk for eight minutes or ten minutes, and then just take questions from the audience, Baldick said. In that setting, Gore's reputed policy-wonkery won over the crowd. In his first town hall meeting, Gore did not flinch even when he fielded a question on the arcane issue of Chilean rose tariffs. "I think it made a mark on people," Baldick said. "People said, 'Hey, he really understands this stuff.'" In addition, Gore seemed better able to relate to voters in the environment of the town hall meeting and engage in the give-and-take that is required of a candidate in New Hampshire. Although the meeting was not scripted, Baldick said, it was "not so casual . . . not like he's sitting down and having a cup of coffee" with a small group of voters. "We brought him back by having him talk about the issues," Baldick said, "not by going to coffee shops."

Nearing the Finish

In the summer of 1999, Gore was down as many as fourteen points to Bradley, Baldick said. The Gore campaign was not hitting the panic button, however, believing that only later in the game would polls really matter. As Baldick put it, "The time you want to be getting people's attention is when most of the voters are finally paying attention. But most of the voters don't care about the New Hampshire primary in September or October. They start paying attention in December and January." In addition, Baldick felt that the push for Bradley was due less to the challenger's strengths than to Gore's weaknesses: "Bradley was moving because Gore had had a lot of bad stories, things hadn't worked well, we had made some mistakes on the campaign, here and elsewhere. And it was all about Gore. . . . It wasn't like there was this huge buzz [about] Bradley."

Gore and Bradley met for the first time at a debate in October at Dartmouth College in Hanover. The rivalry between the two campaigns was most obvious at this public event, as both campaigns waged "sign wars" on the streets surrounding the site of the debate. The scuffling continued at future events.

Inside the hall, Gore went on the attack against Bradley, criticizing his recently unveiled proposal to increase the number of Americans covered by health insurance.[18] For the first time in the campaign, Bradley was on the defensive. Gore's attack that night was the first of many designed to turn the tables on the insurgent; confronted with a deficit in the polls, the Gore campaign proceeded to "eviscerate" Bradley's health care plan, Baldick said. For instance, the Gore campaign began passing out pill boxes in order to highlight that Bradley's health care plan would not cover the cost of prescription drugs. "The Bradley campaign responded by calling us liars, handing out flyers that called Gore a liar. It got ugly," Baldick said. "To be honest, that was good for us, because [until then] his campaign was high and mighty and not slugging it out in the mud with us. And that made it just two campaigns slugging it out in the mud."

For the Bradley campaign, the fun days of run-and-gun campaigning and tweaking the establishment were at an end. Just a few months before the primary, the two candidates were in close quarters. "We were duking it out, it was trench warfare," Scourfield McLauchlan said. The race was "within the margin of error for months," she added.

The Gore campaign from the beginning was uniquely suited for grinding out a victory. Those strengths provided the vice president with a much larger margin of error than his competitor, and his campaign displayed an ability to weather storms that served the candidate well in the final weeks of the campaign.

First and foremost, the Gore operation had "probably . . . the Cadillac of field plans," Scourfield McLauchlan said. Iowa and New Hampshire were the two best-developed Gore organizations after the months of effort poured into them. (In contrast, when Scourfield McLauchlan was sent to Maine after New Hampshire, she had only four weeks to get an operation up and running with the help of just two staffers in order to win both the caucuses and the primaries held there.)

In New Hampshire, the Gore campaign conducted a voter identification program during the fall of 1999, calling registered Democrats to ask them who they would vote for if the election were held today. Night after night, two thousand calls were made to voters in the cities of Manchester and Nashua; all told, tens of thousands, possibly hundreds of thousands, of calls were placed. The voter identification program was coupled with a voter contact operation that used phone banks every night and canvassing every weekend. Voter files indicating Democrats' voting history allowed the campaign to identify those more likely to come out to the polls for a primary.

The success of field organization is defined very simply, Scourfield McLauchlan said: A campaign has succeeded if, on Election Day, "more of your people are going to the polls than their people. So you need a machine that is going to get those people out to the polls. And we had that machine." Field operations count in a close race, as much as three to five percentage points on election day. (Scourfield McLauchlan suspects that fieldwork will be important in 2004; in a big field, 35,000 to 40,000 people would be a strong showing.) New Hampshire "isn't like Texas or California or New York," she said. When a campaign is competing in a voter universe so small, "with a strong field operation, you can call those people on the phone, you can identify, you can persuade the undecideds, you could knock on their door six times, more than that, probably."

In the opposing camp, Bradley was still enjoying the fruits of the summer and early fall work. Now, however, Bradley's organizers in New Hampshire had to turn their attention from creating growth to managing it. January was like a whole new campaign, said field organizer Mica Stark. College students came to work in droves. Seventy-five to one hundred people were always in Manchester headquarters, doing work such as phone-banking. Managing that growth was a huge challenge, and the Bradley campaign was caught off guard. Stark summarized the dilemma: "Wow, what an amazing problem to have, and we really don't know what to do with it."

In the weeks before the primary, the small circles of core supporters had multiplied and expanded, Calegari said. Each of Bradley's field directors, for instance, had begun the campaign with responsibility for an entire congressional district—in other words, half the state. As the campaign grew, that territory was broken up into smaller regions. Interns who excelled became paid hires. Interns were sent out into the field. Out-of-staters, such as students recruited over the Internet, had to be matched up with Bradley supporters in the local communities in order to provide aid and shelter. Logistics became an increasingly important problem. Calegari recalls asking locals, "Do you think you could take five people home with you tonight, and we'll find a place for them to stay tomorrow?"

Both campaigns also had to contend with the velocity of information a campaign has to receive and process on any given day. Each day was like a three-ring circus, Calegari said, with new incoming bulletins. It was one staffer's job to rise early in the morning to collect all the articles from various newspapers so that by seven in the morning there would be a stack of clippings to review. In 1984, the Hart campaign had perhaps one computer. By 2000, all voter registration lists were kept on computer. Walking lists that volunteers carried from house to house were bar coded so that walkers could quickly record data on whether the recipient of a visit was a supporter, an opponent, or an undecided voter. Another innovation was the cell phone; all organizers had them. The Bradley campaign had a "phone bank in a box," Calegari said, literally twenty to thirty cell phones in a box. Bradley operatives also used e-mail to spread information and to organize; advance teams used wireless Palm Pilots to communicate, Stark said.

The Bradley campaign did not have as many traditional storefronts as Gore's campaign, said field organizer Matt Rodriguez, and even in a high-tech campaign, it makes sense to have storefronts where the volunteers are. Store-fronts can be key links in a campaign's logistics, especially for a doorstep campaign that relies on communicating with voters one-on-one as opposed to mass communication. A nearby storefront can save a volunteer or field operative up to one and a half hours of driving time.

Late in any campaign, the emphasis shifts from spurring growth to managing growth and that transition is difficult, Rodriguez said. In the last weeks, the Bradley campaign organization was groaning under the weight of the flood of volunteers. Using the people in the state to maximum efficiency became a problem: Where do the volunteers go? How should we manage the influx? Who is making those decisions? How will volunteers be moved from office to office and from task to task? Although volunteers were numerous, Rodriguez said the campaign's system for putting them where they were needed the most was not all it could have been.

Field organizers on each side criticized aspects of their opponent's organization. On one hand, Gore field operatives such as Scourfield McLauchlan dismissed the Bradley efforts as "all smoke and mirrors" with no real bone and muscle to back up all the hype. Baldick said that Longabaugh, his opposite number on the Bradley campaign, essentially started with no infrastructure and with a candidate running against an incumbent vice president. Therefore Longabaugh concentrated on issues and on acquiring a few key supporters. Bradley's campaign did not have a big get-out-the-vote program but, Baldick argued, they "didn't really have to. Their voters were educated, college graduates, relatively affluent. Guess what—they were going to vote."

Bradley operatives defended their effort as an authentic New Hampshire grass-roots operation, compared to their rival's organization, which was bought and paid for by political insiders and special interests. The Bradley operation, contends Calegari, outmaneuvered the Gore campaign on the ground with more active volunteer phone banks, volunteer canvassing, and in January over a hundred interns from colleges all over the country. Necessity breeds invention and creativity in insurgent campaigns, she said.

Will the Real Insurgent Please Stand Up?

Bradley had to contend not only with Gore in New Hampshire but also with Senator John McCain of Arizona, who was staging an insurgent campaign against Republican front runner George W. Bush, governor of Texas. McCain, Baldick argued, was proof that a candidate's skills at communication and interactions with voters ultimately are more important than a candidate's ideology. It is possible for a candidate to be too ideological—that is, too far to the left or the right—because such candidates find it difficult to display an independent streak and thus to gain the support of voters in the middle. But "John McCain, ideologically, wasn't moderate," Baldick said. "It's the fact that he looked like he was independent in principle" that attracted voters.

McCain's surge in New Hampshire added to Bradley's struggles in a very difficult month prior to the January 27 primary. Bradley began the month with a lead in New Hampshire, but his margin shrank and disappeared with one bad news cycle after another. For one, Bradley revealed that he had had a recurrence of heart palpitations, news that diverted attention from the campaign and conjured up memories of Paul Tsongas's health problems from the 1992 campaign.

In addition, the Bradley campaign split the candidate's time and resources between New Hampshire and the Iowa caucuses, a gambit that backfired when Bradley was badly defeated in Iowa. The Bradley campaign had polled in Iowa early in 1999 and thought he stood a chance of winning the caucuses there, a notion that Bradley's New Hampshire team disputed. The Bradley national campaign clung to that hope into the final months of 1999 even after the AFL-CIO had endorsed Gore in October. They decided to spend time and money in Iowa even though polling in early January 2000 showed that their candidate was leading in New Hampshire and down two-to-one in Iowa. Longabaugh said that Bradley's reformer profile did not fit as well in Iowa, a populist liberal state, as it did in New Hampshire. Bradley had a terrible debate performance in Iowa and, Longabaugh said, generally "wasted all this time out there, just floundering around" instead of being in New Hampshire delivering his message.

Gore's thrashing of Bradley in Iowa was coupled with McCain's surge among independents. At the Bradley phone banks in January, operatives noted a drop-off in Bradley's support among those leaning Democratic as well as among independents. The movement in the race was not so much from Bradley to Gore, Rodriguez said, as it was from Bradley to McCain. After Iowa, the Gore-Bradley contest was relegated to the number-two story in New Hampshire, overshadowed by McCain's challenge to Texas governor and front runner George W. Bush, said longtime observer Dayton Duncan.[19] Bradley's viability depended on the support of a large number of independents, and as that support drained away, so did Bradley's chances of carrying New Hampshire.

Independent (or undeclared) voters are a critical force in the primaries, in a way they were not many years ago, observed Demers, and their votes can make or break a campaign. Independents in 2000, for instance, were shopping. They had decided against the two front runners, Gore and Bush, and were choosing between Bradley and McCain; most eventually decided to go with McCain.[20]

Longabaugh maintains that the movement of independents to McCain was not inevitable, but that the Bradley campaign had squandered its opportunity. Bill Bradley could have been John McCain, he said: Bradley had the persona and the message (not only on campaign finance reform, but on health care and poverty) to be the Democratic insurgent. But Bradley was not able, or perhaps not willing, to fulfill the role of the insurgent on the campaign trail.

Insurgents have to be feisty, Longabaugh said, but Bradley showed a reluctance "to defend himself, to fight for himself," and that made him look weak, "lumbering," and "plodding." Bradley supporter Randy Benthien recalled telling Bradley that he had to ask for people to vote for him and support him. Bradley, however, was too genteel and too scholarly to be successful at this, Benthien observed. The candidate was inspirational, but in an intellectual way, not an emotional way. "People who got inspired, were a lot of bright people who liked listening to a bright guy talk about being a bright president," Benthien said. New Hampshire voters liked the Bradley campaign for the same reason they like National Public Radio, said Mica Stark; both provided high-quality, thoughtful material, rather than pulling at emotional heartstrings.

From the Gore campaign's perspective, Nick Baldick agreed that when Bradley was taking hits on his health care plan, he could have fought back, but "They didn't really fire back." Voters gain an intuitive sense of whether candidates are up to this test, Longabaugh said, from how the candidate reacts to the pressures of a campaign: "If he's not going to fight for himself, or fight for his ideas," voters doubt he has the right stuff. "Voters didn't care about what kind of campaign you were running. Voters care about, 'Are you going to fight for me?' And is the president, the guy we're going to elect as president, is he tough enough and strong enough? Is he going to be able to answer that call in the middle of the night?" Gore managed to convert his fight for his political life into a theme that was larger than his personal struggle and resonated with voters, McCarley said. Time after time, Gore told audiences that he was willing to fight for all of them; in the process, McCarley said, Gore's image shifted from the figure of the vice president to someone who aspired to be president.

The Bradley campaign fixated on the idea that voters do not like nasty campaigns, "and instead of taking the kind of campaign Gore was running and turning it around on him, we sort of said, 'No, no, no, we're above the fray.

We're not going to answer these charges,'" Longabaugh said. This was a complete misreading of what voters cared about, he observed. What Bradley needed to do was to turn around Gore's attacks and point out that these were the kind of "negative, attack politics" that voters were tired of seeing.

Bradley's advertising also was not well focused, Longabaugh said, and failed to capitalize on the insurgency and reform message. McCain was taking individual messages and framing them in an overall theme of reform while Bradley, Longabaugh said, was "plodding through health care" in a way that did not serve the overall dynamic of reform. Longabaugh offered a scenario of how Bradley could have become the Democrats' John McCain and could have capitalized on the character issue:

> Had we fought it out on health care, we actually could have turned health care into a virtue. I always argued with Bradley and the folks in Jersey that we needed to take health care and Gore's attacks upon it and make it part of our insurgency message, and say: "This is why we don't have universal health care. The fact that a Democrat like Al Gore, who ought to be the standard-bearer of the Democratic Party, was walking away from traditional commitments of this party to the less advantaged, to those in need, is a travesty. And my candidacy is not about that. You want to know why Al Gore is not going to be for insuring every American . . . ? Because he's bought into the Washington establishment, the interests-that-be."

A stronger counterattack accusing Gore and his campaign of distortions would have given Bradley the chance to capitalize on the character issue, Longabaugh argued, but Bradley and the operatives running the national campaign would not go for it. "They just completely were distorting the health care plan and what was in it, and they weren't telling the truth," Longabaugh said. "Bill would never stand up and say it." He continued: "We used to joke in New Hampshire that the guys in New Jersey were drinking Kool-Aid . . . they bought into this whole thing that they were running a different kind of campaign: 'We were different. We were going to do it differently.' . . ." "Running a different kind of campaign" meant staying above the fray and refusing to slug it out with Gore.

Bradley's national campaign spokesman Eric Hauser said Longabaugh was generally right that the candidate needed to be feistier and articulate what he was about more aggressively.[21] Hauser was still not convinced, though, that going on the attack would have accomplished this. The Bradley campaign had tried to depict a leader who was beholden to no one and possessed a plain-spoken, reform-minded liberalism; that image, they believed, would be especially attractive to New Hampshire primary voters.

Those running the national campaign believed that responding to what Hauser called the Gore campaign's specious claims, on a tit-for-tat basis, was not in keeping with the new kind of politics the candidate was espousing, Hauser said.

As a result, John McCain, not Bill Bradley, became "the sexy candidate for the independents," Longabaugh said. There was much debate, he said, about whether these independent voters knew that McCain was against abortion or that as a senator he had voted as a conservative Republican. Issue positions were beside the point for most independents. The motive of these voters, said Longabaugh, was to find someone "who wants to shake it up, they're looking for somebody who has got a little bit of dynamism . . . the insurgent candidate who wants to upset the apple cart." McCain was perceived as the stand-up guy of integrity who better expressed these sentiments. McCain held the character advantage with his biography as a prisoner of war in Vietnam, a man of integrity who was willing to take on establishment interests with his campaign finance reform bill. The character issue emerged in New Hampshire in the form of a clean government theme, particularly centered around the issue of campaign finance reform, a plank in the Bradley campaign. While evidence is scarce that voters used campaign finance reform as a litmus test, the issue fed into a theme that resonated with voters.

The Last Week

His back against the wall after the Iowa debacle, Bradley finally got feisty in a debate the week before the primary, and things began to turn around for him. Heading into New Hampshire, Gore was up eight points. Then Gore was asked about his opposition, as a Tennessee congressman, to Medicaid funding for abortions. Gore's response "wasn't quite as clear as it could have been," said Baldick, especially concerning his support for the pro-choice position; instead, Gore tried to talk about his answer in terms of the lines of distinction on the issue at the time. "The Bradley people were able to feed it into this perception that Gore sometimes exaggerates or plays with the truth," Baldick said. That last week, the Gore campaign began to bleed away its lead, losing a point a day to Bradley.

The Bradley campaign had cut a comparative ad highlighting editorials that supported Bradley and criticized Gore. The Bradley campaign held a meeting the Thursday night before the primary to discuss whether to run the ad. Longabaugh recalled:

> I distinctly remember arguing for the spot, and saying, "Look, I think we're going to get close, but I don't think it's going to be enough. We need to pop this thing, and change the dynamics, really drive this the last few days. I think if we make this focus on Al Gore, we will win this thing. If we don't, we won't."
>
> The Kool-Aid crowd made a decision that we couldn't, we pledged to run a different kind of campaign, we couldn't possibly run that ad, the press would take us to task. I think the press actually was just dying for us to mix it up and to take him to task because they thought he was exaggerating the health care record; they thought he hadn't told the truth on a whole bunch of things; they thought his nonsense about the Internet, "Love Story," and every other goofy thing that he said . . . they wanted somebody to mix it up with him.

If they had run the ad, Longabaugh maintains, instead of losing by four points, Bradley would have won by three to five points.

Longabaugh described the last week before the primary as a "cacophony." The week before the primary, Baldick said, proves that being state director is all about management because "you can't do all the jobs that need to be done." The vice president and his wife were in New Hampshire every day; one team accompanied them and another team set up events for them. Field people focused on turnout operations. The press team concentrated on getting publicity for campaign events, as well as pushing back against their opponent on issues. "You just try to make sure that the right people are responsible for the right things," Baldick said. "You have to have good people, and we had great people," all the way up to the vice president and his wife, who "worked their butts off" on eighteen-hour days. "The last thing you want to do is be working your tail off, and the candidate isn't," Baldick said. "That wasn't a problem for us."

Part of the challenge of the last week is running an effective get-out-the-vote (GOTV) operation. Massive phone banking does not work well, Longabaugh said, because of volatility among the electorate. "People move up there in a split second," supporting one candidate and then another, he said. In early January, for example, Bradley had an eleven-point lead in New Hampshire; a couple of weeks out from the primary, Bradley found himself down eight to ten points. In the face of such volatility, Longabaugh contended, it just was not possible for the Gore campaign to accurately target their vote—identifying Gore voters and then pulling those voters out in the weekend before the primary.

Baldick countered that despite the volatility in the New Hampshire electorate, the Gore campaign was confident it knew where to go to find votes for the candidate. "We were always winning working families big," he said. "What varied was how much we were getting beaten by [among] college-educated to white-collar families." Around Labor Day that gap had been large, but it had narrowed during the course of the fall; in January that gap reemerged.

Gore also relied on institutional motors, such as the state party establishment and labor unions, to drive his campaign, while the Bradley campaign looked to independent voters to provide the spark, said Bradley field operative Matt Rodriguez.

One of those institutional motors was the Democratic governor of New Hampshire, Jeanne Shaheen. The governor's campaigning and popularity were huge assets, Baldick said. Shaheen publicly endorsed Gore in December 1999, and in the last days of the campaign, she went on the radio and also made phone calls on behalf of Gore. "I don't think we could have won without her," Baldick said.

Another important institutional motor working for Gore was organized labor. Although only 24 percent of New Hampshire Democratic primary voters reported having a union member in their household,[22] the unions were able to provide organized manpower to the vice president's campaign. Labor was solidly behind Gore, who had eight years of good relations with labor while vice president, said Bill Stetson, secretary-treasurer of the New Hampshire AFL-CIO. In particular, Gore formed a tight bond with the Professional Firefighters of New Hampshire, an organization comprising 38 local unions and 1,200 active members, said David Lang, the president of the union.[23] Firefighters, by the very nature of their job, put a premium on loyalty; supporting one's friends is written into their DNA, Lang said. They base their judgments of candidates on three questions: What have you done? Where have you been? And what do you stand for? Gore had passed all three questions on the exam, proving himself time and again to be a supporter of organized labor on a wide variety of issues. Throughout the primary campaign, the firefighters provided high-visibility support to Gore.

But despite the engine power of Gore's institutional motors, the campaign found itself losing in the early hours of primary day, according to all four exit polls being conducted. Bradley operative Rodriguez recalled that his campaign felt that Bradley was doing very well until midafternoon. In the late afternoon and evening, though, the campaign sensed that Gore had seized the final momentum swing.

"We won it in the field on election day," Baldick said. On the day of the primary, Scourfield McLauchlan said, the Gore campaign had a full-blown get-out-the-vote operation (GOTV), complete with poll checkers, phone banks, runners, and poll teams.

The one piece of good news for the Gore campaign was that a large number of undeclared voters were requesting Republican ballots, not Democratic ones. The assumption in the Gore campaign was that the independents would swing toward McCain, not Bradley. Among the independents, there were those who tended to lean Republican, those who leaned Democratic, and those who were attracted to the race with the high energy. Independents displayed more enthusiasm and energy for the Republican and his straight talk, Baldick said; if they had not, "there was no way to do the math" for a Gore victory. If there had not been a Republican primary and independent voters had been channeled toward the Democratic primary instead, "they would all have voted for Bradley," Baldick said, "not all, but it would have been huge, and we would have lost by thousands and thousands of votes."

Labor played a very important role in the effort to reach working-class voters, Baldick said, by both persuading their members and getting their own membership out to vote. Union members were particularly important, said Jeanne Shaheen, in GOTV efforts on primary day.[24] Gore activist Jane Clemons described the mechanics of a last-minute GOTV drive. The day of the primary, campaigns will carry out a "knock-and-pull": Get-out-the-vote calls produce lists for the poll checkers, who will stand at the polls and check off a candidate's supporters as they come to vote. Updated lists are taken from the poll checkers to the phone banks, where those remaining on the list are called again—and again, if necessary. By 4 P.M., with just a few hours remaining until the election is over, a campaign will have a list of voters who have indicated their support for the candidate but have not yet cast ballots. Campaigns will then send people out on the streets to knock on the doors of remaining supporters and try to pull them out of their homes to vote. A knock-and-pull operation is "very successful if it's done well," Clemons said. "The funny thing is, we never know what we're doing well that day, because it's . . . very chaotic."

Amid the chaos, however, Gore's people knew where their voters were. Gore political director Caroline McCarley was recruited to make phone calls to voters in the traditionally blue-collar cities of Somersworth and Rochester; a good number of those voters told her they already had received calls. In a contest that was "unbelievably tight," Gore's field operatives had identified their voters well enough to know that there were still Gore supporters in these two cities who had not yet turned out to vote. Field operations may indeed have made the margin of victory for Gore that day—and victory in New Hampshire went a long way toward securing the vice president his party's nomination. Gore's victories in the first two contests of the nomination season succeeded in sucking the oxygen out of Bradley's insurgency. Once again, a campaign which managed to weld together a coalition of elite and working-class voters in New Hampshire proved to have greater staying power than an insurgency that depended on elite voters alone.

CHAPTER SEVEN

Stormwatchers: The Primary and the Media

Part of the mystique of the New Hampshire primary has been the apparently splendid isolation of the state and its citizens. Tucked away in the north of New England, its citizens once seemed insulated from the corrupting techniques of modern political campaigning, such as sound bites and thirty-second commercials. Here in New Hampshire, presidential candidates were compelled to campaign as if they were running for sheriff, as journalist John Milne put it.[1] Candidates had to talk with voters one at a time and build their organizations from the grass roots up because there was simply no other way of running a campaign. New Hampshire "offers the only opportunity for someone who might be the next president of the United States to actually have to answer more than one or two questions from an average citizen," said longtime observer Dayton Duncan.[2] Thus, the first-in-the-nation primary has taken on the status of an endangered natural habitat, a political wildlife preserve of national value—or as activist Terry Shumaker said, the last bastion of true democracy against the onslaught of campaigns run on television screens and candidates who only see voters from airport tarmacs.[3]

Although there is truth to this image, as with any image it is also a distortion. Even the earliest New Hampshire primaries were not unaffected by the influence of mass media. After all, Senator Estes Kefauver of Tennessee, the original grassroots presidential campaigner in 1952, made his name via televised Senate hearings on corruption. And in 1968, radio advertising was a significant part of Gene McCarthy's grassroots insurgency. But during the last three decades in particular, the ever-increasing presence of media ever earlier in the process has made the grassroots refuge sometimes resemble a national forest overcrowded by summer tourists. Seeking a glimpse of authentic politics, the media by their very presence inevitably affect the environment they seek to experience and describe for their audience.

In addition, once-isolated New Hampshire, formerly without a television station worth calling its own, is now wired into the nation's virtual body politic. Almost three of four adults have access to the Internet, on which they spend two hours a day on average.[4] To understand how connected New Hampshire is to the national mass media, one need look no further than one's doorstep, said Mark Bodi of the Manchester advertising firm O'Neil Griffin Bodi.[5] As recently as five or ten years ago, for example, one could find the *New York Times* in a handful of outlets in the city of Manchester, each of which carried just a few copies. Now New Hampshire is no longer isolated from out-of-state and national media as advances in communication and printing technology bring the *Times*, the *Boston Globe*, as well as the *Manchester Union Leader* to one's front door by 6:30 in the morning. The advent of cable television and the twenty-four-hour news cycle have also significantly increased the speed of the flow of information into New Hampshire. As a result, New Hampshire voters are much more connected to and perhaps more influenced by nonlocal media than ever before.

Presidential candidates in New Hampshire today undertake the rigors of grassroots politics in a much different environment from their forebears, an environment in which they are on the record from the moment they step off the plane at Manchester International Airport. While no candidate can afford to skip out on traditional grassroots politicking in favor of more modern methods of reaching voters, candidates must understand the distinction between the image of the New Hampshire primary and the reality of how it actually works, said Duncan.

One major misconception is that the primary is all about grassroots politics and meeting voters face-to-face. This misconception goes hand-in-hand with the erroneous assumption that everybody who votes in the primary bases that vote either on a personal relationship or at least a personal connection to the candidate, Duncan said. To a significant extent, a New Hampshire campaign has much in common with those in other states in that most of the voters decide based on what they see on television or read in the newspaper. Grassroots politicking is getting a little less important each cycle, Duncan said, as the state increases in population: "There's just only a certain number of people you're actually going to meet and touch with your grassroots organization." On the other hand, campaigns sometimes make the mistake of believing that running in New Hampshire is exactly like running in other states. The truth of New Hampshire, said Duncan, exists somewhere between those two extremes. A successful candidate needs to campaign as if he believes that the primary is all about grassroots, face-to-face politicking but cannot buy in to this wholeheartedly. For example, candidates campaign "the New Hampshire way" because they will be seen on television meeting people and answering their questions. In other words, the appearance of a grassroots connection is important, Duncan said, "particularly early on, and particularly if you are not a candidate of any initial standing, because otherwise you might get dismissed." This chapter focuses on that interplay among candidates, voters, and the media in the first-in-the-nation primary.

Political Advertising in New Hampshire: Is the Book as Good as the Movie?

The problem for all types of media advertising in New Hampshire, as he has seen firsthand in focus groups from the Granite State, is the voters' expectation of retail politicking, said advertising executive Pat Griffin.[6]

> We have an expectation here that retail politics will play an integral role in our making a final choice. It's like interviewing a daughter-in-law or son-in-law. You really want to have the person come in, see how the dog likes him, see if

the children warm up to him. What did Grandma think? There's this real sense of, What kind of houseguest would this guy be?—not just, What kind of leader of the free world?

Thus candidates must compete in a very sophisticated political community, in which even sixth-graders are savvy enough to ask two-part questions, said activists John and Mary Rauh.[7] New Hampshire voters are accustomed to making electoral choices frequently, in a state where the governor and more than 400 legislators are chosen every two years. "It's our sport," said John Rauh. Citizens of New Hampshire are also influenced by a strong tradition of local government, in which voters are proactive in holding their representatives personally accountable, said longtime activist Ramsey McLauchlan.[8]

In a large state like California, Griffin said, candidates' television ads define who they are, because the chances of a voter actually meeting a candidate are so slim. In New Hampshire, however, a candidate has to deliver on the promise displayed in his television advertising. In New Hampshire, candidates are judged against the ads, and voters decide "if the book is as good as the movie."

Reaching New Hampshire voters via paid media or advertising is very expensive, and there are a limited number of outlets available for a campaign to use, said Griffin, a veteran of the New Hampshire campaigns of George H. W. Bush in 1992, Lamar Alexander in 1996, and George W. Bush in 2000. In the last twenty years, a very important development in New Hampshire's media environment has been the emergence of WMUR-TV as a significant commercial television outlet. WMUR's signal is now received in almost all of New Hampshire's ten counties; signal repeaters and cable penetration have made possible wide distribution of its signal and improved the circulation of its news programming within the state. A campaign could reach New Hampshire voters just by buying spots at WMUR, although now perhaps Channel 31 in the state's upper valley and WNDS-TV based in Derry have to be taken into account as well, Griffin said. An underdog campaign without the money to run ads on Boston television can still reach a significant portion of the state by using just New Hampshire media.

WMUR has played a significant role in past primaries, said Bodi, and surely will continue to do so in 2004 and beyond. The station also has been traditionally aggressive in running political commercials and willingly cut down its news time in order to fit in more ads, Griffin said. When WMUR built its new facility in Manchester, it became known as "the house that Forbes built," because the millionaire Republican candidate in 1996 and 2000 spent so much money running political ads on the station. Under the new ownership of Hearst-Argyle, the station has tightened its rules for running political commercials, Griffin said.

Advertising on New Hampshire television alone, however, is not enough to reach all of the state's voters. New Hampshire is nestled close to the Boston market, the sixth largest in the country, and receives significant overflow from the Boston media, said Bodi. (On its own, New Hampshire's media market ranks approximately about 250th in size, Bodi estimated.) Boston media have a significant influence on a state that has over 70,000 of its residents commuting to Massachusetts for work every day, many of whom were former Massachusetts residents. "They may live here," Griffin said, "but their culture, their work, their family may still be in Massachusetts . . . even though they pay taxes here, even though their kids go to school here, to them, it's still about [Boston news anchor] Natalie Jacobsen, it's still about Channel 7. Those habits are very hard to break." Though they may turn on WMUR occasionally, such voters still naturally gravitate toward Massachusetts.

Therefore, campaigns with sufficient resources will buy air time on WMUR and on Boston television stations because the latter reach households in New Hampshire that WMUR will not despite its increased range. Underfunded candidates face the daunting prospect of paying the cost of advertising in the Boston market—about ten times the cost of advertising on New Hampshire television, Bodi estimated—in order to reach the portion of the heavily populated southern tier of the state that tunes in to Boston media.

During New Hampshire's 2002 general election season, campaigns spent "scads of money" to air ads on WMUR, until there were simply no more units of air time left to buy, said Griffin. But New Hampshire political ads were also plentiful on Boston television stations; Griffin said Boston stations almost did better selling ad time to New Hampshire political campaigns than they did on ads for the Massachusetts gubernatorial race. Airing New Hampshire political ads on Boston television means wasting the message on a lot of uninterested Massachusetts viewers—although, in the case of the New Hampshire primary, those viewers will be voting in their own primary just several weeks later. In presidential primaries, however, only a portion of the money New Hampshire campaigns spend advertising on Boston television stations counts against their Federal Elections Commission spending cap in New Hampshire because only 30 percent of the Boston signal reaches New Hampshire.

A good supplement to television advertising in New Hampshire is local radio, Griffin said. Back in the 1960s and 1970s, before the emergence of WMUR and cable television, radio was the best way to reach the state's voters. In the 1968 campaign, Eugene McCarthy's ad man, Merv Weston, ran 7,200 ads on various New Hampshire radio stations at a cost of $36,000, or just under 30 percent of the campaign's advertising budget for the last three weeks before the primary.[9]

Another major change in the New Hampshire media environment over the last two decades was the homogenization of New Hampshire radio, said Kevin Landrigan of the *Nashua Telegraph*.[10] When Landrigan started covering the presidential primary back in 1980, fifteen to twenty local news organizations were operating. And for those local operations, coverage of presidential candidates was a staple; like the twenty-four-hour cable news stations of today, these local news outlets had lots of time to fill. A presidential candidate was able to walk into a radio station in a relatively distant town such as Lebanon, Berlin, or North Conway and get a half-hour interview—something he could not get from the local newspaper or from WMUR.

Back before the 1976 primary, for instance, the Carter campaign depended on small local outlets to try to make news for their candidate. The media rarely if ever covered Carter events, so the Carter campaign instead went to the media, Carter activist Katherine Rogers recalled.[11] Rogers would pick up Carter's wife, Rosalynn, at the airport, armed with a map and a list of radio stations and newspapers. "And we would drive to every newspaper and radio station," Rogers recalled, "knock on the door, and say, 'Hey, how are you doing? Don't you want to interview us?'" It got to the point that the staff at most radio stations and newspapers knew members of the Carter family on a first-name basis, Rogers said. "They didn't always use the interview, but if it was a slow day, you might get something in it, and every little piece counts." For candidates like Carter, those small stations were a training ground where they could find their voice in politics.

Currently, though, with corporations acquiring local stations, programming at these stations has become much more formulaic and packaged, with air time consumed by syndicated programs (such as Rush Limbaugh) designed to get national advertising dollars. New Hampshire Public Radio has filled some of the gap in local news coverage, but as the influence of WMUR grew exponentially, it replaced radio as the medium of choice for presidential candidates seeking exposure. Instead of going to twenty radio stations as in 1980, candidates now try to pull off 30 seconds of air time on WMUR, Landrigan said. Less expensive than television, radio now is used only to fill in the holes in a paid-media strategy to reach the smaller towns in the North Country that cannot be penetrated via other media, Griffin said.

Radio is also a place to put up a negative or comparative ad as a complement to a series of sunny, positive ads on television. In the 1996 primary, for example, the Alexander campaign ran two days' worth of radio ads statewide directed at Governor Pete Wilson of California, who was making noises about running for president and would have been a threat to Alexander. The spot focused on Wilson's pledge, during his run for reelection as governor, to serve a full term and not run for the presidency. The ad concluded, "Governor Wilson needs to understand that in New Hampshire, we hold politicians to their word. If we can't trust Pete Wilson on that, we can't trust him on anything." The Alexander campaign also ran newspaper ads to the same effect. "That poor guy got off the boat, and he had a press crowd he kept waiting for two hours in the hot sun who were pissed off to begin with," Griffin recounted. "He got off the boat and was greeted by, 'Governor Wilson, you broke your word' . . . that was it. Wilson never recovered."

Sometimes a campaign will use newspapers to convert a paid-media buy into earned media, that is, press coverage of debates created by ads. Griffin observed that "there's a little jujitsu you can do with the media, too. It's not just about running ads. It's using advertising in a way that creates an effective selling environment for you and not a very good environment for your opponents . . . using the media as effectively as you can, and driving earned media from the paid stuff."

For example, the weekend before the 1988 Republican primary, Bush ran an ad against Senator Bob Dole of Kansas that accused him of straddling on taxes. The ad was widely credited with putting Bush over the top, but it did not run nearly often enough and at the time WMUR's signal did not have enough range to reach enough voters to make a difference. The ad did, however, provide "wonderful fodder and great copy," Griffin said, and it drove the news cycle all the way to the day of the primary—prompted, in part, by Dole's fierce denials, which only magnified the original charge. The night of the primary, Dole infamously snarled at Bush, "Stop lying about my record."

The Honor Roll Students: Local Media and the Primary

New Hampshire's tradition of grassroots politics means that, unlike most states, the impact of earned media outweighs that of paid media. While a campaign's advertising is an important element, it is media coverage of the candidate's activities, events, movements, and issue positions "that create[s] the excitement and combustion that will either propel him to victory or, in some cases, will bring him down to the flames of defeat," Bodi said. Despite its recent growth, New Hampshire is still a very small state, and a campaign is still able to reach the community, make news, and get a lot of people out to events in a relatively short time frame with a modest amount of effort. In contrast, organizing events in bigger states such as Massachusetts is a costly logistical nightmare, and the events themselves compete with so many other events and activities. In bigger states, paid media is the most efficient way of reaching voters. But in New Hampshire, grassroots campaigning and earned media are still important parts of the mix, and presidential primary commercials still remain secondary or tertiary elements in success, Bodi said.

The New Hampshire media believe that their audiences, because they live in the first-in-the-nation primary state, possess a higher level of interest in political dialogue, Bodi said. As a result, New Hampshire media begin to cover the candidates earlier and more comprehensively than media in other states. So, while it is unclear that the state voters want to discuss the presidential primary two years before it happens, the media nevertheless are talking about it, Bodi said.

New Hampshire newspapers strive to be the "honor roll student" in state politics, said Landrigan. They always strive to cover serious candidates, even when the duty appears onerous months, if not years, before the primary. The editor may swear out loud in the newsroom about the idea of covering a campaign years before the primary is to be held, but he will grit his teeth and make room for the story in the paper's news hole for the next day. They do so, Landrigan said, because they see it as "part of their responsibility . . . sort of protecting the franchise" of New Hampshire's first-in-the-nation primary.

That sense of local civic duty was echoed by Scott Spradling, political reporter for WMUR-TV. The role of the New Hampshire media, said Spradling, is to give candidates a chance to deliver their message. "I sort of take the face value approach to every idea that they bring forward," he said. "I accept, when I'm hearing the first idea for the first time at face value, that they've done their homework, that one and one is two, and . . . allow time and the review of information to dictate where the coverage goes from there." [12]

The national media, in contrast, watches events in New Hampshire with the context of what is happening elsewhere—just one color in a gigantic mural, Spradling said.

> The guy from *Newsweek* that's standing next to me, that works in Washington full time, has a Washington scope on all that's going on, and has a different level of understanding of the issues. . . . Maybe he's a policy-wonk that follows Congress, so his is a policy-wonk, congressional-type piece. Mine is the perspective of [a woman] from Hudson, who e-mailed me the other day and said, "Why don't you ask this, because I've got three kids and no health insurance, and need some help?"

A number of reporters who work for national media know New Hampshire well and appreciate what issues register here with voters, Landrigan said. Those who do not know the state well, he said, tend to fall back on the campaign–as–horse race story line: "If the candidate's more than a million dollars a month behind [in fund-raising], they don't bother with him, or they give him very little attention. If the candidate is more than fifteen points behind in the polls, ditto."

The state media, in contrast, try to give all campaigns equal amounts of attention "because that's what we're known for, and that's what we're supposed to do," Landrigan said. Campaigns, especially those that are trailing the front runner, are aware of the different approaches to campaign coverage. In the mind of a press person for a lagging campaign, the state media are its lifeline, Landrigan said; a campaign spokesperson will think

> As bad as it gets, I know they'll talk to me, because they want to talk to me, and because they have to talk to me. And the *L. A. Times* can blow me off, and the [*Washington*] *Post* won't return my calls or go to my events because I'm fifth or sixth in the polls. But that won't happen to me at the *Keene Sentinel*. And I'll get as much column-inches as Gore will.

But a key fact of life for fledgling presidential campaigns is that in New Hampshire, they are not automatically considered news—even by the local media, Landrigan said.

Quite the contrary. For the state political media, the presidential campaigns are unknown quantities as they get started. So these campaigns "have to do a lot of spade work" with the local media for months before they actually generate good coverage on a consistent, day-to-day basis. Editors at local newspapers, for instance, are unconvinced that the baby steps of the presidential campaign of an out-of-state politician are actually news, Landrigan said. "Your editor is constantly beseeching reporters with, 'It's three and a half years out. . . . What's [the candidate] got to say to people in New Hampshire that's really relevant right now?'"

As a result, presidential campaigns have to strive for creativity and innovation just to get their names in the local papers. The decision of the campaign of North Carolina senator John Edwards, for example, to donate computers to state Democratic parties in Iowa and New Hampshire for their 2002 campaigns was a "brilliant stroke," Landrigan said. It made Edwards, an "otherwise irrelevant figure," part of the story line for the 2002 state elections, as well as earning him a fair-sized amount of goodwill from party activists. Lots of campaigns give money or lend staff to local and state party campaigns, but the Edwards campaign had found a new wrinkle. "They have to be patient, they have to be willing to put up with the fact that they're going to have to expend a lot of perspiration and time without a lot of results early on," Landrigan said.

Formerly, "if the tree fell in the woods, and New Hampshire didn't notice it, then you didn't make news campaigning in New Hampshire," he observed. But now the advent of twenty-four-hour cable news has provided a fallback position for presidential candidates. For instance, CNN's *Inside Politics* might cover a little-known presidential aspirant on a day when the New Hampshire media does not. National cable coverage sometimes ends up having an echo back in New Hampshire, Landrigan said: "The editor will go home at night, he'll see *Inside Politics*, he'll see . . . a story that the New Hampshire media hasn't covered, and it might get him thinking, 'Maybe we should be covering this guy. What's he up to?'"

Agenda-setting for the media occurs from the local level up as well as from the national level down, Landrigan said. In 1991, for instance, Republican president George Bush was riding sky-high approval ratings after the conclusion of the Persian Gulf War. But New Hampshire was in dire economic straits: the failures of five banks and the state's largest utilities, thirty-five consecutive months of state revenue shortfalls. "We were telling the story about an economy in the tank, at a time when Bush was at an all-time high in his popularity. . . . I think the national media took that story from us, and in the last sixty days of the presidential primary, told that story, which was 'Bush out of touch with the economy.'"

New Hampshire reporters like Landrigan and John DiStaso of the *Manchester Union Leader* (whose Thursday "Granite Status" column is must-reading for the state's political junkies) focus on the process of the primary. That focus sometimes can be an uncomfortable experience for the establishment candidate because "they're going to say, 'This guy screwed up at this particular Rotary event, and this is what he did,'" said Griffin. The local media understand that the primary is their opportunity to write a prize-winning story, Griffin said.

The National Media: Stuck Inside the Campaign Tunnel

In his chronicle of the 1976 presidential campaign, Jules Witcover compared the New Hampshire primary to baseball's spring training.[13] For the national political media, it was a time to watch the presidential candidates as they limbered up for a long season of campaigning. Normal conduct for reporters was to hang out with candidates, "horsing around in New Hampshire," said John Milne, who covered his first New Hampshire primary in 1972 for United Press International wire service. Newspaper reporters liked to cover the early primaries, Milne said, because it afforded them the opportunity to ride around New Hampshire with the candidate stumping in the state and to have a drink with him at the end of the day. During those low-intensity encounters, a reporter could actually get to know the candidates, as well as learn a lot of insider information on an informal basis, which he could use (or at least allude to) in his stories. In addition, the reporter on the campaign trail had the luxury of spending a couple of hours in a local diner talking with voters on a slow news day. "You really were more informed about the broader campaign. You got a much better sense of who this candidate is and a better sense of how this candidate resonates this side of the Beltway," Milne said. "You didn't have to rely on a poll. You had two hours in a diner to talk to real people. I'm not suggesting that this was scientific, but you got an inferential opportunity" to inform yourself about voters' feelings.

Beginning roughly in the middle of the 1980s, primary coverage became much more professionalized, said Milne. In part, technological innovations to the reporter's equipment, such as the microrecorder a reporter could put in his pocket and the laptop computer, were catalysts for change. The computer with a modem allowed reporters quicker access to their editors back at the newspaper's home office and vice versa, as faster communication shrank the isolating distance of the reporter from the editor.

In addition, the relationship between reporters and candidates has become much more formal and distant over the years, Milne said. Nowadays, when the media cover the candidates in New Hampshire, both groups often find themselves inside a "campaign tunnel," on the record from the minute they get off the plane thanks to national media such as C-SPAN or local media such as WMUR. News stories are much more focused on the candidate and less on what is on the mind of the average voter. And while reporters are in contact with the candidate all day, they do not socialize with him. Campaign staffers and reporters do not go out to dinner as frequently as they once did; if they do, it is for an interview in which the staffers stick to the party line.

In addition, the advent of the twenty-four-hour news cycle has placed much more pressure on media and campaigns alike to create and control the news. The speedier cycle, for instance, has created the need for campaigns to develop the capacity for rapid response. In the past, candidates would have the opportunity to adjust their messages in response to activities of other candidates. And, if the candidate made some sort of mistake or gaffe one day, there was time to consider its political implications and develop an appropriate response, Bodi said. Today a candidate stumping for the vote out in relatively isolated western New Hampshire might nevertheless be asked for an immediate response to a national or world event. "The advent of the public's thirst for instant news, as it happens, has dramatically changed the dynamic" of political campaigns, according to Bodi. A single miscalculation could cause a five- to fifteen-point decline in the candidate's poll rating over the subsequent forty-eight hours. In addition, candidate controversies have the potential to escalate dramatically and lead to what Bodi called the "spontaneous combustion of media frenzy," such as the Gennifer Flowers story during Bill Clinton's 1992 New Hampshire campaign. During the 2000 primary, Bradley campaign operative Susan Calegari recalled, when Bradley and Gore were in New Hampshire at the same time, the Bradley campaign would receive reports from across town of Gore's remarks at an event. In the van, on the way to the next event, the Bradley team would consider whether to respond to Gore there and what should be said.[14]

Finally, traditional grassroots activities, such as coffees held in people's homes, are increasingly planned events staged for the benefit of the media, Milne said. Not just anybody is invited; rather, the invitation list is composed of activists leaning toward the candidate and reporters. As a result, questions at the coffees tend to shed light on what political insiders are thinking rather than average voters' thoughts, to revolve around the latest poll results, or to be planted by the campaign. "It has become increasingly a stage show," Milne said, which makes spontaneous encounters between candidate and voter increasingly rare. He recalled one such unscripted moment during the 1980 primary season involving Senator Edward Kennedy of Massachusetts. Kennedy was at a barn full of people in Conway, Milne recalled, when one of the patrons asked, "Listen, how can I possibly support you when you haven't answered questions about that poor girl that died in the car?" (referring to Mary Jo Kopechne, who died while riding with Kennedy at Chappaquiddick). "It was just a classic, this-guy-has-no-clothes question," Milne said, "and those questions don't get answered anymore because it's a stage set." Spradling echoed Milne's sentiments, noting how difficult it is for reporters to catch an unscripted, genuine moment on the campaign trail:

> The most unpredictable is when it's the true grassroots campaigning, where they're going to a place that they didn't have time or opportunity [to]—or just didn't—set up their own people and their own supporters to fill the room for that image . . . that doesn't happen very often. Those genuine moments don't happen too often on the campaign trail. Everything nowadays is structured down to the last letter.

Activist Katherine Rogers, for instance, found herself on stage when she went door-to-door through her Concord neighborhood with Al Gore a couple of weeks before the 2000 primary. First, the street was blocked off. Gore walked down the street accompanied by dozens of press people who arrived by bus, as well as by Secret Service agents. Gore and Rogers went to just six houses, she recalled. The Secret Service and Gore's press people both urged her not to go inside anyone's home out of sight of the cameras. "When we advertise [that] New Hampshire's the personal primary, I don't think that's quite what we're talking about. There's going to be the occasional person that'll ask a tough question. . . . But realistically, what's going to happen? They're going to come to your door, you're going to shake their hand, and say, 'Oh, this is great! Can I take a picture of you with my kids?'" Back in 1984, Mondale did some door-to-door campaigning with a limited number of press people, and the candidate actually engaged in conversation with voters, Rogers said. But press involvement has made such voter contact increasingly difficult.

And while field operatives still want to turn out a big crowd for candidate events, their motives are not in keeping with the grassroots traditions of New Hampshire. Now, for instance, when a candidate holds a house party, he cannot afford to have a small crowd for fear that the media will view the size of the group as a sign of lack of support. The key question for a campaign's field operations is not how many voters the candidate can meet. Nor is it how the campaign can gain the support of those voters present at the event. Nor how the campaign can ensure they get out the vote on Election Day. Rather, the key question is "What press do I get? What picture do I want on Channel 9? Channel 9 is the be-all and end-all. It's Mecca," Rogers said. Therefore, the goal for a campaign's field operatives is to get lots of people out to these events—in order to serve as backdrop for the media coverage: "You've got to have a field operation to get the people there to get the press." The voters who turn out for these events, then, are not the real objects of attention for the campaign. Instead, the real objects of attention are the media, who will write the favorable stories that will get voters to think about the candidate and possibly vote for him.

Scott Spradling agreed that campaigns are aware that the most effective way to make a big media splash is with WMUR or the *Manchester Union Leader*. Presidential campaigns do not ignore other, smaller media outlets, including local radio stations and regional newspapers such as the *Nashua Telegraph*, the *Concord Monitor*, the *Keene Sentinel*, and the *Portsmouth Herald*. Candidates also pay attention to public radio and public television, including New Hampshire Public Radio's morning call-in show "The Exchange" and New Hampshire Public Television's news program "New Hampshire Outlook." Among New Hampshire media, however, WMUR-TV and the *Manchester Union Leader* are the only two news organizations that regularly reach a statewide audience and thus are always the two "800-pound gorillas in the room," said Spradling.

Reaching voters via media is probably a more efficient way of contacting voters than traditional one-on-one, grassroots techniques. This is especially true given the modern realities of the nomination process, such as the large amounts of money being spent and the tightly packed primary calendar. The new techniques, however, cast doubt on the hallowed image of the New Hampshire primary, one in which individual contact with voters makes a difference. As Rogers lamented: "We still in New Hampshire seem to clutch to this idea that we're this personal, one-on-one primary. And we're not, I really don't think we are. We're no different now than in Ohio, or in New York state . . . the New Hampshire primary is like a myth now."

More often than in the past, the candidates who carry the day in New Hampshire are those with the most money, more of the establishment on their side, and high standings in the early polls, said reporter Kevin Landrigan. But while the importance of big media has increased, grassroots politicking and local activists still matter. Landrigan pointed to the 2000 primaries as an example: "Who spent three times more than the other guy in New Hampshire? Bush. But who spent five percent of the time McCain spent in New Hampshire? Bush. Well, what happened to Bush? Who had all the heavies, and who had all the names, who had all the establishment? . . . Bush. And so did Gore, by the way— he almost got his clock cleaned here."

The 1992 Republican primary, which pitted conservative Patrick Buchanan against the incumbent president George H. W. Bush, was another display of the power of a grassroots insurgency, Landrigan said. He recalled walking into Buchanan's campaign offices, situated above the Merrimack Restaurant in downtown Manchester, late one evening about six months before the primary. He found dozens of Buchanan volunteers, placing calls to conservative Republican voters. "That still happens, that still matters, that's still powerful in New Hampshire. And the reason is because it's not New York, because it's not California, because there's a finite number of voters here. . . . That kind of energy can move mountains here."

The 2000 Primary

In the run-up to the 2000 Democratic primary, Bill Bradley found himself in an odd three-way competition for the media's attention and favorable coverage. On one hand, Bradley seemed to enjoy the advantage over his opponent in the primary, Vice President Al Gore. Early on, the vice president's campaign showed all the symptoms of a front runner intent on protecting his lead, including tight access to the media, which put him at odds with the reporters covering his campaign. On the other hand, Bradley found himself in a race with a fellow insurgent on the Republican side, Senator John McCain of Arizona, who was fighting a similar uphill battle against front runner George W. Bush, the governor of Texas.

In this three-way battle, Bradley eventually came up short on both fronts. As reporters who covered the campaign explain, neither Bradley nor his media advisors seemed willing to cater to media wishes; indeed, they cultivated what became a distant, if not outright hostile, relationship. Meanwhile, over the months preceding the primary, Gore's media campaign, headed by Governor Jeanne Shaheen's former press secretary Doug Hattaway, made significant efforts to meet the needs of the media pack following the candidate. And the other insurgent, McCain, eventually became *the* insurgent of the 2000 primary, a star who far outshined Bradley with a one-two punch of grassroots politicking and easy access for the media on the back of his "Straight Talk Express" bus.

Inside the Scrum

The biggest difference between covering a presidential candidate and a candidate running in a New Hampshire state election, said WMUR reporter Scott Spradling, is the size of the group following each candidate. In a typical New Hampshire campaign, even in a race for governor or U.S. senator, no more than half a dozen reporters would follow a candidate, all of whom would be familiar with each other. But when the presidential candidates come to the state, Spradling said, "We all have to do our jobs differently, locally . . . because you're talking about national press: the print, the radio, the many TV cameras, everything is bigger, everything is grander, everything takes longer to do, because you're talking about big numbers." Running with the pack makes the local reporter's job more difficult, he said. In a local race, for instance, obtaining one-on-one time with a candidate is not a difficult matter. But during the presidential primary, reporters have to work harder to coordinate their operations separately from the "mass gaggle" of their peers, in order to have a distinctive story that day. When the national media arrive in New Hampshire, things become more competitive, "more dog-eat-dog"—but at the same time, coverage becomes more rote and mechanical, Spradling said, because of the sheer numbers of media involved: "You're running with the pack of nationals, and you're jockeying for space, and you're shouting over other people. . . . You don't get your one-on-one, you don't get within twenty-five feet."

As a result, local reporters reach out independently to each campaign, to establish a "sidebar relationship," to distinguish themselves from the national media and ensure unique access. That special access is deserved, Spradling said, as long as the candidates are in "our backyard": ". . . the New Hampshire voter, most likely, gets most, if not all, of his or her information about a candidate from local TV, the local papers, the local radio. So, it's sort of a no-brainer that we should be afforded that access, regardless of whether or not the national media is here." The local media tries to be the "anti-pool," Spradling said, sometimes mirroring what the national media are doing, and sometimes presenting the uniquely New Hampshire angle.

An additional complication for reporters in a presidential campaign is the number of intermediaries between the media and the object of their attention, the candidate. Statewide campaign organizations are "lean and mean," Spradling said, with perhaps a half dozen operatives at the top running the show. A national campaign might well have a "labyrinth of leadership" behind the candidate that can make it difficult for the media to obtain access to and information about the candidate. This is especially true of a candidate who already holds an office, such as Gore, said reporter Jennifer Donahue, who covered the 2000 primary for WNDS-TV in Derry and did political analysis for MSNBC.[15] Such candidates already have media handlers who tend to make more attempts to control the press. They also want only one message to get out, such as a sound bite, and frown on giving reporters exclusives with candidates or even putting the candidate in a less formal setting. Such attempts often worked against the candidates, Donahue said, because they were at odds with the media's need for access.

In addition, larger campaign organizations are often run from outside of New Hampshire, and they have to balance the need for centralized operations with the requirement of tailoring a campaign to the unique environment of New Hampshire, Spradling said. One way to achieve such balance is by getting local activists on board, suggested Landrigan. Presidential campaigns that succeed in signing up activists, especially activists who have worked on winning campaigns in the past, gain a good reputation among the media, Landrigan said, and campaigns that fail to attract well-known activists "are behind the eightball here."

Having local activists on board can also help the presidential candidate from out of state avoid another pitfall: inadvertently displaying ignorance of New Hampshire and demonstrating that he has not done his homework. If the candidate mispronounces the North Country city of Berlin as Ber-LIN, instead of BER-lin, or refers to the White Mountains in Hanover, "that's a killer," Landrigan said. "That can be fatal . . . if a candidate gets identified as being out of touch with what the state is, then you don't want to work for that campaign."

Campaign staffers with previous experience in the New Hampshire primary can help to repair a candidate's reputation, Landrigan said, by providing a "reassuring quality" to the media. The local media might adjust their judgment of a candidate with no experience in New Hampshire politics if they see behind him someone who knows the state and how to run a campaign there. An experienced staffer working for a candidate inexperienced in the ways of New Hampshire politics might take members of the media aside, Landrigan said, and ask for their indulgence: "He's never even been up here before," the staffer might say. "Give him a couple of months, let him get to know the place. He readily admits New Hampshire's a foreign country . . . but he's willing to take a graduate course."

Gore and the Media: A Billion Secret Service Guys

As Al Gore began the New Hampshire campaign, he was already the object of skepticism from the media, said his New Hampshire political director, Nick Baldick.[16] "We got in trouble, I think unfairly, because there was this very negative caricature of Gore, because of campaign finance," he said, referring to Gore's explanation that there had been "no controlling legal authority" governing past fund-raising activity that had been called into question. "So he was viewed as rigid," Baldick said, a portrayal he described as "slightly exaggerated, to be honest."

When asked about covering the Gore campaign, Donahue recalled the Secret Service agents, rope line barriers, and the "heavy, heavy handling" of the candidate by his media advisors. "The media beat him down," Donahue joked. "The first task for the media was to knock him off of the formal perch upon which he was standing." Spradling echoed Donahue's sentiments, noting that Gore had what seemed like "a billion Secret Service guys" surrounding him. Reporters did not come close to him, he recalled, unless it was orchestrated beforehand, or if the candidate specifically beckoned to a particular reporter.

In such situations, the media following the candidate turn to the campaign staff to try to renegotiate the rules of the game about access. Staffers are more or less in tune with helping the media to gain access to the candidate, said Donahue. It is the job of the press secretary and senior advisors on the campaign to find the balance and to work for the reporter or producer to help them gain access to the candidate—"or at least to make them feel that way," Donahue added. Those less savvy about influencing the media are those who tend to speak for the candidate or block the media from the candidate. That liaison, said Donahue, "is a very important link. They can help the candidate have a good relationship with the media, or they can inhibit it, based on their own behavior."

Despite the difficulties in gaining access to Gore, the state's political media found Doug Hattaway, the Gore campaign's New Hampshire press secretary, to be an asset, not a liability. Hattaway had worked as Governor Jeanne Shaheen's press secretary before joining the Gore campaign. Hattaway was "somebody that everybody already knew," Spradling said. "He knew all of us. He knew the angles, and he knew New Hampshire politics." Gore's team, not coincidentally, was more accessible, understood the media's needs better, and "at least gave you a feeling of working with you."

By September, the Gore campaign had revamped its strategy to make the candidate more accessible, a gradual change that jelled only in the last weeks before the primary, Donahue said. Early on in the campaign, Hattaway recalled, Gore's advance people from Washington tended to keep the press away from the candidate, and reporters complained of being bullied and treated rudely.[17] The Gore campaign created a New Hampshire advance team composed of members more familiar with the state, Hattaway said, and made sure local media had access to the candidate.

Gore's New Hampshire campaign also made sure that the media had access to news with a local angle. Gore's support from local establishment figures such as state senators and business leaders aided the campaign in continuing to drive the campaign's message, even in the absence of the candidate, Hattaway said. This was especially helpful because in a front-loaded primary schedule, candidates cannot spend as much time in New Hampshire as they once did.

The focus of Gore's attacks was Bradley's health care proposal. Under the Bradley plan, Medicaid beneficiaries would be sent into the mainstream health care system, Hattaway recalled. The Gore campaign teamed up with activists for the disabled community in New Hampshire, which is very organized because of its need to petition government for services. Together, they held press conferences to call attention to the Bradley plan. The way to drive a message on the "comparative track," said Hattaway, is to pick an issue and stick with it, and to include local surrogates with a genuine concern for the issue.

Bradley and his campaign had put themselves on a pedestal, above the back and forth of politics, Hattaway said. Thus, when the Gore campaign vigorously conveyed comparisons unflattering to Bradley, the opposition had nowhere to go but down off the pedestal. Occasionally the Bradley campaign fell off the pedestal with a bump. The Gore campaign launched yet another salvo, highlighting the vice president's plan to lower the price of prescription drugs and charging that Bradley had sided with the pharmaceutical industries in their desire for extensions on patents for drugs that would keep cheaper, generic drugs off the market. Gore's field staff did "visibilities," appearing outside drugstores with flyers comparing the two candidates' records and handmade signs, along with local supporters. The visibility gained pictures in most of the state's daily papers and made the local news on WMUR. Bradley's people responded, Hattaway recalled, with a flyer of their own, calling Gore a liar; the Bradley campaign eventually apologized for the flyer.

By the end of the campaign, Gore had become almost too accessible, holding four-hour-long town meetings and staying until he had spoken to the very last voter, "boring them, boring the press, keeping people way beyond the limits of the event," Donahue said. The unscripted nature of the town meeting actually gave Gore an advantage with the press, Hattaway said. When the candidate was always presented in a controlled setting, the press tended to be on the alert for a slip. In an uncontrolled environment, where the candidate talked like a real person, there was no "off-script" moment that made news.

Bradley and the Media: Militant in Its Operation

As a rule, front runners such as Gore are more in demand from the media and tend to be less available, Donahue said, in part because they have more to lose and are less willing to take risks. In contrast, lesser-known candidates, less in demand early in the process, have the opportunity to establish a relationship with the press following them that lasts well into the campaign and results in favorable coverage and more earned media. According to state political reporters, though, the Bradley campaign failed to capitalize on these opportunities—especially compared to the other insurgent in the 2000 New Hampshire primary, John McCain.

The surest way to a reporter's heart is to grant access to the candidate. The media "loves the royal treatment. They love the access. They love to be made to feel special," Spradling said. "You're talking about a bunch of people with type A personalities here, across the board, so of course they love the positive attention." Therefore, the media are sharply critical behind the scenes when they are denied that access, he said. And when access is difficult, the campaign's coverage suffers—not so much because of outright media bias in the stories written and produced, he said, but because a campaign was not able to get its message out as effectively as it might have due to its poor relations. A case in point was the Bradley campaign, whose insistence on strict regulation of the media caused problems for their coverage: "Because when you don't get a chance to ask the question of the candidate, or get close enough to them, you're not getting your information," Spradling said. "So it may very well mean unanswered questions, stories that don't go on, an accusation that is unanswered, things like that."

Bradley's media relations were "militant in its operation," Spradling said, "the quintessential example of what can go wrong" because the campaign tried to micromanage the media. He recalled orders from the Bradley campaign such as "You will stand *here* to get your video. You will meet us *here* to get this. You will only ask *these* topical . . . questions." The Bradley campaign treated the media as an enemy rather than as a means to an end. Spradling continued, this

> is not [meant] to be a pitch for all candidates to just love thy neighbor and the media with a microphone and trust us implicitly. Because . . . I have plenty of peers that still, to this day, will play the "Gotcha!" politics, or screw you if they've got a chance. . . . But there's a happy medium, and the Bradley people didn't reach it, and it left us all with a bad taste in our mouths.

The Bradley campaign made a mistake, said national campaign spokesman Eric Hauser, in failing to invest early in connecting with the New Hampshire media on an everyday basis; this was something the campaign tried to correct in the winter.[18] Hauser also agreed that the Bradley campaign put a premium on controlling media access, an emphasis that he said came from the candidate himself. While Bradley liked individual reporters, he did not like the press as a whole, he said, and was not interested in mixing it up with them as McCain did. Given the candidate's attitude, campaign operatives decided not to push a strategy that was not going to work. The result was control of access. As a result, when the Gore campaign began to attack Bradley, the press provided coverage in part because they were getting more news to cover from Gore than from his opponent.

At first, the reporting on the Bradley phenomena in New Hampshire was unaffected by the candidate's discomfort. But as the campaign wore on, the media became disenchanted with Bradley, said Jennifer Donahue. She recalled that a story made its way around the press corps about a reporter, newly assigned to the Bradley campaign, being alone in an elevator with the candidate. The reporter introduced himself but Bradley did not bother to "really acknowledge" the introduction. On the other hand, Bradley occasionally would display flashes of warmth and irreverence toward reporters. Donahue recalled a day on the trail when Bradley spotted her doing a stand-up in front of the camera, walked over, kneeled down, put his arm around her, and said on camera, "This is Jen Donahue, reporting from the seacoast with Bill Bradley," and then got up and walked away.

Bradley, like other insurgents such as McCarthy and Hart, was a candidate who marched to the beat of his own drummer, Donahue said. "Bradley didn't warm up to the press, and so they didn't warm up to him. He didn't play the game on the press's terms."

While he could be irreverent and spontaneous, Donahue said, ultimately "he was not able to play that game, or not willing. . . . He had boundaries past which he wouldn't go." When Bradley was asked if he had used illegal drugs, he said that he had smoked marijuana a couple of times and added, "People have a right to know if I'm a crook, but they don't have the right to know if I'm a sinner since we're all sinners."[19] During the campaign, he had an agenda and knew which issues were important to him, and seemingly thought that if he just discussed the substance, that would be enough without tailoring them to the media. "And I think if he had allowed more of that spontaneous side to come out with the media, or allowed some more warmth to come out toward the media," he could have countered the perception that he lacked warmth, Donahue said.

McCain and the Media: Buddying Up at the Back of the Bus

In contrast to Bradley's operatives, John McCain's campaign team took an anything-goes attitude toward media access, reasoning that the candidate needed attention to break from the pack of second-tier candidates challenging Governor George W. Bush of Texas for the Republican presidential nomination. As a result, McCain was extremely available to media, "And the press liked that; he became a media darling," Donahue said. "Everybody wanted to do interviews with McCain because he gave you half an hour, you could ask anything. You could ask him what he thinks about the trees in New Hampshire, and he'd go on at length." McCain also displayed a "natural camaraderie" with the media, and was welcoming and comfortable with them in the back of the campaign bus. In contrast, reporters were lucky to get two minutes with George W. Bush, Donahue said.

McCain's shoot-from-the-hip style appealed to New Hampshire voters as well as to the media. The candidate held dozens of town meetings, which were held up as a hallmark of the New Hampshire old-style, grassroots politicking. Kevin Landrigan compared the town meetings, at least in their final, fully realized form, to a Broadway production, with "so much preparation that goes into the performance." The town meetings served McCain well, Landrigan said, showcasing his compelling personal story as a Vietnam prisoner of war, his ability to take on any question, to handle hecklers and critics. But as the campaign drew closer to the primary, Landrigan said, all the accessories that went with a McCain town meeting—the Straight Talk Express bus, the media entourage, the logistics—became almost a burden on the campaign. Although New Hampshire voters are a hardy lot, some people will not stand up and ask a question in an environment of four or five hundred people and fifteen TV cameras in a hall. "They don't want to look stupid on C-SPAN," Landrigan said.

McCain figured out what was happening, and his campaign scheduled up to ninety minutes of extra time for the town meetings. McCain would linger after the meetings and wade into the crowds, sign autographs, and ask voters if they had any questions or opinions on issues of the day, without the glare of the television lights. "He'd create a dialogue, his version of the village square, leaving the performance and just sort of walking the village square," Landrigan said.

As the pack of media grew around McCain and demands on the candidate's time increased, access became a bone of contention, especially for the local media. One problem, Landrigan said, is that operatives joining the various campaigns for the last couple of months are often thinking nationally, not locally:

> They haven't been here for the last two years with the candidate. You have to remind them, "Hey, I'm the second-largest paper in the state. The *Dallas Morning News* is not voting in this election, their readership doesn't matter in this election. So, you need to call me back, and you need to tell the boys on the bus to chill out for fifteen minutes while you get my candidate to answer the questions." And more often than not, it's just a reminder, they already know that.

A good example of conflict between the boys on the bus and the local media came during the homestretch of the McCain campaign. The maverick senator's campaign was a phenomenon not just among voters but among the national media that came to cover the primary. Every day that McCain toured the state in his Straight Talk Express, national journalists were clamoring to travel with him; McCain was "a great storyteller, a great joke-teller, and a fun guy to be around," Landrigan said. Not surprisingly, McCain got high marks from the national media for his accessibility, especially compared to the restricted access to the front runner, George W. Bush. Meanwhile, the state media was trying to cover the candidate and found their colleagues in the national media in the way. It took a number of weeks, Landrigan said, for the New Hampshire media to convince the candidate and his campaign that all the national media attention might be getting in the way of the candidate's goals in the state.

All in all, though, McCain succeeded in obtaining the star appeal that made him a candidate that attracted independents, "a whole new group of consumers to democracy that don't usually come to the table," Pat Griffin said. This group tends to be less cynical, less ideological, and less interested in politics. "Something's made it interesting," said Griffin, "and that tends to be something novel, something new. And McCain became the new flavor. There was something about McCain that was really interesting—'Straight Talk: yeah, that's what we need is some straight talk, damn it!' You find a totem that everyone can hang on to. It's a little bit like saying, 'A mind is a terrible thing to waste' or . . . 'we love to see you smile.'"

McCain's straight talk hit a chord with voters, and in his town meetings, the premise lived up to the promise, Griffin said. At these meetings, McCain excelled. He was very good on his feet, in an uncontrolled, no-holds-barred environment, and stayed until the last question was answered. He was funny, self-deprecating, and indefatigable. "He could afford to say anything he wanted to," Griffin said, while the Bush campaign, focusing on the big picture, played it more cautiously.

Bradley, in contrast, had plenty of intellectual heft as well as the proper liberal credentials but was "boring," Griffin said. "This guy made Al Gore look like the belle of the ball." When Bradley spoke about various issues, it struck voters as important but not necessarily interesting; McCain managed to be both. McCain's success at playing both the grassroots game and the media game in New Hampshire catapulted him, for a brief time, into the national political spotlight as George Bush's main challenger for the Republican nomination. Meanwhile, Bill Bradley and his insurgency slipped onto the back pages.

CHAPTER EIGHT

New Hampshire as a Barometer of Presidential Primary Success

While critics of New Hampshire's first-in-the-nation presidential primary have had no success in dislodging the Granite State from its place at the front of the line, they have had something to smile about in recent years. For decades, New Hampshire boasted of its ability to choose presidents; no candidate had been elected president without first weathering a New England winter and emerging victorious in New Hampshire. The first blemish on that clean slate appeared in 1992: Bill Clinton finished second to former Senator Paul Tsongas of Massachusetts in the Democratic primary yet went on to win his party's nomination and ultimately the presidency. Advocates of the primary (and there are many) chalked this up to Tsongas's supposed status as a favorite son candidate. A second blemish on New Hampshire's record appeared in 2000, however, when George W. Bush suffered an eighteen-point loss to John McCain yet recovered to win his party's nomination and the presidency. Disparagers of New Hampshire's quadrennial status (and there are many) doubtless took these failures in prediction as more ammunition for their argument that New Hampshire is too small and demographically unrepresentative a state to have so much influence in winnowing out candidates in the presidential nomination process.

Looking ahead to the 2004 Democratic primaries (and making the apparently safe assumption, at this writing, that no serious candidate will emerge to challenge President Bush for the GOP nomination), New Hampshire again is front and center in the so-called invisible primary, the period of time between the last presidential election and the first contests for the nomination in the next election cycle. Prospective candidates for the Democratic nomination have already made many visits to the Granite State (and to Iowa, where caucuses will be held a week before the New Hampshire primary), contributed money to state Democratic candidates, and put staffers on the ground to work for state candidates in 2002 in order to learn the political terrain for 2004.

All of these presidential hopefuls, of course, enter New Hampshire with the assumption that a good showing there in the winter of 2004 will translate into momentum, rocketing a campaign to victories in later primaries and eventually to the nomination. Gauging how much of a bump a candidate gets from New Hampshire, however, often seems more of an art than an exact science. In 1972, George McGovern won just 37 percent of the vote and lost the New Hampshire presidential primary by nine points to Edmund Muskie, yet Muskie faltered and McGovern surged in later contests. In 1992, Clinton managed just 24 percent of the vote in New Hampshire but nonetheless pronounced himself the "Comeback Kid" on primary night and trounced Tsongas in later contests. In 2000, Bill Bradley lost in New Hampshire by just four points to a sitting vice president—and had absolutely nothing to show for his efforts in terms of "momentum" in later primaries, which Gore won handily.

It is doubtlessly true that the varying amounts of momentum each of the above candidates received had something to do with the expectations of success for each candidate, markers laid down by the national political media. Bradley's 46 percent showing, for example, did not seem so impressive after polls released five months earlier had him dead even with Gore. Clinton's second-place finish, however, looked mighty indeed after allegations of sexual scandal and draft dodging had apparently put his campaign on life support. From the expectations perspective, the only thing important about New Hampshire's voting returns is that they are the first actual results received after months of media speculation

TABLE 8.1

An Overview of the New Hampshire Primary, 1968-2000

Year	Leading Mainstream Candidate	Leading Elite Candidate	Winner of New Hampshire Democratic Primary	Winner of Democratic Party Nomination
2000	Al Gore (0.76)	Bill Bradley (1.56)	Gore	Gore (0.76)
1992	**Bill Clinton** (0.78)	Paul Tsongas (1.80)	Tsongas	**Clinton** (0.78)
1988	Richard Gephardt (0.69)	**Michael Dukakis** (1.04)	Dukakis	**Dukakis** (1.04)
1984	Walter Mondale (0.69)	**Gary Hart** (1.20)	Hart	Mondale (0.69)
1980	**Jimmy Carter** (0.91)	**Edward Kennedy** (1.04)	Carter	**Carter** (0.91)
1976	**Jimmy Carter** (0.82)	Morris Udall (2.26)	Carter	**Carter** (0.82)
1972	**Edmund Muskie** (0.81)	George McGovern (1.57)	Muskie	McGovern (1.57)
1968	Lyndon Johnson (0.62)	Eugene McCarthy (1.62)	Johnson	Hubert Humphrey (did not compete in NH)

Boldface = coalition candidate   (Elite scores in parentheses, see p. 53.)

about the prospects of various candidates. From this perspective, the only interesting question about the actual New Hampshire vote is how the results fit the media's "over-under," that is, whether the candidate has exceeded media expectations, met expectations, or failed to meet expectations.

This book, rather than focusing on media expectations as the key to momentum, instead concentrated on the fundamentals of the New Hampshire Democratic primary vote as key predictors of success in subsequent presidential primaries. (This is something akin to picking stocks based on old-fashioned measures of value such as price-earnings ratios, as opposed to buying whichever stocks have the best buzz from various brokers on CNBC.) By focusing on how well candidates did with particular segments of the New Hampshire Democratic primary vote, such as the working class and the liberal elite, we can see which candidates showed sound fundamentals—that is, evidence of a broad-based coalition composed of both the liberal elite and the working-class base—and which candidates showed weak fundamentals—or support from just one faction of the party with little evidence of the ability to build a coalition among the Democratic Party electorate. In five of the last seven contested primary cycles since 1972 (including the last three in 1988, 1992, and 2000), it has been the coalition candidate, not the candidate of a particular faction, who has left New Hampshire and proceeded to win the Democratic Party nomination.

A look at the New Hampshire "elite scores" of candidates who proceeded to win the nomination, in sequence from 1972 to 2000, is revealing:

McGovern	1.57
Carter	0.82
Carter	0.91
Mondale	0.69
Dukakis	1.04
Clinton	0.78
Gore	0.76

Clearly, one of these scores, George McGovern's 1.57 in 1972, sticks out as the fluke in this series of seven primary cycles. McGovern is the only Democratic candidate who went on to win the nomination of the party whose support came primarily from the New Hampshire Democratic elite. Only one candidate since McGovern, Michael Dukakis, had an elite score (barely) above 1.00 in New Hampshire and went on to win his party's nomination.

In sum: *No candidate since McGovern has rallied elites in New Hampshire and then proceeded to build a coalition of other factions in the party and win the nomination.* The only other "factional" candidate since McGovern who has defeated a coalition candidate was Walter Mondale, who managed to beat back Gary Hart's challenge by relying heavily on labor and African American support in subsequent primaries. (See table 8.1.)

Candidates for the presidential nomination of their party (as well as the media that cover them) often approach New Hampshire as the dispenser of that magical elixir known as momentum. In the frantic process of winnowing that begins with the Iowa caucuses and ends with New Hampshire and its immediate aftermath, pundits often draw a cause-and-effect relationship between a candidate's ability to exceed the expectations of conventional media wisdom and his potential to convert performance in these first two contests into success in subsequent primaries. Excessive focus on the media expectations game leads to a narrow reading of the vote totals, with a lack of serious thought about what those votes represent in terms of core party constituencies.

Shifting the focus to the core fundamentals of a candidate's performance in the New Hampshire primary—that is, how the candidate performed among elite communities and working-class communities—offers a perspective that tempers "irrational exuberance" regarding the significance of a strong candidate performance in New Hampshire. Concentrating on the core fundamentals of a candidate's support also puts perspective on the effects of media spin on a candidate's performance.

Put simply: *Candidates who are competitive in New Hampshire and display coalition or crossover potential there (appealing both to elite voters and working-class voters) are much more likely to win the Democratic Party's nomination than candidates who appeal to only one faction.*

Twenty years ago, Nelson Polsby, in his pioneering work on the primary-centered nomination process, made the case that candidates for a presidential nomination must try to mobilize factions, rather than build coalitions, in order to win. "The task of a presidential hopeful, threading a path through the minefield of successive primary elections, is not to win a majority but rather to survive," he argued.[1] In order to survive, a candidate must achieve as high a ranking as possible among his competitors. To accomplish this, one must win an early primary in order to gain exposure and media attention as a contender and to raise more money to compete in subsequent contests. A win in an early state might depend on defeating a rival by just several thousand votes, as it did for Jimmy Carter in the 1976 New Hampshire primary. Therefore, a candidate should try to distinguish himself from his competitors, build organizations, and get more of his supporters out to vote—all while hoping that his rivals wind up competing for the same share of the vote in a particular wing of the party. Again, such a strategy worked for Carter in 1976; early on, most of his rivals were fighting to be the candidate of the liberal wing of the party while Carter had the conservative wing mainly to himself in Iowa and New Hampshire.

In 1988, 1992, and 2000, however, the eventual nominee of the Democratic Party was the candidate who did the best job of building coalitions in New

Hampshire, not the one who mobilized a particular faction. In 1988, Michael Dukakis was the only candidate to draw equally well from both elite and working-class communities, defeating two factional candidates, Richard Gephardt (who did very well among working-class communities, considerably worse among elite communities) and Paul Simon (strong performance among elite communities, weak performance among working-class communities). Al Gore, who aborted his 1988 New Hampshire campaign to pursue a southern strategy, showed some potential for achieving crossover status but received only 7 percent of the overall vote. Dukakis, the coalition candidate in New Hampshire, proved to have much more staying power in the primaries than either of his factional rivals.

The 1992 primary cycle provides the most compelling evidence that the ability to form coalitions in New Hampshire is a good predictor of success in subsequent primaries. In 1992, Bill Clinton succeeded in disproving the maxim that every president must first win the New Hampshire primary; despite finishing second to Paul Tsongas in New Hampshire, Clinton succeeded in winning the Democratic Party's nomination and eventually the presidency. (Jerry Brown also drew equally well from both elite and working-class communities, but like Gore, he received under 10 percent of the statewide vote.) Again, looking at the core fundamentals of Clinton's and Tsongas's respective votes in New Hampshire casts doubt on the conventional analysis of the 1992 primary. One piece of conventional wisdom was that Tsongas won the primary because of his favorite son status as a Massachusetts senator who hailed from Lowell, right next to the border between the two states. Geography played some part in Tsongas's success, but a comparison of his core fundamentals with those of another Massachusetts candidate, Michael Dukakis, indicates that the two had very different bases of support. While Dukakis drew support almost equally well from elite communities and working-class communities, Tsongas's base came mainly from elite communities.

Another piece of conventional wisdom on that New Hampshire primary is that Clinton stole the night (and the all-important momentum) from Tsongas, by getting on the airwaves first with his declaration that New Hampshire had again made him the Comeback Kid. Again, a look at the fundamentals of Clinton's vote indicates that he actually had good reason to be confident that evening, regardless of when he got on the air: He had drawn well from both elite and working-class communities, an early indication that his vote-getting potential in subsequent primaries would be much greater than Tsongas's.

The most recent New Hampshire primary studied here, the 2000 contest between Gore and Bradley, provides one last piece of evidence for the potential of candidates who prove their ability to form coalitions in New Hampshire. One of the great what-ifs in New Hampshire primary history concerns the hypothetical future potential of the Bradley campaign if only it had managed to turn a few thousand more votes its way in the Granite State. Again, this what-if scenario is based on the expectations game: Bradley had been running even with Gore in New Hampshire polls as early as Labor Day 1999; therefore, nothing less than a win in New Hampshire would have met or exceeded media expectations. In a variation on this, Bradley's strong second place in New Hampshire was overshadowed by John McCain's stunning first-place finish; in effect, McCain became the insurgent of the 2000 primary cycle, sucking all the media oxygen out of Bradley's campaign.

No doubt a Bradley victory in New Hampshire would have given his campaign a much-needed second wind. A look at the fundamentals of Bradley's vote, however, compared to the broad base of Gore's support, indicates that the insurgent's campaign was based on the support of the elite faction of the party, not a coalition. As a result, even a narrow Bradley victory in New Hampshire would not have overcome his relatively poor fundamentals compared to those of his rival. (See table 8.1.)

Several possible explanations exist for why coalition candidates, not factional candidates, have been more successful of late. One is the front-loading of numerous primaries, scheduled increasingly early in the election calendar, close to Iowa and New Hampshire. As a result, candidates do not have the luxury of beginning the primary cycle with the support of just one faction of the party and the hope of adding other factions later in the process. Coupled with front-loading is the need to raise large amounts of money (at least $20 million, conventional wisdom dictates) before the primaries even begin; in a front-loaded process, an insurgent candidate can no longer live off the land, counting on upset victories to bring more funds into campaign coffers in order to fight and win another day. Perhaps the need to raise large amounts of money early forces a candidate to appeal to diverse interests in the party. The recent success of coalition candidates

TABLE 8.2

Manchester, Nashua, Concord, and Portsmouth, and Their Collar Towns, 1976-2000

	2000	1992	1984	1976
Manchester	15,190	18,311	14,235	15,409
Hooksett	1,220	1,328	595	784
Candia	489	512	197	184
Auburn	570	594	291	279
Londonderry	2,430	2,765	1,202	753
Litchfield	800	800	407	217
Merrimack	3,021	3,254	1,298	1,299
Bedford	2,170	1,963	989	809
Goffstown	2,062	1,764	1,411	1,355
Total, collar towns	12,762	12,980	6,390	5,680
RATIO city:collar votes	**1.19**	**1.41**	**2.23**	**2.71**

	2000	1992	1984	1976
Nashua	11,175	13,870	8,780	7,816
Hollis	980	866	480	360
Amherst	1,526	1,258	682	525
Merrimack	3,021	3,254	1,298	1,299
Litchfield	800	800	407	217
Hudson	2,588	2,940	1,579	653
Total, collar towns	8,915	9,118	4,446	3,054
RATIO, city:collar votes	**1.25**	**1.52**	**1.97**	**2.56**

in New Hampshire may be supporting evidence for the hypothesis that party leaders have recovered their ability to control presidential nominations, despite the vagaries of the primary process; one would expect party leaders to coordinate their efforts on behalf of a candidate who appeals to various factions of the party.[2]

Where's the Vote Going?

What storms lie ahead in the 2004 New Hampshire Democratic presidential primary? Long-range forecasts are notoriously inaccurate but one factor that may

TABLE 8.2 (Continued)

	2000	1992	1984	1976
Concord	6,430	6,235	3,468	2,686
Bow	404	439	249	179
Pembroke	849	1,132	532	548
Chichester	302	279	110	73
Loudon	452	504	191	157
Canterbury	390	380	185	105
Boscawen	404	439	249	179
Webster	206	192	113	69
Hopkinton	978	832	430	265
Total, collar towns	3,985	4,197	2,059	1,575
RATIO, city:collar votes	**1.61**	**1.49**	**1.68**	**1.71**

	2000	1992	1984	1976
Portsmouth	4,317	4,265	3,072	2,447
New Castle	211	178	137	147
Rye	889	925	567	383
Greenland	468	477	264	229
Newington	101	106	71	84
Total, collar towns	1,669	1,686	1,039	843
RATIO, city: collar towns	**2.59**	**2.53**	**2.96**	**2.90**

be forecast with some accuracy is the balance of power between the two main blocs of Democratic primary voters in New Hampshire: wealthy, highly educated elites and traditional working-class constituencies. In order to offer a glimpse of the demographic trends that will shape the 2004 Democratic presidential primary, I examined the Democratic primary turnout from 1976 to 2000 (in eight-year increments) in four major New Hampshire cities— Manchester, Nashua, Concord, and Portsmouth—and compared it to the turnout in the suburban ring of collar communities surrounding these cities.

In all four cases, the ratio of city turnout to collar-community turnout has decreased since 1976. The most striking shifts in turnout appeared in the cases of the Manchester and Nashua metropolitan areas, where turnout in the collar communities exploded while turnout in the cities remained stagnant or experienced smaller growth. Smaller shifts from city to collar town occurred in Concord and Portsmouth and their environs. All in all, it may fairly be claimed that as New Hampshire has become more prosperous and more suburban over the past quarter century, so have Democratic presidential primary voters.

And as Democratic voters become increasingly upscale in New Hampshire, the opportunities for reform-minded candidates increase here—as well as the dangers. On one hand, candidates with a message of reform have historically attracted the support of voters from the elite zones of the New Hampshire Democratic electorate. Those zones have only increased over time, both absolutely and as a relative proportion of the Democratic primary universe. In contrast, working-class voters have shrunk as a portion of that universe of voters. It is no wonder, then, that candidates such as Paul Tsongas in 1992 and Bill Bradley in 2000 did so well in New Hampshire.

On the other hand, like exotic plants taken out of the greenhouse, both Tsongas and Bradley wilted once they left New Hampshire for states in which the income and education levels of the average primary voter dropped significantly. Given the amount of attention devoted to candidates during their New Hampshire campaigns, it is easier said than done for reform-minded candidates to tack away from elites and build a coalition with other factions of the party after New Hampshire.

Although a victory in New Hampshire can no longer be declared essential to ascending to the presidency, a strong case can still be made that a candidate must perform well in the Granite State to be a serious contender. An examination of recent New Hampshire primary results, however, indicates that one must be careful how strength of performance is measured. In 2004, New Hampshire again could be a hothouse for candidates who appeal to the party's elite. But campaigns that grow well in Granite State soil often wither when exposed to the harsher voting environment of subsequent primary states, where the socioeconomic status of the average primary voter is most likely significantly lower. In contrast, candidates who do not necessarily finish first but build a broad base of support in New Hampshire could do much better than expected in subsequent primaries and have a better chance of winning the ultimate prize: the nomination of their party.

Notes

Chapter One

1. Memo obtained from Joseph Keefe, dated January 29, 1999.
2. Ibid.
3. Ibid.
4. Memo obtained from Keefe, dated September 14, 1999. Keefe's observation here was borne out by the results of the primary season. Bradley lost the New Hampshire primary by four percentage points—an impressive performance against the sitting vice president—yet he did not reap the benefits of a "bounce" or shift in momentum. Five weeks later, after a string of losses on March 7, he bowed out of the competition.
5. Ibid.
6. Keefe memo, January 29, 1999.
7. New Hampshire has since moved up its primary date several times, in part to stay ahead of other states' electoral contests. The 2004 primary is expected to take place on January 27, although that date is not yet confirmed as of July 2003.
8. For a short summary of the history of the American presidential nomination process, see Dante Scala, "The Evolution of Nominating Conventions," pp. 32-39, in *American Presidential Campaigns and Elections: A Reference Guide*, edited by Ballard C. Campbell and William G. Shade (Armonk, N.Y.: M.E. Sharpe, Inc., 2003). For an extended treatment, see James W. Ceaser, *Presidential Selection: Theory and Development* (Princeton, N.J.: Princeton University Press, 1979); William Crotty and John S. Jackson III, *Presidential Primaries and Nominations* (Washington, D.C.: Congressional Quarterly, 1985); James W. Davis, *U.S. Presidential Primaries and the Caucus-Convention System* (Westport, C.T.: Greenwood Press, 1997); Gerald Pomper, *Nominating the President* (Evanston, I.L.: Northwestern University Press, 1966); Howard L. Reiter, *Selecting the President: The Nominating Process in Transition* (Philadelphia: University of Pennsylvania Press, 1985).
9. Charles Brereton, *First in the Nation: New Hampshire and the Premier Presidential Primary* (Portsmouth, N.H.: Peter E. Randall, 1987), p. 3.
10. Scholars of the New Hampshire primary have mentioned different motives for the change. Charles Brereton attributes this change in date to "Yankee frugality," stating that "someone with an eye for the dollar calculated that if the date were moved up to coincide with Town Meeting day it would be necessary to hold one less election in a presidential year" (Brereton, pp. 3-4). Niall Palmer argues that the change was for the convenience of the "large rural population, much of which would be engaged in ploughing in late April" (Niall Palmer, *The New Hampshire Primary and the American Electoral Process* [Boulder, C.O.: Westview Press, 2000], p. 1).
11. Theodore H. White, *The Making of the President 1960* (New York: Atheneum, 1961), pp. 79-80.
12. Brereton, p. 4; Palmer, p. 2. New Hampshire voters chose both convention delegates and presidential candidates from 1952 to 1976. In 1977, the state dropped the convention delegate selection from the ballot, leaving only the "beauty contest" portion.
13. Brereton, pp. 21-23.
14. Nelson W. Polsby, *Consequences of Party Reform* (Oxford: Oxford University Press, 1983), p. 12.
15. Brereton, p. 23; Palmer, p. 5.
16. Brereton, p. 24.
17. Palmer, p. 5.
18. William L. Dunfey, "A Short History of the Democratic Party in New Hampshire" (master's thesis, University of New Hampshire, 1954), pp. 216-18.
19. Interview by the author, July 17, 2002.
20. Brereton, p. 30.
21. Dunfey, p. 221.
22. Brereton, pp. 27-30.

23. Brereton, p. 243; Dunfey, p. 221.

24. Brereton, p. 31.

25. Polsby, pp. 10-11.

26. Brereton, p. 107.

27. Ibid., p. 108.

28. Ibid., pp. 120-21.

29. Michael G. Hagen and William G. Mayer, "The Modern Politics of Presidential Selection: How Changing the Rules Really Did Change the Game," in *In Pursuit of the White House 2000*, edited by William G. Mayer (New York: Chatham House, 2000).

30. In a contest for which neither campaign expended much effort, Muskie won 35.5 percent to McGovern's 22.6 percent after the first round of the caucuses. See Nelson Polsby and Aaron Wildavsky, *Presidential Elections* (New York: Chatham House, 2000), p. 103.

31. Interview by the author, August 9, 2002. For a thorough discussion of New Hampshire's continued efforts to retain the first-in-the-nation primary, see Palmer. According to a recent study commissioned by the Library and Archives of New Hampshire's Political Tradition, the one-year economic impact of the 2000 primary, including $33 million in publicity benefits, was $264 million, or six-tenths of 1 percent of the state's $42 billion gross state product.

32. The Federal Election Commission's ceiling on state-by-state spending is computed by multiplying the state's voting age population times 16 cents, with adjustments for inflation. In 2000, a candidate receiving public funding was limited to spending $675,600 on the New Hampshire primary campaign. For more details on FEC rules, see Anthony Corrado and Heitor Gouvea, "Financing Presidential Nominations under the BCRA," in *The Making of the Presidential Candidates 2004*, edited by William G. Mayer (Lanham, M.D.: Rowman & Littlefield, 2003), pp. 45-82.

33. Specifically, a candidate who succeeds in raising at least $5,000 in contributions of $250 or less from individuals in at least twenty states, qualifies to receive matching public funds for all individuals' contributions up to $250.

34. Hagen and Mayer, pp. 4-5.

35. Jules Witcover, *Marathon: The Pursuit of the Presidency* (New York: Viking Press, 1977), pp. 128-31.

36. Ibid., p. 114.

37. Interview by the author, July 16, 2002.

38. Polsby, p. 65.

39. Ibid.

40. Ibid., p. 66.

41. Ibid., pp. 67-68.

42. For example, New Hampshire will send 27 delegates to the 2004 Democratic national convention, out of a total of 4,320. California will send 440 delegates.

43. Polsby and Wildavsky, p. 106.

44. John Aldrich, *Before the Convention* (Chicago, I.L.: University of Chicago Press, 1980). Also on the phenomenon of momentum, see Larry Bartels, *Presidential Primaries and the Dynamics of Public Choice* (Princeton, N.J.: Princeton University Press, 1988).

45. Aldrich, p. 103.

46. Polsby and Wildavsky, p. 106.

47. Aldrich, p. 103.

48. Polsby and Wildavsky, p. 106.

49. Aldrich, p. 101.

50. Ibid., p. 104.

51. Ibid., pp. 104-106.

52. Ibid., p. 106.

53. Ibid., p. 106.

54. Ibid., p. 108.

55. Polsby and Wildavsky, p. 102.

56. Rhodes Cook, "The Nominating Process," in *The Elections of 1988* (Washington, D.C.: Congressional Quarterly, 1989).

57. Cook, p. 32.

58. Ibid., p. 31.

59. For a full discussion of presidential campaign finance, see Anthony Corrado, "The Changing Environment of Presidential Campaign Finance," in *In Pursuit of the White House: How We Choose Our Presidential Nominees*, edited by William G. Mayer (Chatham, N.J.: Chatham House, 1996), pp. 220-53.

60. Interview by the author, October 20, 2002.
61. Interview by the author, November 11, 2002. All quotes from Dayton Duncan in this chapter are from this interview.
62. Interview by the author, July 1, 2002.
63. Polsby and Wildavsky, p. 102.
64. Ibid., p. 109.
65. Interview by the author, December 17, 2002.
66. Cook, p. 35.
67. Ibid.; Polsby and Wildavsky, p. 109.
68. Hagen and Mayer, pp. 32-41.
69. Ryan J. Barilleaux and Randall E. Adkins, "The Nominations: Process and Patterns," in *The Elections of 1992* (Washington, D.C.: Congressional Quarterly, 1993), pp. 32-33; Cook, pp. 35-36.
70. Polsby and Wildavsky, pp. 110-11.
71. Ibid., p. 111.
72. Cook, p. 37.
73. Interview by the author, August 9, 2002.
74. William G. Mayer, "Forecasting Presidential Nominations," in *In Pursuit of the White House*, pp.44-71. Also see Randall E. Adkins and Andrew J. Dowdle, "How Important Are Iowa and New Hampshire to Winning Post-Reform Presidential Nominations?" *Political Research Quarterly* 54, no. 2 (June 2001): 431-44; and "Break Out the Mint Juleps? Is New Hampshire the 'Primary' Culprit Limiting Presidential Nomination Forecasts?" *American Politics Quarterly* 28, no. 2 (April 2000): 251-69.
75. Marty Cohen, David Karol, Hans Noel, and John Zaller, "Beating Reform: The Resurgence of Parties in Presidential Nominations, 1980 to 2000" (presented at the 2001 meeting of the American Political Science Association).
76. Ibid.
77. Interview by the author, July 22, 2002.

Chapter Two

1. Interview by the author, October 20, 2002.
2. The work of Ronald Brownstein of *Los Angeles Times* offered much food for thought when I began to examine this subject during the 2000 primary cycle. See, for example, "To Challenge Gore, Bradley Needs to Look Beyond Volvo Democrats," the *Los Angeles Times*, May 17, 1999.
3. Interview by the author, November 11, 2002. All quotes from Dayton Duncan in this chapter are from this interview.
4. William L. Dunfey, "A Short History of the Democratic Party in New Hampshire" (master's thesis, submitted to the University of New Hampshire, 1954), p. 228.
5. The state's executive council is a group of elected officials that acts as a check on the governor.
6. Dunfey, p. 17.
7. Ibid., p. 19.
8. Ibid., pp. 30-31.
9. Ibid., pp. 28-29.
10. Ibid., pp. 29-30.
11. Neal R. Peirce, *The New England States* (New York: W. W. Norton, 1976), p. 289.
12. Nancy Coffey Hefferman and Ann Page Stecker, *New Hampshire: Crosscurrents in Its Development* (Grantham, N.H.: Tompson & Rutter, 1986), pp. 144-45.
13. Duane Lockard, *New England State Politics* (Princeton, N.J.: Princeton University Press, 1959), p. 63.
14. Ibid., p. 64.
15. Ibid., p. 62.
16. Ibid., p. 67.
17. Dunfey, pp. 124-29.
18. Ibid., p. 233.
19. Ibid., p. 133.
20. Ibid., p. 237.
21. Jules Witcover, *Marathon: The Pursuit of the Presidency* (New York: Viking Press, 1977), p. 222.
22. New Hampshire Office of State Planning, *Statistical Profile of New Hampshire 1970-1990,* 1992, p. 1.
23. Hefferman and Stecker, pp. 186-87.

24. Michael Dupre and Dante Scala, "Border Crossings: The Impact of Migration on the New Hampshire House of Representatives," New Hampshire Institute of Politics, Research Center Working Paper Series No. 1, 2002, pp. 3-4.

25. Interview by the author, November 18, 2002.

26. Interview by the author, July 11, 2002. All quotes from Kathy Sullivan in this chapter are from this interview.

27. Interview by the author, July 16, 2002. All quotes from Bill Shaheen in this chapter are from this interview.

28. Interview by the author, July 1, 2002.

29. Interviews by the author, July 22, 2002, and August 20, 2002. All quotes from Peter Burling in this chapter are from these interviews.

30. The idea to separate the state into "zones of influence" belongs to my colleague Michael Dupre of the Department of Sociology at Saint Anselm College.

31. In 1972, this working-class zone included the towns of Farmington, Middleton, Milton, New Durham, the city of Rochester, Rollinsford, and the city of Somersworth. (See note 45 for an explanation of how the author targeted working-class areas and elite areas.) In 1984, this zone included the towns of Farmington, Middleton, Milton, and the cities of Rochester and Somersworth. In 2000, this zone included Farmington, Middleton, Milton, and the author was able to use census block-group data to target working-class wards in Rochester—Wards 1, 3, 4, and Somersworth—Wards 2, 5.

32. In 1972 and 1984, the author looked at the entire city of Manchester; in 2000, the author was able to use census block-group data to target working-class wards (4, 5, 7, 9, 11).

33. Interview by the author, November 23, 2002.

34. In 1972, this zone included Gilsum, Hinsdale, Marlow, Roxbury, Surry, Troy, Westmoreland, and Winchester in Cheshire County; and Acworth, Charlestown, the city of Claremont, Croydon, Goshen, Grantham, and Langdon in Sullivan County. In 1984, this zone included Hinsdale, Roxbury, Troy, and Winchester in Cheshire County; and Charlestown, Claremont, Croydon, Langdon, Lempster, Newport, and Unity in Sullivan County. In 2000, this zone included Gilsum, Troy, and Winchester in Cheshire County; and Charlestown, Claremont, Croydon, Goshen, Langdon, Lempster, Newport, and Unity in Sullivan County.

35. In 1972, this zone included Alexandria, Benton, Dorchester, Ellsworth, Grafton, Groton, Haverhill, Lincoln, Lisbon, and Warren; in 1984, this zone included Alexandria, Bath, Benton, Grafton, Groton, Haverhill, Landaff, Lincoln, Lisbon, Littleton, Monroe, Warren, and Woodstock. In 2000, this zone included Alexandria, Ashland, Bath, Benton, Dorchester, Groton, Lisbon, Orange, Warren, and Wentworth.

36. In 1972, this zone included the city of Berlin, and the towns of Clarksville, Columbia, Dalton, Dummer, Errol, Gorham, Jefferson, Northumberland, Pittsburg, Stark, Stewartstown, Stratford, and Whitefield. In 1984, this zone included Berlin, Carroll, Clarksville, Colebrook, Columbia, Dalton, Errol, Gorham, Milan, Northumberland, Pittsburg, Stark, Stewartstown, Stratford, and Whitefield. In 2000, this zone included Berlin, Clarksville, Colebrook, Columbia, Dalton, Dummer, Errol, Milan, Northumberland, Pittsburg, Stark, Stewartstown, and Stratford.

37. Interview by the author, February 5, 2003.

38. In 1972, this zone included Durham and Lee in Strafford County, and Brentwood, Chester, Deerfield, Exeter, Greenland, Hampton, Hampton Falls, Kensington, New Castle, Newfields, Newington, North Hampton, Rye, and South Hampton in Rockingham County. In 1984, it included Durham, Lee, and Madbury in Strafford County, and Greenland, Hampton, Hampton Falls, New Castle, North Hampton, Nottingham, Rye and Stratham in Rockingham County. In 2000, it included Dover—Ward 3, Durham, Lee, and Madbury in Strafford County, and Chester, Deerfield, East Kingston, Exeter, Hampton, Hampton Falls, Kensington, New Castle, Newfields, North Hampton, Portsmouth—Wards 1, 2, and 5, Rye, and Stratham.

39. In 1972, this zone included Hollis in Hillsborough County, and Atkinson and Windham in Rockingham County. In 1984, it included Brookline, Hollis, and Merrimack in Hillsborough County, and Atkinson, Hampstead, Londonderry, and Windham in Rockingham County. In 2000, it included Brookline, Hollis, Litchfield, Mason, Merrimack, Nashua—Wards 1, 2, 8, and 9 in Hillsborough County, and Atkinson, Hampstead, Londonderry, and Windham in Rockingham County.

40. Interview by the author, July 1, 2002.

41. In 1972, this zone included Dublin, Rindge, and Stoddard in Cheshire County, and Amherst, Bedford, Francestown, Hancock, Lyndeborough, Mont Vernon, Peterborough, and Temple in Hillsborough County. In 1984, this zone included Dublin and Harrisville in Cheshire County; and Amherst,

Bedford, Francestown, Hancock, Mont Vernon, Peterborough, Sharon, and Temple in Hillsborough County. In 2000, this zone included Chesterfield, Dublin, Harrisville, Keene—Ward 4, and Westmoreland in Cheshire County, and Amherst, Bedford, Francestown, Lyndeborough, Mont Vernon, New Boston, Peterborough, Sharon, Temple, and Wilton in Hillsborough County.

42. In 1972, this zone included Bow and Hopkinton; in 1984, it included Bow, Canterbury, Dunbarton, Henniker, and Hopkinton; and in 2000, it included Bow, Canterbury, Concord—Wards 5, 7, 10, Dunbarton, Henniker, Hopkinton, and Newbury.

43. In 1972, this zone included Hanover and Lyme in Grafton County; in 1984, it included Hanover and Lyme in Grafton County, and Grantham and Plainfield in Sullivan County; in 2000, it included Hanover, Lebanon—Ward 1, Lyme, and Orford in Grafton County, and Grantham and Plainfield in Sullivan County.

44. Rhodes Cook, "New Hampshire Introductory Essay," http://www.rhodescook.com/analysis/presidential_primaries/nh/intro.html.

45. To ascertain whether towns and wards qualified as working-class communities or elite communities, the author used information available from the U.S. Bureau of the Census. Three measures of socioeconomic status were considered: educational attainment, median family income, and occupational status (when readily obtainable). Towns and city wards with socioeconomic status levels significantly below the national average were classified as working-class communities; and conversely, towns and city wards with levels significantly above national averages were classified as elite communities.

For the 1968 and 1972 primaries, 1970 census data were used. For the 1976, 1980, and 1984 primaries, 1980 census data were used. For the 1988 and 1992 primaries, 1990 census data were used. Finally, for the 2000 primary, 2000 census data were used.

Determining the socioeconomic status of New Hampshire's city wards proved especially difficult, because census data is not provided for these units as they are for towns. In addition, city ward boundaries change every decade, and in some cases, the number of city wards shrinks or grows. For 1990 and 2000, the following procedure was used: (1) Census block groups belonging to a particular ward were identified, using the 2000 census maps available online at http://www2.census.gov/plmap/pl_blk/st33_NewHampshire; (2) demographic data on these block groups were obtained from census records; (3) block-group data were compiled and aggregated to provide an approximate demographic profile of the city ward.

This procedure was not without its difficulties. First, the 2000 census maps take into account the redrawing of city wards in the early 1990s. Thus, for purposes of analyzing the 1988 and 1992 New Hampshire returns, the author made the assumption that only minor changes in city ward lines were made in the early 1990s—in other words, that no ward was changed so drastically that it would lose its status as an elite or working-class ward. An exception to that case was made for the city of Concord, which shifted from eight wards to ten in the early 1990s; in this case, information was obtained on wards from the city's Community Development Department.

The difficulty of obtaining block-group data for city wards in 1970 and 1980 made demographic profiles of city wards infeasible. Therefore, for primaries using 1970 and 1980 census data, I placed the traditional blue-collar cities of Berlin, Claremont, Franklin, Manchester, Rochester, and Somersworth in the working-class category.

For more details on methodology, contact the author at dscala@anselm.edu.

1970 elite areas: *Belknap County:* Gilford, New Hampton; *Carroll County:* Eaton, Sandwich, Tuftonboro; *Cheshire County:* Dublin, Rindge, Stoddard; *Coos County:* None; *Grafton County:* Bethlehem, Franconia, Hanover, Lyman, Lyme, Monroe, Plymouth, Sugar Hill, Waterville Valley; *Hillsborough County:* Amherst, Bedford, Francestown, Hancock, Hollis, Lyndeborough, Mont Vernon, Peterborough, Temple; *Merrimack County:* Andover, Bow, Danbury, Hopkinton, New London, Salisbury; *Rockingham County:* Atkinson, Brentwood, Chester, Deerfield, Exeter, Greenland, Hampton, Hampton Falls, Kensington, New Castle, Newfields, Newington, North Hampton, Rye, South Hampton, Windham; *Strafford County:* Durham, Lee, Strafford; *Sullivan County:* Washington.

1970 working-class areas: *Belknap County:* Alton, Belmont; *Carroll County:* Albany, Chatham, Wakefield; *Cheshire County:* Gilsum, Hinsdale, Marlow, Roxbury, Surry, Troy, Westmoreland, Winchester; *Coos County:* Berlin (all wards), Clarksville, Columbia, Dalton, Dummer, Errol, Gorham, Jefferson, Northumberland, Pittsburg, Stark, Stewartstown, Stratford, Whitefield; *Grafton County:* Alexandria, Benton, Dorchester, Ellsworth, Grafton, Groton, Haverhill, Lincoln, Lisbon, Warren; *Hillsborough County:* Bennington, Greenville, Manchester (all wards), Windsor; *Merrimack County:* Allenstown, Boscawen, Bradford, Franklin (all wards), Hill, Loudon, Newbury, Pittsfield; *Rockingham*

County: Auburn, Danville, Epping, Fremont, Newmarket, Nottingham, Raymond, Seabrook; *Strafford County:* Farmington, Middleton, Milton, New Durham, Rochester (all wards), Rollinsford, Somersworth (all wards); *Sullivan County:* Acworth, Charlestown, Claremont (all wards), Croydon, Goshen, Grantham, Langdon.

1980 elite areas: *Belknap County:* Gilford; *Carroll County:* Brookfield, Jackson, Wolfeboro; *Cheshire County:* Dublin, Harrisville; *Coos County:* Randolph, Shelburne; *Grafton County:* Ellsworth, Hanover, Hebron; *Hillsborough County:* Amherst, Bedford, Brookline, Francestown, Hancock, Hollis, Merrimack, Mont Vernon, Peterborough, Sharon, Temple, Windsor; *Merrimack County:* Bow, Canterbury, Dunbarton, Henniker, Hopkinton, New London; *Rockingham County:* Atkinson, Greenland, Hampstead, Hampton, Hampton Falls, Londonderry, New Castle, North Hampton, Nottingham, Rye, Stratham, Windham; *Strafford County:* Durham, Lee, Madbury, Strafford; *Sullivan County:* Grantham, Plainfield.

1980 working-class areas: *Belknap County:* Belmont; *Carroll County:* Chatham, Ossipee, Wakefield; *Cheshire County:* Hinsdale, Roxbury, Troy, Winchester; *Coos County:* Berlin (all wards), Carroll, Clarksville, Columbia, Dalton, Errol, Gorham, Milan, Northumberland, Pittsburg, Stark, Stewartstown, Stratford, Whitefield; *Grafton County:* Alexandria, Bath, Benton, Grafton, Groton, Haverhill, Landaff, Lincoln, Lisbon, Littleton, Monroe, Warren; *Hillsborough County:* Bennington, Greenville, Hillsborough, Manchester (all wards); *Merrimack County:* Allenstown, Boscawen, Danbury, Franklin (all wards), Pittsfield; *Rockingham County:* Epping, Raymond, Seabrook; *Strafford County:* Farmington, Middleton, Milton, Rochester (all wards), Somersworth (all wards); *Sullivan County:* Charlestown, Claremont (all wards), Croydon, Langdon, Lempster, Newport, Unity.

1990 elite areas: *Belknap County:* None; *Carroll County:* Eaton; *Cheshire County:* Dublin, Keene—Ward 1; *Coos County:* None; *Grafton County:* Hanover, Lebanon—Ward 1, Lyme, Sugar Hill, Waterville Valley; *Hillsborough County:* Amherst, Bedford, Brookline, Francestown, Hancock, Hollis, Litchfield, Lyndeborough, Manchester—Wards 1, 2, Mason, Merrimack, Mont Vernon, Nashua—Wards 1, 2, 3, 5, 8, 9, New Boston, Peterborough, Sharon; *Merrimack County:* Bow, Canterbury, Concord—Wards 4, 8, Dunbarton, Henniker, Hopkinton, New London; *Rockingham County:* Atkinson, Greenland, Hampstead, Hampton Falls, Londonderry, New Castle, North Hampton, Portsmouth—Wards 2, 5, Rye, Stratham, Windham; *Strafford County:* Dover—Ward 3, Durham, Lee, Madbury; *Sullivan County:* Grantham.

1990 working-class areas: *Belknap County:* Alton, Laconia—Wards 2, 3, 4, 5; *Carroll County:* Chatham, Effingham, Wakefield; *Cheshire County:* Gilsum, Marlow, Stoddard, Sullivan, Troy, Winchester; *Coos County:* Berlin (all wards), Clarksville, Colebrook, Columbia, Dalton, Dummer, Errol, Jefferson, Milan, Northumberland, Pittsburg, Stark, Stewartstown, Stratford, Whitefield; *Grafton County:* Alexandria, Ashland, Bath, Benton, Groton, Landaff, Lisbon, Littleton, Lyman, Monroe, Warren, Wentworth; *Hillsborough County:* Bennington, Greenville, Hillsborough, Manchester—Wards 5, 6, 7, 9, 10, 11, Nashua 6; *Merrimack County:* Allenstown, Concord—Wards 1, 5, Danbury, Franklin—Wards 1, 2, 3, Hill, Northfield, Pittsfield; *Rockingham County:* None; *Strafford County:* Farmington, Middleton, Milton, New Durham, Rochester—Wards 1, 2, 3, 4, 5, 6, Somersworth—Wards 1, 2, 3, 4, 5; *Sullivan County:* Acworth, Claremont—Wards 1, 2, 3, Croydon, Langdon, Lempster, Newport, Unity, Washington.

2000 elite areas: *Belknap County:* None; *Carroll County:* Jackson; *Cheshire County:* Chesterfield, Dublin, Harrisville, Keene—Ward 4, Westmoreland; *Coos County:* Randolph; *Grafton County:* Easton, Hanover, Holderness, Lebanon—Ward 1, Lyme, Orford, Sugar Hill, Waterville Valley; *Hillsborough County:* Amherst, Bedford, Brookline, Francestown, Hancock, Hollis, Litchfield, Lyndeborough, Manchester—Wards 1, 2, Mason, Merrimack, Mount Vernon, Nashua—Wards 1, 2, 8, 9, New Boston, Peterborough, Sharon, Temple, Wilton; *Merrimack County:* Bow, Canterbury, Concord—Wards 5, 7, 10, Dunbarton, Henniker, Hopkinton, New London, Newbury; *Rockingham County:* Atkinson, Chester, Deerfield, East Kingston, Exeter, Hampstead, Hampton, Hampton Falls, Kensington, Londonderry, New Castle, Newfields, North Hampton, Portsmouth—Wards 1, 2, 5, Rye, Stratham, Windham; *Strafford County:* Dover—Ward 3, Durham, Lee, Madbury; *Sullivan County:* Grantham, Plainfield, Sunapee.

2000 working-class areas: *Belknap County:* Barnstead, Belmont, Laconia—Wards 4, 5, Tilton; *Carroll County:* Albany, Effingham; *Cheshire County:* Gilsum, Troy, Winchester; *Coos County:* Berlin—Wards 1, 2, 3, 4, Clarksville, Colebrook, Columbia, Dalton, Dummer, Errol, Milan, Northumberland, Pittsburg, Stark, Stewartstown, Stratford; *Grafton County:* Alexandria, Ashland, Bath, Benton, Dorchester, Groton, Lisbon, Orange, Warren, Wentworth; *Hillsborough County:* Greenville, Manchester—Wards 4, 5, 7, 9, 11, Nashua—Ward 4, Windsor; *Merrimack County:*

Allenstown, Boscawen, Danbury, Franklin—Wards 1, 3, Hill, Northfield, Pittsfield; *Rockingham County*: Raymond, Seabrook; *Strafford County*: Farmington, Middleton, Milton, Rochester—Wards 1, 3, 4, Somersworth—Wards 2, 5; *Sullivan County*: Charlestown, Claremont—Wards 1, 2, 3; Croydon, Goshen, Langdon, Lempster, Newport, Unity.

46. David C. Hoeh, *1968, McCarthy, New Hampshire* (Rochester, Minn.: Lone Oak Press, 1994), p. 493.
47. Ibid., pp. 334-37.
48. Ibid., pp. 15-16.
49. Charles Brereton, *First in the Nation: New Hampshire and the Premier Presidential Primary* (Portsmouth, N.H.: Peter E. Randall, 1987), p. 146.
50. Theodore H. White, *The Making of the President 1972* (New York: Atheneum, 1973), p. 121.
51. Ibid., p. 121.
52. Ibid., p. 79.
53. White, p. 83; also, see summary of Muskie presidential campaign briefing books, part of the George J. Mitchell Papers at Bowdoin College.
54. White, p. 81.
55. Interview by the author, November 22, 2002.
56. Brereton, p. 213.
57. Interview by the author, July 31, 2002.
58. Susan Berry Casey, *Hart and Soul: Gary Hart's New Hampshire Odyssey . . . and Beyond* (Concord, N.H.: NHI Press), pp. 278-79.
59. Interview by the author, July 22, 2002. All quotes from Jim Demers in this chapter are from this interview.
60. Interview by the author, June 12, 2002.
61. Interview by the author, August 15, 2002. All quotes from Arnie Arnesen in this chapter are from this interview.
62. John DiStaso and Michael Cousineau, "Forbes Has Good Night, but Bradley Doesn't," *Manchester Union Leader*, January 25, 2000.
63. Brereton, pp. 154-56.
64. Emmett Buell, "The Changing Face of the New Hampshire Primary," in *In Pursuit of the White House 2000*, edited by William G. Mayer (New York: Chatham House, 2000).
65. Ibid., pp. 111-18.
66. Data from exit polls conducted at 2000 New Hampshire primary; for further details, see http://abcnews.go.com/sections/politics/2000vote/exitpoll_nh_dem.html.
67. Berlin, Claremont, Dover, Franklin, Keene, Manchester, Nashua, Rochester, Somersworth.
68. Those towns, in alphabetical order: Acworth, Amherst, Andover, Dublin, Durham, Easton, Eaton, Francestown, Franconia, Gilsum, Grantham, Hancock, Hanover, Hebron, Holderness, Lyme, Nelson, New London, Orford, Plainfield, Plymouth, Sandwich, Sharon, Sugar Hill, Waterville Valley.
69. Interview by the author, July 17, 2002.
70. Interview by the author, December 17, 2002. A recent study of New Hampshire voters concludes that there is little evidence that undeclared voters in the state behaved much differently from registered party voters in the 2000 presidential primary. Primaries are volatile, they state, because "voters and candidates are operating in a low-information environment in which new facts and new impressions count heavily"; both undeclared voters and registered party voters are subject to these same uncertainties. Allowing undeclared voters to participate, they conclude, "does not seem to make an already unstable situation decidedly worse." Linda L. Fowler, Constantine J. Spiliotes, and Lynn Vavreck, "Sheep in Wolves' Clothing: Undeclared Voters in New Hampshire's Open Primary," *PS: Political Science and Politics* 36, no. 2 (April 2003): 159-63.

Chapter Three

1. Interview by the author, December 17, 2002.
2. Interview by the author, August 5, 2002.
3. David C Hoeh. *1968, McCarthy, New Hampshire* (Rochester, M.N..: Lone Oak Press, 1994), p. 113.
4. Interview by the author, November 25, 2002. All quotes from Jean Wallin in this chapter are from this interview.
5. Charles Brereton. *First in the Nation: New Hampshire and the Premier Presidential Primary.* (Portsmouth, N.H.: Peter E. Randall, 1987), pp. 120-21.

6. Interview by the author, August 27, 2002. All quotes from William Farrell and Merv Weston in this chapter are from this interview.
7. "A Stranger in Our Town," *Manchester Union Leader*, March 18, 1964.
8. Brereton, pp. 106-107.
9. Ibid., p. 107.
10. Hoeh, p. 125.
11. Ibid., p. 125.
12. Ibid., pp. 124-25.
13. Interview by the author, July 11, 2002. All quotes from Pat Morris in this chapter are from this interview.
14. Interview by the author, August 27, 2002.
15. Hoeh, p. 336.
16. Ibid., pp. 324-25.
17. Ibid., pp. 336-37.
18. Ibid., p. 335.
19. Ibid., p. 409.
20. Ibid., p. 415; Weston interview.
21. Hoeh, p. 413.
22. Brereton, p. 128.
23. Ibid., p. 128.
24. Ibid., pp. 121-22.
25. Hoeh, pp. 411-12.
26. Brereton, p. 129.
27. Hunter Thompson, *Fear and Loathing: On the Campaign Trail '72* (New York: Warner Books, 1973), p. 242.
28. Interview by the author, February 26, 2003. All quotes from Joseph Grandmaison in this chapter are from this interview.
29. Michael G. Hagen and William G. Mayer, "The Modern Politics of Presidential Selection: How Changing the Rules Really Did Change the Game," in *In Pursuit of the White House 2000*, edited by William G. Mayer (New York: Chatham House, 2000), pp. 22-25.
30. Theodore H. White, *The Making of the President 1972* (New York: Atheneum, 1973), p. 121.
31. Brereton, pp. 142-43.
32. Ibid., p. 142.
33. Ibid., p. 143.
34. Ibid., p. 138.
35. Interview by the author, February 26, 2003.
36. Brereton, p. 146.
37. Interview by the author, November 23, 2002. All quotes from Joseph McQuaid in this chapter are from this interview.
38. Brereton, pp. 152-53.
39. Ibid., p. 153.
40. Ibid., pp. 155-56.
41. Ibid., p. 161.
42. Ibid., p. 162.

Chapter Four

1. Interview by the author, July 16, 2002. All quotes from Bill Shaheen in this chapter are from this interview.
2. Interview by the author, November 22, 2002. All quotes from Katherine Rogers in this chapter are from this interview.
3. Jules Witcover, *Marathon: The Pursuit of the Presidency* (New York: The Viking Press, 1977), p. 225.
4. Ibid., p. 198.
5. Interview by the author, February 21, 2003. All quotes from Jeanne Shaheen in this chapter are from this interview.
6. Carter's last visit before the 1980 primary was in April 1979; Brereton, p. 210.
7. Brereton, p. 209.
8. Interview by the author, July 17, 2002.

9.   Interview by the author, November 11, 2002.
10. Brereton, p. 208-209.
11. Ibid., p. 211.
12. Ibid., p. 212.

Chapter Five

1.   Interview by the author, November 11, 2002. All quotes from Dayton Duncan in this chapter are from this interview.
2.   Prior to the 2004 New Hampshire primary, politicsnh.com, a website devoted to coverage of New Hampshire politics, displayed a scoreboard of exactly how many prominent activists were signed up with each of the candidates.
3.   Interview by the author, November 22, 2002. All quotes from Katherine Rogers in this chapter are from this interview.
4.   Jack W. Germond and Jules Witcover, *Wake Us When It's Over* (New York: Macmillan, 1985), pp. 36-48, 58.
5.   Ibid., p. 54.
6.   Interview by the author, June 24, 2002.
7.   Susan Berry Casey, *Hart and Soul* (Concord, N.H.: NHI Press, 1986), p. 50.
8.   Interview by the author, August 5, 2002. All quotes from Ned Helms in this chapter are from this interview.
9.   Casey, p. 52.
10. Ibid., p. 53.
11. Interview by the author, February 21, 2003. All quotes from Jeanne Shaheen in this chapter are from this interview.
12. Casey, pp. 42-43.
13. Interview by the author, July 22, 2002. All quotes from Debbie Butler in this chapter are from this interview.
14. Interview by the author, June 13, 2002.
15. Casey, p. 69.
16. Interview by the author, July 1, 2002. All quotes from Raymond Buckley in this chapter are from this interview.
17. Interview with Jeanne Shaheen; Casey, pp. 132-35.
18. Casey, pp. 193-94.
19. Interview by the author, December 17, 2002.
20. For a political scientist's perspective on New Hampshire voters' level of knowledge about primary candidates, see Tami Buhr, "What Voters Know about the Candidates and How They Learn It: The 1996 New Hampshire Republican Primary as a Case Study," in *In Pursuit of the White House 2000*, edited by William G. Mayer (New York: Chatham House, 2000), pp. 203-53. Buhr concurs with Griffin to some degree: "While the New Hampshire primary campaign is clearly an educating experience for the electorate," she states, "it fails to provide the same level of education for all of its members" (p. 244).
21. Elizabeth Drew, *Campaign Journal: The Political Events of 1983-1984* (New York: Macmillan, 1985), pp. 352-53.
22. During the final days of the campaign, Hart made a campaign stop in Berlin and participated in the ax throw at a woodsmen competition. He hit the target on the second try, and his throw made headlines and newscasts. For a description, see Casey, pp. 219-20.
23. *Campaign for President: The Managers Look at '88*, edited by David R. Runkel (Dover, Mass.: Auburn House, 1989), p. 18.
24. Interview by the author, July 31, 2002. All quotes from Susan Calegari in this chapter are from this interview.
25. Jack W. Germond and Jules Witcover, *Whose Broad Stripes and Bright Stars? The Trivial Pursuit of the Presidency 1988* (New York: Warner Books, 1989), p. 218.
26. Ibid., pp. 222-23.
27. Interview by the author, July 22, 2002. All quotes from Jim Demers in this chapter are from this interview.
28. Germond and Witcover, *Whose Broad Stripes and Bright Stars?* p. 272.
29. Ibid., p. 272.

30. Interview by the author, August 26, 2002. All quotes from Jane Clemons in this chapter are from this interview.
31. Germond and Witcover, *Whose Broad Stripes and Bright Stars?* p. 220.
32. Interview by the author, July 17, 2002. All quotes from Jeff Woodburn in this chapter are from this interview.
33. Germond and Witcover, *Whose Broad Stripes and Bright Stars?* p. 266.
34. Ibid., pp. 258-59.
35. Ibid., p. 266.
36. Interview by the author, August 29, 2002.
37. Germond and Witcover, *Whose Broad Stripes and Bright Stars?* p. 276.
38. Jack W. Germond and Jules Witcover, *Mad as Hell: Revolt at the Ballot Box, 1992* (New York: Warner Books, 1993), p. 96.
39. Germond and Witcover, *Mad as Hell*, p. 83.
40. Ibid., pp. 126-28.
41. Ibid., pp. 93-94.
42. Ibid., pp. 79-80, 98.
43. Ibid., p. 99.
44. Ibid., p. 83.
45. Eight months after dropping out of the 1992 race, Tsongas was again diagnosed with lymphoma. He died from liver failure and pneumonia in 1997.
46. *Campaign for President: The Managers Look at '92*, edited by Charles T. Royer (Hollis, N.H.: Hollis Publishing Company, 1994), pp. 2-3.
47. Interview by the author, November 25, 2002.
48. See pollster Stan Greenberg's description of the evolution of Clinton's populism in *Campaign for President . . . '92*, pp. 14-15.
49. Ibid., p. 15.
50. Interview by the author, February 5, 2003.
51. Interview by the author, November 1, 2002. All quotes from John Broderick in this chapter are from this interview.
52. Germond and Witcover, *Whose Broad Stripes and Bright Stars?* pp. 230-38.
53. Interview by the author, November 22, 2002. All quotes from Terry Shumaker in this chapter are from this interview.
54. John DiStaso, "DLC and Spirou Almost Mend All Party Fences," *Manchester Union Leader*, August 6, 1991, p. 7.
55. Interview by the author, June 12, 2003. All quotes from George Bruno in this chapter are from this interview.
56. Interview by the author, July 16, 2002.
57. Germond and Witcover, *Mad as Hell*, p. 162.
58. Interview by the author, February 26, 2003.
59. Interview by the author, February 26, 2003. All quotes from Peter Sullivan in this chapter are from this interview.
60. *Campaign for President . . . '92*, p. 38.
61. Ibid., pp. 38-39.
62. Ibid., p. 39.
63. Germond and Witcover, *Mad as Hell*, p. 159, 161.
64. Interview by the author, August 15, 2002. All quotes from Arnie Arnesen in this chapter are from this interview.
65. *Campaign for President . . . '92*, p. 40.
66. Ibid., pp. 39-40.
67. Ibid., p. 35.
68. Germond and Witcover, *Mad as Hell*, p. 103; *Campaign for President . . . '92*, pp. 33-36.
69. *Campaign for President . . . '92*, p. 33.
70. Ibid., pp. 34-37.
71. Germond and Witcover, *Mad as Hell*, p. 162.
72. *Campaign for President . . . '92*, p. 307.
73. Ibid., p. 308.
74. Germond and Witcover, *Mad as Hell*, pp. 194-95.
75. Interview by the author, July 11, 2002.

76.   Interview by the author, October 24, 2002.
77.   Interview by the author, November 18, 2002.
78.   Interview by the author, July 9, 2002.

Chapter Six

1.   Interview by the author, August 29, 2002. All quotes from Mark Longabaugh in this chapter are from this interview.
2.   Interview by the author, July 31, 2002. All quotes from Susan Calegari in this chapter are from this interview.
3.   Interview by the author, fall 2002. All quotes from Matt Rodriguez in this chapter are from this interview.
4.   Interview by the author, August 12, 2002.
5.   Interview by the author, October 23, 2002. All quotes from Randy Benthien in this chapter are from this interview.
6.   Interview by the author, October 23, 2002. All quotes from Mica Stark in this chapter are from this interview.
7.   Interview by the author, October 20, 2002. All quotes from Nick Baldick in this chapter are from this interview.
8.   Interview by the author, July 17, 2002. All quotes from Jeff Woodburn in this chapter are from this interview.
9.   Interview by the author, July 2, 2002. All quotes from Judith Scourfield McLauchlan in this chapter are from this interview.
10.   Interview by the author, August 26, 2002. All quotes from Jane Clemons in this chapter are from this interview.
11.   Interview by the author, November 22, 2002.
12.   Interview by the author, June 13, 2002.
13.   Interview by the author, June 12, 2002.
14.   Interview by the author, July 22, 2002. All quotes from Jim Demers in this chapter are from this interview.
15.   Interview by the author, August 16, 2002. All quotes from Caroline McCarley in this chapter are from this interview.
16.   Interview by the author, July 16, 2002. All quotes from Bill Shaheen in this chapter are from this interview.
17.   Interview by the author, September 4, 2002. All quotes from Bill Stetson in this chapter are from this interview.
18.   In September 1999, Bradley unveiled a $65 billion, detail-rich plan to provide Americans with universal access to health insurance. The plan offered subsidies to families unable to afford insurance, required parents to obtain coverage for their children; and allowed nineteen to sixty-four-year-olds to buy into the health insurance plan provided to members of Congress. The Gore campaign harshly criticized the plan, charging that it would not cover prescription drugs for senior citizens; that Medicaid patients would lose benefits; that it would not ensure the solvency of Medicare; and that it was generally indifferent to the needs of the poor and uninsured. Health insurance became the key policy issue of the Democratic primaries. See "Bradley unveils $65 billion plan for universal health care," CNN.com, September 28, 1999; and "Gore, Bradley spar over negative ads, health care in Manchester debate," Ian Christopher McCaleb, CNN.com, January 27, 2000.
19.   Interview by the author, November 11, 2002.
20.   Of the 111,013 undeclared voters who cast ballots in the 2000 New Hampshire primary, 68,492 took Republican ballots and 42,521 took Democratic ballots.
21.   Interview by the author, April 7, 2003.
22.   See chapter 2, note 66.
23.   Interview by the author, August 26, 2002.
24.   Interview by the author, February 21, 2003.

Chapter Seven

1. Interview by the author, December 17, 2002. All quotes from John Milne in this chapter are from this interview.
2. Interview by the author, November 11, 2002.
3. Interview by the author, November 22, 2002.
4. University of New Hampshire Survey Center, "The New Hampshire 2000 Survey," released August 22, 2000.
5. Interview by the author, December 12, 2002. All quotes from Mark Bodi in this chapter are from this interview.
6. Interview by the author, December 17, 2002. All quotes from Pat Griffin in this chapter are from this interview.
7. Interview by the author, October 24, 2002.
8. Interview by the author, August 21, 2002.
9. Charles Brereton, *First in the Nation: New Hampshire and the Premier Presidential Primary* (Portsmouth, N.H.: Peter E. Randall, 1987), p. 126. The campaign also spent $31,000 on newspaper ads, and just $20,000 for television time in Maine, New Hampshire, and Boston.
10. Interview by the author, November 25, 2002. All quotes from Kevin Landrigan in this chapter are from this interview.
11. Interview by the author, November 22, 2002. All quotes from Katherine Rogers in this chapter are from this interview.
12. Interview by the author, November 18, 2002. All quotes from Scott Spradling in this chapter are from this interview.
13. Jules Witcover, *Marathon: The Pursuit of the Presidency 1972-1976* (New York: Viking Press, 1977), p. 223.
14. Interview by the author, July 31, 2002.
15. Interview by the author, December 4, 2002. All quotes from Jennifer Donahue in this chapter are from this interview.
16. Interview by the author, October 20, 2002.
17. Interview by the author, June 20, 2003. All quotes from Doug Hattaway in this chapter are from this interview.
18. Interview by the author, April·7, 2003.
19. Lorna Colquhoun, "Bradley's Illegal Drug Was Marijuana, Twice," *Manchester Union Leader*, August 30, 1999, A8.

Chapter Eight

1. Nelson W. Polsby, *Consequences of Party Reform* (Oxford: Oxford University Press, 1983), pp. 10-11.
2. Marty Cohen, David Karol, Hans Noel, and John Zaller, "Beating Reform: The Resurgence of Parties in Presidential Nominations, 1980 to 2000," presented at the 2001 meeting of the American Political Science Association.

Index

DATE DUE